New Perspectives in German Studies

General Editors: Michael Butler is Emeritus Professor of Modern German Literature at the University of Birmingham and Professor William E. Paterson OBE is Professor of European and German Politics at the University of Birmingham and Chairman of the German British Forum.

Over the last twenty years the concept of German studies has undergone major transformation. The traditional mixture of language and literary studies, related very closely to the discipline as practised in German universities, has expanded to embrace history, politics, economics and cultural studies. The conventional boundaries between all these disciplines have become increasingly blurred, a process which has been accelerated markedly since German unification in 1989/90.

New Perspectives in German Studies, developed in conjunction with the Institute for German Studies and the Department of German Studies at the University of Birmingham, has been designed to respond precisely to this trend of the interdisciplinary approach to the study of German and to cater for the growing interest in Germany in the context of European integration. The books in this series will focus on the modern period, from 1750 to the present day.

Titles include:

Matthew M.C. Allen
THE VARIETIES OF CAPITALISM PARADIGM
Explaining Germany's Comparative Advantage?

Peter Bleses and Martin Seeleib-Kaiser
THE DUAL TRANSFORMATION OF THE GERMAN WELFARE STATE

Michael Butler and Robert Evans (*editors*)
THE CHALLENGE OF GERMAN CULTURE
Essays Presented to Wilfried van der Will

Michael Butler, Malcolm Pender and Joy Charnley (*editors*)
THE MAKING OF MODERN SWITZERLAND 1848–1998

Paul Cooke and Andrew Plowman (*editors*)
GERMAN WRITERS AND THE POLITICS OF CULTURE
Dealing with the Stasi

Wolf-Dieter Eberwein and Karl Kaiser (*editors*)
GERMANY'S NEW FOREIGN POLICY
Decision-Making in an Interdependent World

Karl Christian Führer and Corey Ross (*editors*)
MASS MEDIA, CULTURE AND SOCIETY IN TWENTIETH-CENTURY GERMANY

Jonathan Grix
THE ROLE OF THE MASSES IN THE COLLAPSE OF THE GDR

Gunther Hellmann (*editor*)
GERMANY'S EU POLICY IN ASYLUM AND DEFENCE
De-Europeanization by Default?

Margarete Kohlenbach
WALTER BENJAMIN
Self-Reference and Religiosity

Charles Lees
PARTY POLITICS IN GERMANY
A Comparative Politics Approach

Hanns W, Maull
GERMANY'S UNCERTAIN POWER
Foreign Policy of the Berlin Republic

Christian Schweiger
BRITAIN, GERMANY AND THE FUTURE OF THE EUROPEAN UNION

James Sloam
THE EUROPEAN POLICY OF THE GERMAN SOCIAL DEMOCRATS
Interpreting a Changing World

Ronald Speirs and John Breuilly (editors)
GERMANY'S TWO UNIFICATIONS
Anticipations, Experiences, Responses

Henning Tewes
GERMANY, CIVILIAN POWER AND THE NEW EUROPE
Enlarging Nato and the European Union

Maiken Umbach
GERMAN FEDERALISM
Past, Present, Future

Roger Woods
GERMANY'S NEW RIGHT AS CULTURE AND POLITICS

New Perspective in German Studies
Series Standing Order ISBN 0–333–92430–4 hardcover
Series Standing Order ISBN 0–333–92434–7 paperback
(*outside North America only*)

You can receive future titles in this series as they are published by placing a standing order. Please contact your bookseller or, in case of difficulty, write to us at the address below with your name and address, the title of the series and the ISBN quoted above.

Customer Services Department, Macmillan Distribution Ltd, Houndmills, Basingstoke, Hampshire RG21 6XS, England

---

Also by same author:

ERNST JÜNGER AND THE NATURE OF POLITICAL COMMITMENT

OPPOSITION IN THE GDR UNDER HONECKER, 1971–85

THE END OF THE GDR AND THE PROBLEMS OF INTEGRATION (*co-edited* with M. Gerber)

UNDERSTANDING THE PAST, MANAGING THE FUTURE: THE INTEGRATION OF THE FIVE NEW LÄNDER INTO THE FEDERAL REPUBLIC OF GERMANY (*co-edited* with M. Gerber)

CHANGING IDENTITIES IN EAST GERMANY (*co-edited* with M. Gerber)

THE CONSERVATIVE REVOLUTION IN THE WEIMAR REPUBLIC

NATIONALISMUS OHNE SELBSTBEWUßTSEIN

Germany's New Right as Culture and Politics

Roger Woods
Professor of German
University of Nottingham, UK

First published 2007 by
PALGRAVE MACMILLAN
Houndmills, Basingstoke, Hampshire RG21 6XS and
175 Fifth Avenue, New York, N. Y. 10010
Companies and representatives throughout the world

PALGRAVE MACMILLAN is the global academic imprint of the Palgrave
Macmillan division of St. Martin's Press, LLC and of Palgrave Macmillan Ltd.
Macmillan® is a registered trademark in the United States, United Kingdom
and other countries. Palgrave is a registered trademark in the European
Union and other countries.

ISBN-13: 978–0–230–50672–5   hardback
ISBN-10: 0–230–50672–0   hardback

This book is printed on paper suitable for recycling and made from fully
managed and sustained forest sources.

A catalogue record for this book is available from the British Library.

Library of Congress Cataloging-in-Publication Data
Woods, Roger, 1949–
    Germany's new Right as culture and politics / Roger Woods.
       p. cm.
    Includes bibliographical references and index.
    ISBN-13: 978–0–230–50672–5 (cloth)
    ISBN-10: 0–230–50672–0 (cloth)
    1. Radicalism–Germany. 2. Political parties–Germany. 3. Nationalism
–Germany. I. Title.

HN460.R3W66 2007
320.520943–dc22   2006051440

10   9   8   7   6   5   4   3   2   1
16   15   14   13   12   11   10   09   08   07

Printed and bound in Great Britain by
Antony Rowe Ltd, Chippenham and Eastbourne

To the memory of my father

Contents

Acknowledgements

I am grateful for travel grants and research leave awarded by the British Academy, the Arts and Humanities Research Council, the German Academic Exchange Service, and the University of Nottingham.

Introduction

The New Right has been around in Germany for over 30 years, and in this time it has provided a loud and persistent voice in cultural and political debate, especially since German unification. The loose network of politicians, writers, academics and journalists that make up the New Right is constantly in the public eye, through the controversial activities of the political parties associated with it (mainly the Republikaner), and through newspapers and journals such as *Junge Freiheit* and *Nation und Europa*. Many organisations promote New Right ideas, for example the Förderstiftung Konservative Bildung und Forschung (Foundation for Conservative Education and Research) under Caspar von Schrenck-Notzing, the Thule Seminar under Pierre Krebs, the Deutschland-Bewegung (Movement for Germany) under Alfred Mechtersheimer, and Karlheinz Weißmann's Institut für Staatspolitik (National Policy Institute), all of which run seminars, summer schools and conferences. These publications and organisations have an Internet presence which is growing in importance for the dissemination of New Right ideas.[1] The New Right also attracts attention through the hotly debated pronouncements of its most prominent intellectuals: Botho Strauß's 'Anschwellender Bocksgesang' (Mounting Tragedy), a highly articulate attack on the foundations of German liberalism, was originally published in *Der Spiegel* in 1993 and provoked a public debate that continued for many months.[2] Its best known advocates make the news by publishing detailed accounts of their political aims and cultural values,[3] and its voice is heard not least because it is the most sophisticated advocate of ideas to the right of mainstream

1

conservatism. Whether the public debate is on German identity or the role of nationalism in post-unification Germany, National Socialism or immigration and multi-culturalism, the New Right is quick to speak out and sure of a sharp response from its left-wing and liberal opponents. The New Right is a notable contributor to public debate in Germany, even if its contributions serve to confirm its notoriety rather than to establish the 'cultural hegemony' it aspires to.

Observers have argued that the New Right has grown in influence. Kurt Lenk sees the New Right gaining ground among those who have been alienated by the party squabbling, scandals, corruption and self-interest that have become the norm in many democratic societies. By contrast the New Right calls for strong leadership, obedience, discipline and service to the state and the people.[4]

Most commentators see a close link between the New Right and right-wing extremism: *Der Spiegel* described the movement as 'brownshirts in pinstripes',[5] and academics and the Office for the Protection of the Constitution regularly express their concern about the New Right's attempts to gain cultural acceptance for a self-assertive nationalism that is uninhibited by the Nazi past and about its attempts to undermine German democracy.[6] Wolfgang Gessenharter counters the image of the New Right as an isolated circle of extremist thinkers when he points out that at the organisational and ideological levels it has been able to chalk up some successes in breaking down the barrier between conservatism and extremism.[7]

The New Right is also in the news because it has a European dimension. As a political phenomenon the German New Right has its counterparts in other Western European countries, and together they are engaged in an effort to establish a network and develop a shared programme based on notions of a Western culture and Western values. Attempts at collaboration from the 1980s to the present day have often turned out to be self-limiting, however, largely due to the clash of interests that inevitably occurs when nationalistic groups from different countries set out their positions. Collaborative initiatives also tend to break down when the New Right in one country feels obliged to distance itself from the New Right in another as it crosses the line of what is publicly acceptable. Thus Franz Schönhuber condemned Jean Marie Le Pen as a racist and brought about the end of the short-lived Technical Group of the European Right formed after the 1989 elections to the European Parliament. The egos of New Right leaders also present an obstacle to collaboration, yet the effort to come together is regularly renewed, for example at a meeting in Austria in the Summer of 2002 of senior politicians from the Freiheitliche Partei Österreichs (FPÖ), members of the Belgian Vlaams Blok, Italy's Lega Nord, Germany's CDU and FDP, and of Scandinavian and Spanish right-wing parties. Here again one of the main barriers to collaboration turned out to be the fear of lining up with right-wing extremists. According to the New Right's own report on the meeting, the General Secretary of the FPÖ ruled out working with the Vlaams Blok even as Jörg Haider described such cooperation as very sensible in view of the over-lapping positions of the two parties.[8]

Seasoned observers point out that the conditions are not in place for the New Right to enjoy the kind of prominence and success achieved by the Conservative Revolution, its acknowledged predecessor in the Weimar Republic. Extreme right-wing parties and their associated ideologies fared well in the Weimar Republic but not in the Federal Republic.[9] The deep concern for the stability of the Federal Republic, expressed in studies of the New Right with titles such as *Kippt die Republik?* (Is the Republic toppling?),[10] is based on an overestimate of the movement's influence. Kurt Sontheimer confirms the sentiment behind the title of the Swiss journalist Fritz René Allemann's 1956 study of the political system of the Federal Republic: *Bonn ist nicht Weimar* (Bonn is not Weimar) when he concludes that despite some irritating successes of the extreme right in Landtag elections the traces of the Weimar Republic and the Third Reich never posed a serious threat to democracy in the Federal Republic. Moreover, New Right authors do not have the originality or the popularity of the anti-democratic thinkers in the Weimar years.[11] This low-key assessment of the New Right seems all the more appropriate since the movement goes out of its way to avoid being labelled extremist, and critics themselves often place the New Right somewhere to the right of mainstream conservatism but not in the extremist camp.

Yet such assessments of the significance of the New Right tend to flow from an understanding of the movement as a political force, and it is clear from the most cursory glance at New Right sources that it is not just a political movement. It addresses broad cultural issues of the kind summarised by Richard Herzinger in his assessment of open societies that are having to find their way without recourse to a clearly definable ethnic, moral, cultural or religious identity.[12] Herzinger detects among the right a fear of the destabilising effects of social division, individualism and cosmopolitanism, and this fear leads to a call for a more homogeneous society under the slogan 'integration'.[13]

The following study takes as its main focus the culture of the New Right and sets out to show how New Right politics can be better understood against the background of New Right culture. The movement's cultural positions need to be studied if the thinking behind its illiberal solutions to the problems it perceives is to be grasped. As a cultural movement the New Right is engaged in a search for identity and purpose, and it is significant as one of the more articulate expressions of a deep-rooted despair and of conservative 'solutions' to the challenges posed by what Herzinger calls a decentred society.[14]

The cultural despair lurking beneath New Right political positions will be studied in all its manifestations. The first chapter sets out a definition of the New Right that embraces culture and is therefore broader than those definitions that interpret the New Right as an exclusively political movement. The broader definition leads to a broader assessment of the movement's significance.

The second chapter examines how the positive version of a German or Western culture presented in many New Right sources has to do battle with a more profound cultural pessimism. This chapter analyses the ways in which the New Right project of gaining cultural hegemony is complicated by the movement's internal tensions over what it stands for. Here too is the place for a consideration of New Right attitudes towards multi-culturalism: while one group of New Right authors and associated politicians labels immigration as an external cause of social disintegration and a loss of cultural identity, other New Right authors take a more philosophical approach which locates the origins of decline within German society itself and, more broadly, within Modernity.

The focus on culture is maintained in Chapter 3 which analyses the New Right's views on National Socialism. Much is made of the New Right's frequent public rejections of Nazi ideology, yet the New

Right remains preoccupied with Nazism. In order to understand why, one must understand the New Right's construction of a cultural model of existence involving just two options: on the one hand, a commitment to a vision which strives for mastery over all aspects of life and the restoration of order; on the other, an uncomfortable acknowledgement of reason which knows no community, only isolation. The New Right project of relativising the Nazi past is also examined and found to be endangered by a cultural understanding of this past as Germany's fate for all time. In its search for a non-Nazi past that can serve as a moral foundation for the future the New Right turns to alternative German traditions that seem to be embodied by the Conservative Revolution of the Weimar years and the aristocratic and military resistance to Hitler. The significance of the cultural dimension again becomes apparent in the tension between the Conservative Revolution's political distance from and its philosophical closeness to National Socialism.

Chapter 4 looks at the potential foundations of a New Right programme: nationalism, religion and post-politics appear at different stages in the history of the New Right as its guiding principles, yet for every New Right thinker who proposes these values, another will show them to be heavily compromised. At the cultural level the New Right displays an acute awareness of a precarious existence with no foundation. One response is to dismiss all politics as an irrelevance; another is to follow the line of the 'active nihilist' and turn to an inflated nationalism as a source of absolute meaning. Here New Right politics and culture are seen in their most revealing configuration, with cultural pessimism in turn undermining and shoring up political commitment. The need for absolutes is also behind the New Right's interest in religion, and a study of its cultural dimension explains how defunct values are revived in order to satisfy this need.

The conclusion examines how applicable Jürgen Habermas's interpretation of German neo-conservatism is to the New Right. At the heart of neo-conservatism Habermas detects an acceptance of technical modernity and a rejection of cultural modernity. In his analysis of the neo-conservative mind the subversive threat of culture is externalised: neo-conservatives, he argues, present the explosive contents of cultural modernity as coming from the left and counter this threat by insisting on the value of tradition. To what extent is this model an accurate reflection of the New Right mentality? To anticipate the outcome of the analysis, the cultural approach to the New Right suggests that the model fails to take into account the fact that New Right culture itself is part of the modernity that causes it such anxiety.

If New Right politics is informed by a cultural dimension the counter-argument to the New Right cannot be narrowly political. The conclusion considers what broad cultural liberal responses are available.

1
What is the New Right?

Definitions and their uses

There is little agreement among observers or representatives of the New Right about what it is. This lack of agreement is partly due to the varying motives of writers on the subject, but it is partly also due to the tensions and ambiguities within the New Right itself. Surveying the definitions of the New Right that have been advanced in recent years and reconsidering the nature and the boundaries of the New Right will help to define the critic's task.

Defining the New Right in terms of its general beliefs sheds light on the movement, but this approach also illustrates a problem. The New Right in Germany is frequently defined as an anti-democratic movement[1] dating back to the late sixties or early seventies and variously referred to as the 'Young Right', 'young conservatism' or 'neo-conservatism'.[2] For this reason it has attracted the attention of the Federal Office for the Protection of the Constitution which defined the New Right in the mid-nineties as an 'intellectual current or ideology that looks to the ideas of the Conservative Revolution and seeks to limit or abolish completely the principles of the free democratic basic order'.[3] Political scientists rightly home in on its rejection of universalism, pluralism, liberalism, parliamentarianism, equality, and multi-culturalism, on its ranking of the collective above the individual, on its wish to see a strong state and a strong leader instead of political decision-making through negotiation and compromise. Many observers define the New Right by pointing to its rejection of the French Revolution and the associated principles of freedom, equality and fraternity.[4] In their place the New Right seeks to establish a 'Volksgemeinschaft' (community of the people), based on a supposed natural inequality of races and on the rule of an elite.[5] The New Right is also said to reject neo-Nazism and racism but is committed to the related concept of ethnopluralism.[6] Underlying all these positions, it is argued, is a self-assertive nationalism. One observer quotes Dieter Stein, editor of the New Right newspaper *Junge Freiheit,* calling for 'the revival of a healthy national consciousness that will make it possible, especially for young citizens, to declare straightforwardly and with a sense of joy their allegiance to their country and their people, to do their duty for the state and to meet other people with pride, openness, and a positive sense of their own history and culture'.[7] For the New Right, it is argued, 1989 marked the end of Germany's post-war history, and Germany should no longer allow itself to be led like a bull by the nose. Germany should overcome its long-established habit of putting other countries' interests ahead of its own, and it should become a culturally, economically, and politically dominant country.[8]

These attitudes are generally ascribed to the New Right as if they had been embraced by a united movement. Gessenharter argues that the New Right represents a clearly delineated set of views, including the aim of creating a homogeneous society based on authoritarian structures, anti-liberalism, and the rejection of individualism in favour of the collective. These views, it is claimed, make it possible to mark the New Right off from other ideological trends.[9]

On closer inspection, however, we see that although the New Right has a set of recurrent themes, it is far from being united in its attitude towards them. The idea of the *Volksgemeinschaft,* for example, is explicitly rejected by one of its leading spokesmen, Karlheinz Weißmann, because of its clear associations with National Socialism,[10] and even the idea that the nation is a central concept of the New Right is called into question by those New Right voices which declare it dead and buried.[11] The leading French intellectual of the New Right, Alain de Benoist, whose work is eagerly seized upon by the German New Right, remarks that the nation state has lost its legitimacy in the post-modern world since it is too large to deal with the everyday concerns of ordinary people and too small to counter worldwide threats.[12] As will be shown, the political concepts used by observers to characterise the New Right do indeed feature in its thinking, but at one point or another they are all called into question by the movement itself. It is therefore misleading to suggest that the New Right has an 'unbending obsession with a series of "noble" collective concepts which provide a kind of foundation for its world view', and that the 'Volk' and the 'Reich' are invoked by the New Right as the fixed points which provide the substance of a new identity.[13] Commentators will not capture the subject-matter in its full complexity if the task of defining the New Right is restricted to working out which fixed positions mark it off from other movements;[14] rather, the New Right must be understood in its tendency to demonstrate a fractured mind, at one point proposing what its core values might be and at another doubting the relevance of these values or even retracting them.

Anyone engaged in the attempt to define the New Right needs to ask how useful any definition will be when it comes to understanding what is going on in political and cultural thought at the far-right end of the spectrum in Germany today, and here it is particularly useful to define and examine the New Right in terms of its claim to newness or, more precisely, its persistent struggle to achieve newness. The self-styled left-wing national revolutionary, Henning Eichberg, writing an open letter in the pages of *Wir selbst* to 'R', possibly Roland Bubik, a regular contributor to the New Right newspaper *Junge Freiheit* and editor of the best-selling *Wir '89er*, underlines this claim to newness as he remembers how R had handed him a copy of the newspaper *Junge Freiheit*, saying: 'have a read of that, it's really getting somewhere, a reformed right is what we need, and we can do it, a right that has got some intellectual depth to it, ..., a right that can cast off the hang-ups of the old right'.[15] The New Right academic, Günter Rohrmoser, describes the New Right as educated, young, and 'not living in the past'.[16]

The New Right claims to be new in two ways: firstly, by having taken leave of the Old Right, which looks back to National Socialism as its model, and secondly, by having come up with a new and substantial set of ideas which do what in the German context seems so difficult to do: to make German nationalism and German self-assertiveness respectable. These ambitions of the New Right have been noted by analysts: Richard Stöss cites the reports of the Office for the Protection of the Constitution from the early seventies onwards which register the emergence of a New Right which is dismissive of the right-wing Nationaldemokratische Partei Deutschlands (NPD), and which distances itself from the 'veterans of the "Old Right", whose efforts are guided by a longing for the past'.[17] This rejection of the NPD is generally regarded as the explanation for the emergence of the New Right around the start of the seventies since it was in 1969 that the NPD failed to secure any seats in the Bundestag elections despite having won some 1.5 million votes.[18] This failure hastened the turn away from organisations that were tainted by ideological and personal connections with National Socialism, and it drove home the point that it was necessary to provide a coherent non-Nazi intellectual tradition and to win support in the pre-political sphere of public debate before any electoral victories could be expected. Connecting the fate of the Right with Germany's fate, Wolfgang Strauss explains in the journal *Europa vorn*: 'If all we have in our ideological kitbag are the Hitler cult and Nazi nostalgia there won't be a Germany in the 21st century,'[19] and Hartmut Lange writes: 'A New Right that sees no problem in taking as its guide old-fashioned, traditional and racist principles rooted in blood and soil Romanticism will never reach new horizons and therefore never acquire any influence'.[20]

In a second wave of defections, a group of NPD members broke with the party and set up the New Right journal *Wir selbst* in 1979. Twenty years on, the editor, Siegfried Bublies, explicitly refers to the 'mother party' they left behind as of the Old Right, given to conspiracy theories and doomed to failure. Bublies's dissatisfaction with the NPD can be traced back to the party's attitude towards the Nazi past:

Es gab immer wieder Bestrebungen vor allem aus den Reihen der Jungen Nationaldemokraten, eine zukunftsorientierte, intellektuell anspruchsvollere Politik zu formulieren und sich einer schon fast zum Parteiritual entwickelten NS-Verklärung zu verweigern. Viele in den Reihen der NPD – ich gehörte zu ihnen – empfanden es als eine Beleidigung des eigenen Intellekts und als moralisch widerwärtig, daß die während des Dritten Reiches begangenen Verbrechen – und zu ihnen gehört der millionenfache Mord an den deutschen und europäischen Juden – bestritten oder bagatellisiert wurden.[21]
(Time and again there were attempts, especially from the ranks of the Young National Democrats, to draw up policies that looked

to the future, policies that showed some intellectual ambition, and to resist what had practically developed into the party ritual of glorifying National Socialism. Many NPD members – and I was one of them – took it as an insult to our intelligence and as morally repugnant that the crimes committed during the Third Reich, including the murder of German and European Jews in their millions, were disputed and trivialised.)

Bublies describes the NPD leadership in the seventies as mainly made up of 'political illiterates' who could only respond to the argument that Germany had forfeited the right to national unity and sovereignty because of the Nazis' crimes by denying any German guilt or responsibility. By contrast he characterises the group around *Wir selbst* as 'undogmatic nationalists'.[22]

Critics have remarked on the difference in tone between the New and the Old Right: Funke quotes the NPD leadership on its commitment to a 'völkisch' community, a racist concept taken over from the Nazis, the use of which contributed to the move to have the party banned in August 2000.[23] The 1995 party manifesto speaks of the new creation of a German 'Reich' as its ultimate goal.[24] Despite this more outspoken style of the Old Right, commentators argue that that there is no clear dividing line between the Old and New Right when it comes to their ideological traditions, the anti-democratic thinkers from the first half of the 20th century who serve as their models, their tactics and their propaganda.[25]

The New Right attempts to put some distance between itself and the Old Right by stressing its affinity with the anti-democratic intellectual and political movement in the years of the Weimar Republic known as the Conservative Revolution. The New Right presents the Conservative Revolution as a non-Nazi intellectual tradition, and this aspect of New Right thought has been used by observers as a defining characteristic: Pfahl-Traughber accepts the New Right's self-image as 'modern-day adherents of the Conservative Revolution', and he agrees with the definition of the New Right offered by Backes and Jesse as 'an intellectually relatively sophisticated branch of right-wing extremism which takes the "Conservative Revolution" of the Weimar Republic as its guide'.[26] This definition certainly points to a key feature of the New Right, but it gives rise to two problems. Firstly, the New Right view of the Conservative Revolution as an alternative German tradition to National Socialism is central to the New Right's effort to present itself as non-Nazi, but it cannot be taken at face value. The overlap not just in terms of people but also in terms of fundamental, political and philosophical positions between the Conservative Revolution and National Socialism is not hard to demonstrate.[27] Moreover, if there is room for doubt about the coherence of the New Right's attitudes, this is just as much the case with the Conservative Revolution. Its many prominent individual thinkers, groups and associated organisations represented a vast range of incompatible political views. The absence of clear goals among the Conservative Revolutionaries complicates the attempt to define the New Right by reference to the Conservative Revolution, a point which is implicitly acknowledged by those observers who favour this approach. Pfahl-Traughber takes up Stefan Breuer's argument that Conservative Revolutionary writers' views on the nation, race, the State, the *Volk*, the enemy, the economy, science and technology are so varied that they cannot be considered under a single heading. Breuer actually concludes that the term 'Conservative Revolution' generates more confusion than clarity and that it should be removed from the list of political movements of the 20th century.[28]

The lack of a clear outcome to the discussion of definitions based on the idea of a break with the Old Right and an affinity with the Conservative Revolution generates one of the basic questions to be examined in this study: if the Conservative Revolution cannot be seen as separate from National Socialism and if it is notable for its lack of programmatic clarity, what does this tell us about the New Right's habit of projecting the Conservative Revolution as its model? Might the appeal of this model lie not in individual items of political thought but rather in its strategies for coping with a failure to produce a clear set of goals? Is this the deeper structural connection between the two movements?

From the discussion so far, it can come as no surprise that a New Right political programme or coherent ideology is not available to serve as the convenient basis of a definition. The lack of unity among New Right thinkers is something they acknowledge themselves.[29] For the sake of clarity research may focus on the political thought of prominent New Right individuals,[30] yet this approach loses sight of important debates within the New Right.[31] Nevertheless, intellectuals play a central role in the New Right, and their involvement gives rise to a further issue: while it is true that, as one observer points out, intellectuals are not necessarily critical in their relationships with political movements,[32] Jürgen Habermas has argued that when it comes to the shaping of a national identity intellectuals may not in the business of providing absolute values. With academics in the humanities ('Geisteswissenschaften') in mind he argues that 'in order to form and maintain a collective identity, the linguistic-cultural life context has to be given representation in the present in such a way as to produce meaning. But the medium in which affirmative pasts are given present representation, the *Geisteswissenschaften*, works against this. Their claim to truth commits the *Geisteswissenschaften* to critique; it stands opposed to the function of social integration'.[33] This suggests that the intellectuals who operate as more or less autonomous agents within the loose structure of the New Right and exercise their critical faculties may be a disruptive presence rather than a homogenising force. Our study of their contributions to debates on the nation and national identity will confirm that this is indeed the case.

One important reason for studying the New Right is to assess how much of a threat it is to democracy. This motivation has produced a strand in the definitions debate which seeks to locate the New Right at a point somewhere on a spectrum between right-wing radicalism and right-wing extremism. German research looks to judgements of the Federal Constitutional Court to set out the difference between these two categories: according to these judgements, which guide the work of the Office for the Protection of the Constitution, parties and organisations may be classified as right-wing extremist if their policies and ideology reject the essential principles of the democratic constitutional state. This means rejection of the basic equality of all people, of human rights and freedoms, of democracy, of the separation of powers, of the right to opposition and of minority rights, of pluralism, and of competition between parties. Right-wing extremism also embraces racism, extreme nationalism, and the leader principle. By contrast right-wing radicalism includes positions that do not clearly aim at removing the free democratic basic order, but that are located at the outer limits of what the Constitution permits.[34]

Taking up this distinction, Pfahl-Traughber classifies the New Right as extremist because it seeks to 'delegitimise the democratic constitutional state', and he sees its ultimate goal as removing it completely.[35] When the North Rhine-Westphalia Office for the Protection of the Constitution kept *Junge Freiheit* under observation, it justified its action in terms of suspecting it of extreme right-wing activities.[36]

For others, however, the New Right is the 'hinge' between conservatism and extremism,[37] or the bridge between the two and the place where conservatives and extremists meet, collaborate and seek to make an impact.[38] While it is clearly important to undertake the work of locating the New Right as a point on a continuum between democratic conservatism and antidemocratic extremism the hinge or bridge image is offered as a way of capturing the more complex reality of how networks of people, groups, organisations and publishers operate, establishing links with extremism at one point and moving towards the political centre at another.[39] The fact that such collaboration occurs is seen as proof of the 'erosion of the barrier' between democratic conservatism and the extreme right.[40] Minkenberg rightly sees the New Right as providing 'a crucial link between established conservatism and the openly anti-democratic extremists on the right by radicalising conservative positions on the one hand, and legitimising extreme right positions on the other'.[41]

If New Right intellectuals complicate the task of defining the movement by their avoidance of political programmes, is the task any easier when it comes to classifying political parties? Gessenharter sees the NPD, Deutsche Volksunion (DVU) and the Republikaner, as the incarnation of New Right ideology at party level.[42] This categorisation is disputed by many observers who see the Republikaner together with the Deutsche Volksunion as belonging to the Old Right.[43] Nevertheless there are more examples of collaboration between the Republikaner and prominent individuals or groups who are generally acknowledged as belonging to the New Right than between the two other parties and the New Right. Gessenharter points out that the New Right journal *Criticón* showed sympathy for the Republikaner when they gained seats in the Berlin Parliament.[44] At various points New Right journals have seen the Republikaner as having the potential to become the party political wing of the New Right. But it is clear that the New Right is more often than not removed from party politics, seeing itself as the provider of ideas and the catalyst for debate, and it was striking how the most prominent New Right journals and newspapers conspicuously avoided endorsing any one party in the run-up to the 2005 Federal elections. For this reason recent research has defined the New Right as a movement which cannot be understood in terms of traditional organisations.[45] It has been described as a particular set of journals and cultural projects, individuals and groups who spread ideas and exert their influence on traditional organisations and parties.[46] While this definition may be rather broad and loose it is particularly important for the purposes of interpretation since it underlines the fact that the New Right is a constellation of political journalists, philosophers, writers, academics and politicians rather than a purely political movement.

The problems of the New Right already demonstrated encourage observers to dismiss it as relatively unimportant: Stöss argues that the New Right has no coherent ideology but is rather composed of intellectuals with very different views. This makes it highly unlikely that it will ever emerge as a significant political force. Moreover, the views that are expressed by some of the most prominent names associated with the New Right could scarcely be described as nationalistic: 'They raise the issue of the "Federal Republic's commitment to the West" without fundamentally calling this commitment into question or offering any alternative, and they talk about a "shift eastwards" for the Federal Republic without drawing any conclusions for the "national question"'. Stöss registers a moderately critical stance on Europe, a call for more effective measures to combat crime, stricter policies on asylum, and law and order, but he concludes that these points hardly differ from what the right in the German Bundestag has to offer. New Right figures are just a little more authoritarian, a little more xenophobic, racist, and keen on the State than their political friends in the mainstream conservative parties. Stöss concludes that this does not add up to a rebirth of nationalist thinking, nor does it threaten democracy.[47] For others, however, the very overlap with mainstream conservatism, particularly when it came to the reform of the Federal Republic's laws on asylum, is a possible sign of a triumph of the New Right,[48] and others quote Edmund Stoiber, the Bavarian Minister-President and CSU Chairman, on the 'German people undergoing a mixing up of the races' and German newspapers and magazines on the 'flood of asylum-seekers' as examples of what they regard as further New Right successes in stretching the limits of public discourse.[49]

The latter assessment of the New Right relies on a causality in political influence which is difficult, if not impossible to prove. More generally, both of these diametrically opposed views of the significance of the New Right emerge within a narrowly political definition of the movement. Pfahl-Traughber rightly explains, however, that the New Right is not concerned with making its mark through party politics or militant action. Rather, it is mainly intent on changing the way people think about basic political issues. It is engaged in a struggle for minds and for 'cultural hegemony'.[50] Thus we see New Right academics using their positions to promote New Right views,[51] New Right organisations running conferences and summer schools, and publishing their own journals,[52] and New Right figures who work in the media encouraging public debate on controversial issues such as remembering the Nazi past.

It is particularly in the cultural sphere that we see the full breadth of New Right thinking. The collection of essays published in 1994 under the title *Die selbstbewußte Nation* (The Confident Nation) may be generally regarded as a kind of New Right manifesto, yet it contains lengthy reflections not just on the contemporary political scene but also on the nature of existence, on religion, literature and philosophy.

This cultural dimension of the New Right is not an arbitrary addition to a political core of thought, and it has to be included in any analysis of the movement. One commentator acknowledges this dimension when he describes the movement as a 'cultural revolution of the Right'.[53] The following study will therefore consider the New Right in the round as a cultural and political movement, as a group of politicians, intellectuals, philosophers, writers, academics and journalists. This approach makes the analytical task more complicated since it must deal with the tensions and contradictions in New Right thought which multiply once one includes cultural sources that are generally more ambiguous, open-ended, and pessimistic than political pronouncements. Yet these cultural sources are inextricably bound up with the politics of the New Right, and they are often more reflective, questioning, tentative, self-analytical and self-critical than the political texts. A more inclusive approach to the New Right may lead to a more complex and subtle characterisation of the movement: far from being just a set of political positions it is the expression of a complex and contradictory mentality which nevertheless contains some basic and recurrent patterns of thought. The link between culture and politics is sometimes portrayed as the interaction between theory and practice. Stöss refers to the tense relationship between New Right intellectuals and politicians, with the theorists accusing the practitioners of having no theory and no principles, and of being too ready to compromise. These shortcomings are then presented as the reason for electoral failure. In return, the practitioners accuse the theoreticians of being remote from reality, and take what theory might be of use while keeping the intellectuals at a distance.[54] In the following study it will become clear that the intellectuals' contribution to the New Right cannot be explained simply in terms of the provision of a theoretical foundation for political action. It can in turns be critical, supportive or, at its most difficult, dismissive of all political activity.

The definition of the New Right which follows from the above discussion is a political and cultural movement which embraces individuals, groups, newspapers, journals, and organisations (including political parties). In terms of the New Right's position on the political spectrum, the absence of a clear programme plus the broad definition of what is to be included in our analysis makes it harder to arrive at a satisfactory formulation, but it is located to the right of the mainstream conservative parties which often distance themselves from it. Individuals from these parties however often collaborate with New Right groups and identify with positions that these parties reject. As it approaches the grey zone between legal radicalism and unconstitutional extremism the more innovative voices within the New Right steer clear of crude racism and aggressive nationalism, and it is these voices with which we shall be primarily concerned. On occasion the philosophical implications of arguments advanced by New Right intellectuals are discussed and given greater depth by thinkers who have little direct connection with the movement. In order to gain a better understanding of New Right thinking our study will pursue these discussions into areas that have hitherto received little or no attention from critics with an exclusively political focus.

The significance of the New Right

The images of the hinge and the bridge to describe the function and location of the New Right point to one measure of its significance: the connection between mainstream conservatism and extreme right-wing thought. Its various projects are often the result of collaboration between the more outspoken and the more moderate groups on either side of the bridge. Politicians and other members of the mainstream conservative parties contribute to New Right publications and work within New Right organisations. Contributors to *Junge Freiheit* include the CDU Bundestag members Axel Fischer, Jochen-Konrad Fromme and Klaus-Jürgen Hedrich, CDU Landtag member Rüdiger Goldmann, and CDU member of the European Parliament, Rolf Berend. The former Berlin senator, Heinrich Lummer (CDU), attended the meeting of extreme right-wing European party leaders in August 2002 in Austria, hosted by Jörg Haider. Albrecht Jebens (CDU) is also a leading member of the Gesellschaft für freie Publizistik (Society for Free Journalism) which the Office for the Protection of the Constitution describes as one of the most important cultural organisations of the extreme right. The co-editor of the New Right journal *Criticón*, Wolfram Zabel, is a member of the CDU, and the owner, Gunnar Sohn, who bought the journal from Schrenck-Notzing, also has a CDU background. Senior journalists from the conservative press and from radio and TV stations also write for New Right publications,[55] and in the academic world the New Right has many supporters: historians, political scientists, sociologists and philosophers produce work that feeds into New Right thinking even as it provides a critical commentary on the movement.[56] The New Right therefore exists not just at the fringe but also in the mainstream of political and cultural thought,[57] with a large group of intellectuals and politicians in the conservative camp who have an important role as multipliers in shaping public opinion in Germany willing to associate themselves with or indeed be part of the New Right. One commentator sees an overlap in the patterns of thought of the New Right and mainstream political culture in an increasing trend to argue in ethnic, cultural and nationalistic categories.[58] Such assessments of how New Right ideas are spreading are often based on loose terminological overlaps, however, and at most they demonstrate the need for definitions that take not just individual statements into account but which approach the New Right as a broader movement whose contours and outer limits become apparent when one examines its cultural hinterland.

It has been correctly pointed out that the New Right does not content itself with communicating within subcultures but instead seeks to reach and influence the majority.[59] In this role the New Right may be regarded as the intellectual movement which provides new ideas for the right in Germany,[60] and here we can detect a parallel between the New Right and the Conservative Revolution. Yet, as the following analysis intends to show, the New Right's significance in this role lies not in any ability to formulate a clear set of beliefs and a programme which might unite all shades of right-wing thinking, but rather in the internal debates and very public soul-searching it engages in as it sets about articulating its vision.

This feature of New Right thought goes to the heart of any discussion about the movement's significance. The New Right's importance as an object of study is bound up with its intellectual ambitions: it offers not just political slogans but also political philosophy, cultural analysis and debate, and the intellectual dimension of the New Right enables the observer to gain an insight into the thinking behind its politics.

Moreover, the New Right cultural and political spheres interact, as, for example, when intellectuals advise politicians: the figure widely regarded as the father of the German New Right, Armin Mohler, was adviser to Franz Schönhuber when Schönhuber was leader of the Republikaner. Schönhuber takes his lead from Mohler on coming to terms with the Nazi past when he describes how he wanted to take the issue out of the ivory towers inhabited by the intellectuals and onto the streets. He wanted to bring his 'old friend Armin Mohler' into the debate since Mohler had shown how the Germans were being led by the nose-ring of historical research that shaped thinking on the subject.[61] Günter Rohrmoser, Professor of Social Philosophy at the University of Hohenheim, was at one time adviser to Franz-Josef Strauß and is now a leading figure of the New Right.[62] Political figures themselves can develop their theories in New Right publications: Johanna Grund, one-time deputy leader of the Republikaner and member of the European Parliament, attacks the European Union's version of democracy in the pages of *Junge Freiheit, Staatsbriefe,* and *Nation und Europa.* As we shall see, politicians and intellectuals also interact in a revealing way when they

take up the same terms in order to set out their vision of the future
or their reasons for rejecting such a vision: concepts such as culture,
tradition, German identity, nationalism, and German values are
made to do political service by the practitioners but subjected to
more critical scrutiny by the theoreticians.

Writers, academics and journalists with New Right sympathies
have been engaged in the project of intellectualising the movement
since the seventies, and their elaborate explorations of New Right
positions enable the observer to understand the mentality of the
movement and the motives behind political commitment.[63] The
New Right embarked upon the project of intellectualising right-wing
thought in order to make its views acceptable and its political representatives electable. Yet when the New Right attempts to articulate
its non-Nazi vision for Germany and thereby gain public acceptance, there is little consensus about the contents of that vision.
The cultural pessimism of the New Right is often at odds with the
need for positive political statements, and establishing a clear distinction between New Right and Old Right thought turns out to be
an ongoing preoccupation rather than a single act of ideological
realignment.

The importance of a link between culture and politics is expressed
by New Right sources themselves in their attack on what is taken to
be a very limited understanding of politics within the mainstream
parties. The New Right promotes a different kind of politics that
claims to offer profound emotional support and fulfilment. Günter
Rohrmoser explains:

Ich glaube nicht, daß man politisch-kulturelle Probleme auf die
Dauer nur technokratisch lösen kann. Natürlich kann man sagen,
die Wählerschichten der Republikaner werden gespeist aus den
Modernitätsgeschädigten oder den Opfern der Modernitätsdefizite,
die aus mangelnder Gestaltungskraft der Politik entstanden sind.
Aber außer dieser neuen sozialen Dimension müssen wir auch
lernen, diese Schichten nicht emotional allein zu lassen. Es gibt
auch einen ganz echten emotionalen symbolischen Bedarf, daß
diese Menschen nicht völlig mit diesen schrecklichen technokratis-
chen Idioten, die wir kultivieren, allein gelassen werden.[64]
(I don't believe that we can solve political and cultural problems
in the long term by purely technocratic means. Of course one

can say that those strata of the electorate who vote for the Republikaner are replenished by those people who have been damaged by Modernity or by the victims of the shortcomings of Modernity which have come about because of the inability of politics to provide structure. But regardless of this new social dimension we also have to learn not to leave these people alone emotionally. It is vital for emotional and symbolic reasons that we do not abandon them entirely to these terrible technocratic idiots that we cultivate).

Expressed more generally, the New Right is engaged in a political and cultural response to Modernity. In this response it finds its inspiration not only in the work of political thinkers but also in philosophy. On occasion the political and cultural dimensions of New Right thought seem to support each other, as when New Right author Karlheinz Weißmann takes up Ernst Jünger's view that nationalism can follow on from nihilism to fill the gap left by the collapse of belief in progress.[65] There is also a clear parallel between the New Right perceptions of political and existential chaos.

The New Right commitment to the process of intellectualisation enables the observer to understand the internal dynamics of New Right thought, for embracing culture means embracing 'functionality' and 'dysfunctionality'. In his reflections on whether modern culture undermines or supports existence, the sociologist Zygmunt Bauman concludes that it does both:

> Zwanghafte Negation ist die Positivität der modernen Kultur. Die Dysfunktionalität der modernen Kultur ist ihre Funktionalität. Der Kampf der modernen Mächte um eine künstliche Ordnung bedarf der Kultur, die die Grenzen und Beschränkungen der Macht der Künstlichkeit erkundet. Der Kampf um Ordnung belebt jene Erforschung und wird seinerseits durch ihre Ergebnisse belebt. In diesem Prozeß verliert der Kampf seine anfängliche Hybris: seine aus Naivität und Ignoranz geborene Streitsucht. Er lernt statt dessen mit seiner eigenen Permanenz, seiner Ergebnislosigkeit – und seiner Aussichtslosigkeit zu leben.[66]
> (Obsessive negation is the positive feature of modern culture. The dysfunctionality of modern culture is its functionality. The

struggle of modern forces to create an artificial order requires culture to probe the limits and limitations of the powers of artificial creation. The struggle for order informs that probing, and is in turn informed by what the probing reveals. In this process the struggle loses its initial hybris: its urge to engage in conflict born of a blend of naïveté and ignorance. Instead, it learns to live with its own permanence, its own lack of results and its own futility).

Bauman thus views culture in Modernity as an exploring, questioning force that may be informed by a struggle to create order but may also demonstrate that there can be no end to this struggle. Hermann Glaser makes a similar case when he examines how the concept of 'cultural authenticity' acknowledges the fragility of one's identity. This 'authentic identity' is at odds with dogmatism and ideological simplification. Culture is characterised by its lack of certainty and its tendency to find questions rather than answers:

> Kultur ist voller Fragwürdigkeiten und Verunsicherungen, voller Antinomien, Ambivalenzen und Aporien. Sie schafft nicht fix-und-fertige Lösungen, sondern macht, dem Geschwindigkeitssog wie den Appellen zur Übereinstimmung sich entziehend, aus Lösungen immer wieder Probleme. ... Kultur hat stets das Doppelgesicht von *clair-obscur*, von hell-dunkel.[67]
> (Culture is full of doubts and challenges to certainty, full of antinomies, ambivalence, and aporias. It does not come up with ready solutions to problems, but rather it resists the speeding maelstrom and the appeal for harmony, and makes problems out of solutions... Culture always presents the two faces of *clair-obscur*, of light and dark.)

These general propositions about the nature of modern culture can be applied to the New Right. The search for absolute values through culture is without a doubt one of the deeper structures of New Right thinking. As we shall see, however, New Right culture does not provide a simple and reassuring message. The move within the New Right towards what one observer calls 'culturalisation of politics', ie the re-presentation of political issues in cultural terms, is also a move towards greater dysfunctionality.[68]

Cultural theorists such as Bauman suggest that modern society actually benefits from having its beliefs challenged in the cultural sphere:

Die Geschichte der Moderne ist eine Geschichte der Spannung zwischen gesellschaftlicher Existenz und ihrer Kultur. Die moderne Existenz zwingt ihre Kultur in eine Opposition zu sich selbst. Diese Disharmonie ist genau die Harmonie, deren die Moderne bedarf.[69]

(The history of modern times is a history of the tension between social existence and its culture. Modern existence forces its culture to oppose it. This disharmony is precisely the harmony that Modernity requires.)

In this study we shall examine the painful gap between what the New Right needs and expects from its culture and what it actually gets. In recent years research on the New Right has started to emphasise the importance of the cultural or pre-political sphere and to direct attention towards its cultural complexity.[70] This echoes earlier calls in historical research to 'give ideas their due'.[71] Cultural complexity is to be found not least within and between the philosophical, literary, political and journalistic texts produced by the New Right. The historian John Pocock considers the potential for texts to perform complex functions: 'we have been giving all our attention to thought as conditioned by social facts outside itself and not enough of our attention to thought as denoting, referring, assuming, alluding, implying, and as performing a variety of functions of which the simplest is that of containing and conveying information'.[72] Homing in on language, he argues that 'the paradigms which order "reality" are part of the reality they order, ...language is part of the social structure and not epiphenomenal to it, and...we are studying an aspect of reality when we study the ways in which it appeared real to the persons to whom it was more real than to anyone else'.[73] Similarly, Robert Darnton points out that historians are becoming more interested in showing 'how thought organized experience and conveyed meaning among the general citizenry'.[74] 'Ordering reality' and 'organising experience' are clearly part of the New Right project, and at the level of political texts the ordering and organising are designed to win over an audience to a view of society in decline and disorder and to gain support for a set of supposed remedies. Other types of New Right sources order reality and organise experience very differently, however, and Pocock's 'variety of functions' manifests itself as an illuminating set of tensions. Coming from a background in intellectual history, Dominick LaCapra refers to the historians' habit of reducing sources to mere documents and not paying sufficient attention to the ambiguous structure of complex texts.[75] This point is highly relevant for any study of the New Right since ambiguity is at the heart of its thinking. The New Right is a rewarding object of study not least because it presents a wide variety of related sources on major issues facing Germany today. If social scientists have used the more straightforwardly political sources in order to characterise the movement, it is the ambition of this study to probe the thought processes which feed into New Right attitudes by embracing and analysing a broader mix of sources.

This ambition is informed not least by the long-running discussion about the 'cultural turn'. David Chaney argues that 'culture and a number of related concepts have become simultaneously both the dominant topic and most productive intellectual resource in ways that lead us to rewrite our understanding of life in the modern world'.[76] This study of the New Right makes no claim on such a scale, but it does seek to make full use of culture as an intellectual resource, and it adopts what has been called the distinctive feature of the research undertaken by historians and sociologists in the wake of the cultural turn: what Bonnell and Hunt refer to as an 'attentiveness to culture'.[77]

2
From Cultural Hegemony to Cultural Pessimism

New Right politics and the project of cultural hegemony

After the NPD's failure in the Bundestag elections of 1969 the more innovative sections of the extreme right set in motion the process generally referred to as the intellectualisation of the right, and this process marked the birth of the New Right. The New Right took up the theories of the Italian communist Antonio Gramsci on the need to achieve 'cultural hegemony' in society before one can expect political success. This means achieving acceptance in civil society, particularly in the education system, the media and mass culture. The New Right thus aims to change the parameters of public debate by discussing issues which are seen as undiscussable, and drawing others into the discussion. In the late sixties and early seventies the New Right concentrated on marking itself off from National Socialism as the first step to gaining wider acceptance. In more recent years it has concentrated on gaining acceptance for an assertive nationalism in which the memory of National Socialism is outweighed by anti-Nazi elements of Germany's past, on setting out German values which are distinctive and in need of protection from multi-culturalism, and winning support for its views within the political mainstream.

Since the 1980s it has been Alain de Benoist, the leading intellectual of the French New Right, who has insisted on the importance of cultural hegemony, and his work has been introduced to the German public by Armin Mohler. Mohler wrote the introduction to de Benoist's *Kulturrevolution von rechts* (Cultural Revolution from the Right) when it appeared in West Germany in 1985, and he mocked

the German right for being behind the times and failing to provide
itself with an intellectual foundation:

Ein zu großer Teil ihrer (the right's) Anhänger versteift sich in
einer markigen Trotzhaltung und hat sich geistig in einen kom-
fortablen Winterschlaf zurückgezogen, der etwas zu lange dauert.
Nur zu oft ist ein burschenhafter Anti-Intellektualismus die
Ausrede, mit der man um die fatal Tatsache herumzukommen
sucht, daß der Geist die Welt regiert.[1]
(Too many of the right's supporters are insisting on all-out
defiance and have withdrawn intellectually into a comfortable
hibernation that has been going on for rather too long. All too
often a boorish anti-intellectualism is the unconvincing response
to the awkward fact that the intellect rules the world).

De Benoist himself insists that action without ideas cannot succeed,
and he makes it clear that the French right is also having to face up
to the challenge of gaining 'cultural power': the 'drama of the right'
– from putschists to moderates – is its inability to realise that long-
term planning is essential. It has not appreciated the importance of
Gramsci's point that cultural power can threaten the state by
influencing the consensus that underpins political power.[2]

De Benoist sees the right either as a collection of splinter groups
or as parliamentary groups preoccupied with the next round of elections. Between them they are steadily losing ground, and for de
Benoist no revolutionary change of political power can happen if it
has not already happened in people's minds.[3] He explains Gramsci's
view that the state exercises control not just through the state appa-
ratus but also through an 'implied ideology' which is based on
values held by the majority. These values are expressed through
culture, ideas, morals, tradition and what is held to be common
sense in any given society. In all these spheres, which are not
directly political, a power is at work to support the state: cultural
power.[4] Seeing Gramsci's views on how to bring about a socialist
society as readily transferable to the right's purposes, de Benoist
explains why achieving power is a lengthy process:

Nach Gramscis Ansicht läßt sich der 'Übergang zum Sozialismus'
in einer entwickelten Gesellschaft weder über einen Putsch noch

über die direkte Auseinandersetzung, wohl aber über die Transformation der allgemeinen Vorstellungen bewerkstelligen, die mit einer langsamen Umformung der Geister gleichbedeutend ist. Und der Einsatz in diesem Stellungskrieg ist die Kultur.[5] (According to Gramsci the 'transition to socialism' cannot be brought about in any developed society by means of a putsch or direct conflict, but it can be brought about by means of a gradual transformation of general attitudes which means a slow transforming of people's minds. And it is culture that is deployed in this war of position).

De Benoist declares that intellectuals today are in a strong position to exercise power. The growth of leisure time, much of which is occupied by cultural activity, and the susceptibility of the public to a 'metapolitical message' provide the starting point. The message, argues de Benoist, is all the more effective and meets with a more favourable reception if its prescriptive and suggestive nature is not clearly recognised. If it is recognised it is more likely to meet with the same kind of rational and conscious resistance that greets an overtly political message. De Benoist sees the process at work in plays, novels, films, and television programmes which are politically all the more influential if they are not immediately recognised as political. They can bring about a gradual shift in people's minds from one set of values to another.[6]

It is clear to see the appeal of this brand of cultural persuasion for the German New Right. Armed with a message that is either unclear or likely to meet with resistance from large sections of the population, it is offered the chance of bypassing rational debate. Significantly, it is Armin Mohler who is responsible for introducing de Benoist's ideas to the German New Right, for it was Mohler who put forward a similar view in his assessment of fascism as a movement whose ideas did not have to add up. Rather, ideas were a mobilising force which were not meant to be analysed.[7]

De Benoist maps out a very specific strategy for taking power in a pluralist society. He points out that liberal Western regimes are by their very nature ill-equipped to counter the infiltration and transformation of people's minds. Indeed, they possess no weapons to stop this. Liberal powers are prisoners of their own principles, guaranteeing free competition between all ideologies, including subversive

ones. The State may ban the possession of arms or the use of explo-
sives, but it has more difficulty in banning a book or a play since it
does not want to be seen restricting freedom of expression, even if
these may be effective weapons directed against it.[8] De Benoist's militant tone is generally not copied in Germany, but the idea of an
intellectual vanguard certainly is. The German New Right has a presence in all the pre-political areas noted by de Benoist: the media,
culture, education. Yet it is also clear that much New Right activity
in these areas is not in the mainstream: although some New Right
figures write for the conservative press, the most outspoken New
Right journalism is to be found in its own non-mainstream papers
and journals. And as we shall show, although the cultural output of
prominent right-wing intellectuals may sometimes serve New Right
political needs, it is just as often at odds with any simple New Right
political message.

Success and failure

The German New Right shows how seriously it takes de Benoist's
message about cultural hegemony by returning time and again to
the need for parties and theoreticians to work together on an intellectual foundation. Gessenharter has convincingly shown how the
so-called *Deutschlandrat* (Council for Germany), which included
many New Right intellectuals, had the ideas it published in journals such as *Mut* in the 1980s taken up by the Republikaner in the
Siegburger Manifest (Siegburg Manifesto), the party's first political
programme of June 1985.[9] Gessenharter also quotes the North
Rhine-Westphalia chairman of the Republikaner saying: 'While the
New Right uses its resources to work out a new model for society
we Republikaner shall convert the theory into politics'.[10] In the
1980s it was common practice for the Republikaner to refer to
themselves as a New Right party,[11] and New Right intellectuals
such as Karl-Heinz Weißmann in turn saw the Republikaner as
potential partners. The NPD has also attempted to engage in the
process of intellectualisation, setting out its 'three pillars' in terms
which indicate an awareness of the need for more than political
slogans: 'fighting for the streets, fighting for parliament and
fighting for people's minds'.[12] *Junge Freiheit* acknowledged these
efforts when it registered a shift in NPD thinking away from 'gut

instinct' and flag-waving, which merely alienated most people, and towards intellectual debate.[13] Out of the many journals that sprang up and attached themselves to the project of shaping a New Right one of the most important was *Criticón*, founded in 1970 as a forum for conservative and New Right intellectuals.[14] Its contents are a mixture of culture and politics, and they are aimed at other intellectuals rather than a mass audience. What it offers at the most general cultural level are glimpses of an alternative, undemocratic order, conveyed indirectly by reference to a German tradition of anti-democratic thought, mainly embodied by the Conservative Revolution and its 'mentor', Friedrich Nietzsche. A simplified Nietzsche is very useful to the New Right, and his attack on democracy is seized upon and quoted at length: 'Who wants to rule? Who wants to obey? Both are too much trouble. No herdsman, just a herd! Everyone wants the same thing, everyone is the same'.[15] For anyone familiar with Nietzsche, and most New Right intellectuals are, his critique of democracy brings its opposite to mind: his praise for the self-assertive noble races, including the Germanic race.[16] The reader is meant to continue the line of thought, but not so far that Nietzsche's criticism of nationalism or his doubts about the self-assertiveness of noble races come to mind, or the fact that he saw no link whatsoever between the ancient Germanic race and the Germans of his day.[17]

One striking feature of the New Right is its drive to set up cultural and political think tanks in order to achieve its goal of cultural hegemony. In 1980 Pierre Krebs, together with a group of young writers and journalists, founded the Thule Seminar in Kassel. At a time, as Krebs puts it, when political parties were multiplying it was necessary to establish a 'party of the mind', a 'school for metapolitics'. This school would deal in philosophies and provide the cultural foundations for political initiatives.[18] Krebs proudly reported in the late eighties that after seven years his school had produced four groundbreaking books, given 200 lectures in Germany and abroad and provided the foundations for a new culture.[19] The Thule Seminar also has its own journal, *Elemente*, modelled on the French New Right's *éléments*, and de Benoist has been a frequent contributor to it. More recently the Thule Seminar has been joined by the Institut für Staatspolitik, founded in 2000 and headed by Karlheinz Weißmann and Götz Kubitschek. The Institute has a programme of publications, public lectures, seminars and summer schools for students, and its own journal, *Sezession*. It covers issues ranging from war, education, population crisis, globalisation, decadence, immigration, the role of the state, but it also organises discussions of strategies for reaching a wide audience through its publications and media work.[20] Commentators have claimed that the New Right has chalked up some notable successes. Gessenharter gives as an example the different fates of Philipp Jenninger and Steffen Heitmann. In 1988 Jenninger had resigned as President of the Bundestag when his party failed to stand by him after his speech to the Bundestag on the fiftieth anniversary of the November 1938 pogroms in which he failed to distance himself clearly enough from the Nazi terms he used. In 1993, however, the CDU supported Heitmann as their candidate for the office of President of the Federal Republic although he had spoken in an interview about the 'foreignisation of the German people' and declared that he was expressing a view shared by many Germans. Gessenharter argues that standards had shifted over the intervening five years and that this shift reflected a wider development in the political culture of Germany over a period of two decades. Gessenharter sees the New Right as a key actor in this process.[21] He also sees *Junge Freiheit*'s themes cropping up in the mainstream papers *Die Welt* and *Frankfurter Allgemeine Zeitung*, and he concludes that the New Right has made considerable headway in the German media.[22] Greß argues that the activities of the New Right are designed to 'cross the cordon sanitaire that had been erected as a supposedly clear dividing line between extremist subcultures and mainstream public discourse by extending the limits of this discourse'.[23] If we locate the New Right between these two poles there are indeed signs of an erosion both in the direction of conservatism and extremism. Hajo Funke quotes Friedrich Zimmermann, CDU Minister of the Interior in 1983, arguing that living together without conflict will only be possible if the number of foreigners in West Germany is limited and in the longer term reduced, especially the number of Turks. Zimmermann repeatedly refers to a threat to German homogeneity.[24] The New Right sees its task as 'reminding the conservative parties in Germany what conservatism means'.[25] New Right authors themselves are eager to point out the overlaps with mainstream parties: Günter Rohrmoser regards Republikaner statements on foreigners in the eighties as almost identical to those made by the CDU in an election campaign of the time.[26] In the other direction Gessenharter sees New Right links with right-wing extremism and even neo-nazism in the work of the Studienzentrum Weikersheim which has guest speakers such as Hans Dietrich Sander, editor of *Staatsbriefe*, for which the neo-nazi Michael Kühnen had written.[27] Funke sees a New Right link with extremism in the 'Bogenhauser Gespräche' (Bogenhaus Discussions), organised by the Munich-based student corporation *Danubia* where extreme right-wing views are aired and links with violent neo-nazis have been investigated.[28]

Yet while there are clear signs of an organisational network which can embrace the two poles of extremism and conservatism and which has a strong input from New Right thinkers, it is not possible to attribute the creation of this network to the New Right. Moreover, ideological overlaps between more outspoken conservatives and the extreme right are nothing new, and the terms in which these overlaps are expressed tend to be vague and in common usage.

A further complicating factor in the discussion about an erosion of the barrier between the extreme right and conservatism is the fact that it is not possible to set out definitively what the New Right stands for. The point becomes clear when one looks at Jörg Schönbohm (CDU), Deputy Prime Minister and Minister of the Interior for Brandenburg, who, commentators have suggested, makes use of New Right models in his thinking.[29] His nationalism and his view that there are too many foreigners in Germany are said to show him building bridges in the direction of the right.[30] Apart from the fact that Schönbohm is airing views that are too common to be ascribed to the New Right in particular, his positive commitment to nationalist values tends, if anything, to mark him off from a New Right hesitancy to commit to simple nationalism. Whereas Schönbohm embraces a national identity made up of German culture, history and language,[31] these are the very values with which New Right thinkers have so much trouble. The idea of Germany as a 'confident nation' may be close to Schönbohm's heart,[32] but the New Right contributors to the volume of that very title actually demonstrate their lack of confidence in their own project. Schönbohm may look with envy at the national pride in evidence in the USA where schoolchildren sing the national anthem each morning,[33] yet his brand of nationalism is at odds with the more complex and self-critical line taken by many New Right intellectuals who cannot themselves manage a simple commitment to the nation.

Schönbohm may adhere to Carl Schmitt's ideal of a national identity based on a 'homogeneity within', and in so doing he is certainly taking up one strand of New Right thought.[34] But the theory of an erosion of the barrier between the extreme right and conservatism tends to disregard the ambiguity and uncertainty within the New Right about precisely what values the New Right can espouse. The ambiguity and uncertainty are reflected in the New Right's pessimistic view that the attempt to intellectualise the movement and gain cultural hegemony is likely to end in failure. If the project of intellectualisation of the right started in the seventies, its spokesmen are still registering failure some 30 years later: just as Bublies had described the NPD leadership in the seventies as mainly made up of 'political illiterates', Karlheinz Weißmann accuses today's German right of being 'illiterate' and repeats with a minor update on political correctness what his predecessors were saying in earlier decades: anyone who believes he stands for the right ideas because of his origins and his common sense will see little point in concerning himself with theoretical matters, but in a pluralist society values are determined by the person who has attained 'cultural hegemony' or who can declare what is politically correct.[35]

Weißmann sees the New Right project of intellectualisation prefigured in the work of the Freiburg historian Rudolf Stadelmann in the 1930s. In a lecture series instigated by Martin Heidegger on the 'Tasks of the Intellectual World in the National Socialist State' Stadelmann's contribution was entitled *Das geschichtliche Selbstbewußtsein der Nation* (The Historical Confidence of the Nation). Not only is the title reminiscent of the New Right volume *Die selbstbewußte Nation*, but Stadelmann's broad purpose, as Weißmann describes it, parallels that of the New Right:

> Stadelmann entwickelte die Auffassung, daß es neben einem naiven, noch ganz selbstverständlichen Selbstbewußtsein, aus dem der kollektive Stolz der Nation folgt, durchaus ein reflektiertes Selbstbewußtsein geben könne, das – ohne die bindende Kraft mythischer Vorstellungen zu zerstören und eine unmögliche

Objektivität der Betrachtung zu behaupten – in die Lage versetze, sich Rechenschaft über die Vergangenheit der Nation abzulegen und Folgerungen für die Zukunft zu ziehen.[36] (Stadelmann developed the idea that besides a naive confidence that is beyond debate and provides the foundation of a collective national pride, there can definitely also be a reflective confidence which, without destroying the binding force of myth and without claiming to offer some impossibly objective perspective, can put people in a position to answer for a nation's past and to draw conclusions for the future).

This extension of national confidence which can be taken for granted to include one which is the product of reflection is remarkably similar to the shift in right-wing thinking towards a reflective yet assertive view of Germany that the New Right is trying to bring about. In practice the New Right gets bogged down in the reflective stage of the project, unable to get beyond the questions it asks itself. Time and time again it laments its 'fragmentation', its lack of 'philosophical coherence'.[37] The German New Right journals look enviously at the electoral successes of Jörg Haider in Austria and Jean-Marie Le Pen in France and reflect on the splits in the German right which prevent it from becoming an alternative to the established parties.[38] At the start of the nineties Günter Rohrmoser criticised those political forces to the right of the conservative parties for being vulnerable to the charge of fascism. They had never made the theoretical or philosophical effort to work out the conceptual basis and the substance of a programme which would have protected them from such a charge.[39] The Republikaner were a typical one-issue party, he argued, and had not the remotest idea of what a society of the future should look like.[40] Roland Bubik finds it objectionable that the extreme right today is essentially based on personalities rather than political programmes.[41]

Henning Eichberg's letter to R on the supposed innovative potential of newspapers such as *Junge Freiheit* poses the basic question: what does the New Right stand for? What has emerged so far and what will tend to be confirmed in the rest of our study of New Right thinking is its failure to generate a coherent set of ideas once it has declared its distance from National Socialism. Eichberg is aware of this failure: in his letter he points out that the paper calls itself conservative but offers no clue about what is to be conserved. It is not green, nor is it multi-cultural. Central to its reporting is the 'image of the enemy', a sure sign for Eichberg that it has tried to make a virtue out of a necessity. In this the paper has taken Carl Schmitt as a guide: for Schmitt the enemy was always at the heart of political thought, says Eichberg, and this 'friend or foe' thinking shows that the paper cannot answer the question of what it represents and what the Right stands for. Eichberg concludes by saying that although some see *Junge Freiheit* as belonging to the New Right, all the paper has to offer is a rejuvenated version of the Old Right.[42]

Eichberg's view of a New Right which tends to fall back into Old Right ways is confirmed by *Junge Freiheit* writer Angelika Willig who agrees with the NPD leaders that it is not enough to express disgust at 'the system'; one has to offer a concrete alternative. Yet this alternative is not available and, she concludes, if it were, it would immediately come into conflict with the free democratic order or the Basic Law.[43]

As Gramsci's notion of cultural hegemony is transferred from the pre-war Italian left to the post-war French and eventually German right it acquires tactical inhibitions of the kind described by Willig, historical inhibitions at the heart of the New Right claim to have broken with National Socialism, cultural inhibitions about the very worth of politics and ideological inhibitions reflecting the internal disputes of the New Right. These inhibitions make the goal of cultural hegemony a particularly difficult one for the German New Right to achieve. In the French context de Benoist may attach an aggressive and unambiguous right-wing ideology to Gramsci's theories on how to prepare the route to power, but the German New Right takes up these theories in a more contradictory, hesitant and self-doubting manner. Gaining support in the pre-political sphere by intellectual means has to contend with the tendency to avoid articulating a message which either meets with the hostility of the majority or, as its spokesmen themselves frequently suggest, does not stand up to close scrutiny.

As we have suggested, intellectualisation is also a problem for the New Right because it involves culture. De Benoist sees two functions of culture: it can be an instrument in the hands of the state to consolidate its power or it can challenge the power of the state.[44] The New Right has a problem with this dual aspect of culture because it needs to draw on both functions. The cultural hegemony which the New Right wishes to achieve draws on the critical function of culture. Yet the New Right also looks to culture as a stabilising force from which it can expect a positive sense of German tradition. What it actually gets is a complex mixture of the two functions. The critical voice of culture is directed not only at the ideological enemy but also at the values which the New Right is meant to espouse. It is to this complex mixture that we now turn.

Feelgood culture or cultural pessimism?

Although critics have made much of the New Right's preference for strong values and traditions beyond question,[45] they do not generally place these against the background of the acute sense of loss that pervades New Right culture. The New Right is reduced to a single unambiguous voice although complex processes lie beneath its affirmations. The following analysis examines the contradictory attitudes of the New Right towards culture: at one extreme it is made to do service as the source of reassuring certainty and the foundation for political values in the midst of uncertainty and loss of direction. Culture in this role we shall call feelgood culture. At the other extreme, culture is the medium for reflecting on chaotic human experience which renders politics irrelevant. It will become apparent that whatever certainty the New Right aims to provide has to coexist with doubt and despair. Moreover, there is a causal connection between certainty and doubt. Although Habermas generally reduces the neo-conservative predecessors of the New Right to a single unambiguous voice, he raises the possibility of a more complex mentality when he describes how the 'need for affirmation that characterises a disenchanted modernity has to be satisfied by a process of reenchantment, by narrative without argument, inspirational literature, the creation of meaning, and empathic historicism'.[46] Here is an interpretation which suggests process rather than position, and it also suggests cause and effect, with a loss of certainty generating a need for reassurance. This is a highly relevant model for our understanding of the New Right, and the following analysis will examine how the need for affirmation is satisfied.

It is clear that culture can be a source of certainty for the New Right. Stefan Ulbrich expresses the reassuring version of culture when he describes it in the pages of *Junge Freiheit* as one means by which the individual establishes roots and becomes at one with oneself and with others:

Kultur ist vor allem das komplizierte Netz aus Verhaltensmustern, welches dem Menschen erlaubt, sich in dieser Welt zu orientieren und gestaltend einzugreifen. Kulturelle Identität beinhaltet Verhaltensmaßregeln genauso wie Ziele des gemeinsamen Lebens. Identität ist deshalb die Verwurzelung des eigenen bewußten Ich in einer Kultur. Es ist dieses rational schwer zu beschreibende Gefühl des Bei-sich-Seins, des Ein- und Mitklangs an gemeinsamen Überlieferungen, an Erlebnissen und Wissenserkenntnissen, an einem überindividuellen System von Werten und Normen.[47] (Above all, culture is the complex network of behaviour patterns that acts as a guide for people and enables them to shape their world. Cultural identity involves rules of behaviour and provides common goals for life. Identity is therefore the rootedness of the conscious self in a culture. It is a feeling that is hard to describe in rational terms, a feeling of being at one with oneself and of existing in harmony and sympathy with shared traditions, experiences and knowledge, of being part of a system of values and norms that is greater than the individual)

The cultural values offered by the New Right are not universal. Pierre Krebs elaborates on the specific aspect of culture in his often quoted *Das unvergängliche Erbe* (The Eternal Heritage):

Unsere Verwurzelung ist territorial, menschlich und kulturell. Territorial im ethnologischen Sinne, nämlich daß der territoriale Instinkt des Individuums in der Personalisierung eines Raumes besteht, innerhalb dessen es sich absichert, sich organisiert und sich eingewöhnt.... Menschlich im anthropologischen Sinne, nämlich, daß ein Individuum sich dann einer bestimmten Gruppe verpflichtet fühlt, wenn es sich mit Menschen, in denen es sich wiedererkennt, identifizieren kann. Kulturell im ethnologischen Sinne, nämlich daß ein Individuum sich durch die Sprache, die Bräuche und die gesellschaftlichen Verhaltensweisen der Menschen, unter denen es sich entfaltet, identifiziert.[48] (Our rootedness is territorial, human and cultural. Territorial in the ethnological sense that the territorial instinct of the individual exists through the personalisation of the space within which he establishes his security, organises himself and settles down. Human in the anthropological sense that an individual feels committed to a group when he can identify with people in whom he recognises himself. Cultural in the ethnological sense that an individual defines himself through the language, customs and social behaviour which are the setting for his development).

In this reading culture is made up of a very particular constellation of language, customs and social behaviour, and it helps the individual to develop roots and shared identity. The historian Karlheinz Weißmann uses similar imagery to convey the non-arbitrary and specific nature of culture when he argues that all proclamations of universality ignore the fact that, unlike animals, human beings do not exist in isolation but always in a particular situation which surrounds them from the start as their cultural sphere. The differences that follow from the 'existence of cultures' are not inconsiderable and cannot simply be shrugged off, because culture is man's 'second nature'.[49] New Right feelgood culture is thus not a random collection of values but rather the sphere in which the individual has a fixed place. Culture is also a plural, non-universalist concept that provides the contents of an exclusive national identity. Pierre Krebs sees identity as rooted in culture, with the right to be different depending on the right to one's culture.[50] Ex-Bundestag member and New Right author Alfred Mechtersheimer takes these arguments one step further by seeing culture as the shared foundation for a political position:

National bezieht sich auf die Nation, das heißt auf eine Willensgemeinschaft von Menschen, die neben ihrem Recht auf Gemeinsamkeit ihr 'Recht auf Unterschied'... politisch in Anspruch nehmen. Das Gemeinsame eines Volkes mag einmal mehr auf Kultur, Sprache, Religion oder Geschichte beruhen; die Nation manifestiert sich erst in einem politischen Bewußtsein der gemeinsamen Wertvorstellungen und Intentionen und der Selbstbehauptung... Offenkundig befriedigt die Nation das soziale Grundbedürfnis des Menschen nach Zugehörigkeit in besonders intensiver Weise.[51]
(National refers to the nation, that is to say to a community based on a political act of will by people who are laying claim not just to

their right to a shared identity but also to their right to be different. What a people has in common may be culture, language, religion or history; the nation manifests itself properly in a political consciousness of common values, intentions and a wish to prevail. It is clear that the nation satisfies in a particularly profound way the basic social need of people for a sense of belonging).

Mechtersheimer's points have a slightly different feel to them, with the wish for rootedness at their heart. His understanding of the link between culture and politics is different from Ulbrich's view of shared and unshakable cultural traditions and values. It is different also from Weißmann's view of culture as 'second nature' which one cannot shrug off. For Mechtersheimer culture is one potential focal point for bringing a nation together. The community based on an act of will indicates not an automatic and irrevocable belonging but rather a conscious commitment, a decision behind the concept of the nation. The need for absolute bonds and a sense of belonging comes first in Mechtersheimer's thinking, and the nation comes second as a means of satisfying the need.

The themes of rootedness and exclusive national identity are to be found in the work of Alain de Benoist. Although his work has often been quoted by the German New Right for its innovative thinking, when it comes to culture he is clearly in the feelgood camp. In the 'Verwurzelung' (Rootedness) chapter of his *Cultural Revolution from the Right* he writes that most living beings are in a state of ecological dependence: there is a close connection between their achievements, their potential for growth and the presence or absence of a specific environment to which they are adapted. Outside this natural environment they perish.[52] For human beings the commitment to one's natural environment may take the form of nationalism or regional identity, and he detects a revival of this commitment:

> Allerorten Wiedererwachen der Regionen und unaufhörlich neuauflebende Nationalismen. Mögen diese Bestrebungen begründet sein oder nicht, eines steht fest: Die Menschen, wer immer sie seien und wo immer sie leben, sind mit einem Land, mit einem Stück Erde verbunden, das sie als das ihre ansehen; sie sind bereit, für die Erhaltung seiner Unabhängigkeit und seiner Integrität zu kämpfen.[53]

(Everywhere a reawakening of the regions and relentlessly reemerging nationalisms. These efforts may or may not be well founded, but one thing is certain: whoever they are and wherever they live, people are bound to a country, to a piece of earth which they regard as theirs; they are willing to fight to preserve its independence and its integrity).

Part of the feelgood culture for de Benoist is continuity and tradition: people are bound to the piece of earth where they are born. When they die they will return to this earth, and their achievements will be remembered by those who come after them. For de Benoist a comforting notion of tradition is still intact.[54]

The politics of Modernity

For the New Right Modernity is the opposite of this feelgood culture: it means the dissolution of cultural bonds and a lack of rootedness, and it is associated with liberalism and social democracy. Conservatism is the counterforce which preserves culture and history, as explained by Alexander Gauland in *Criticón*: unlike liberals and social democrats, conservatives insist on preserving the forces that maintain society's equilibrium. Anything that slows down the rate of decay is therefore right and proper: tradition and myth, confessions of faith and cultures, ethnic groups and borders. Even prejudice has its place for Gauland, as long as it does not tip over into violence or racism, since it can be a force for stability. Modernity is only tolerable, he declares, if those who are homeless in economic terms find compensation in the security of culture and history. The conservative, he concludes, cannot therefore be in favour of treating neighbour and stranger alike; he has to favour his own community over outsiders.[55]

The New Right sees the culture of Modernity as characterised by a 'creative destruction' that leaves humankind without fixed points to guide its thoughts and actions. There is no 'unchanging store of customs and habits, institutions and symbols, signposts and cultural landmarks to which we can turn for guidance and reassurance that we are doing things right'.[56]

The collection of essays by the younger generation of the New Right, *Wir 89er* (We 89ers), largely fails as a statement of positive

New Right ideas, yet it succeeds in conveying the profound unease associated with Modernity. Simone Satzger asserts the impossibility of creating a sense of community between people when all norms of behaviour are called into question. The individual no longer feels part of a greater whole. This has given greater freedom to the individual, but the consequences are isolation, indifference towards others, and selfishness. Liberal society is without a clear hierarchy of values, and the relativisation of all values renders people incapable of action. Authority, discipline, and order, which she regards as the pillars of any functioning community, have gone out of fashion. The social isolation she describes tips over into an existential desire for some kind of philosophical unity as she expresses her distaste for a world without myth, heroism, or transcendence. People want to sacrifice themselves for a belief in order to find meaning and purpose.[57] Despite its lack of subtlety this collection of essays does convey the political and existential unease that runs through New Right thinking, and one gains an insight into thought processes that are characterised by a sense of loss and the need for bonds.

The philosopher Günter Figal is one of the figures on the periphery of the New Right who has written at length about the threat posed by Modernity in a way that reflects New Right perceptions. Modernity, he argues, is characterised by change, and he sees Friedrich Nietzsche as one of the first thinkers to register this.[58] The pace of change means that it cannot be understood within any existing framework. Moreover, although change presents us with greater choice it also makes us more dependent:

> Irgendwann wird klar, daß man Veränderungen nicht nur bewirkt, sondern daß man ihnen auch unterworfen ist. Die veränderbare Welt ist zugleich die Welt, in der man selbst unübersehbaren Veränderungen unterliegt. So ist man in den Wirbel eines Geschehens geraten, in dem es keinen festen und zuverlässigen Halt gibt. Die Welt läßt sich auf keinen letzten Grund zurückführen. Vielmehr unterliegt sie, wie Nietzsche es einmal nennt, dem 'souveränen Werden'.[59]
> (Sooner or later it becomes clear that we do not just bring about change; we are subject to change. The changeable world is also the world in which we are the objects of undeniable change. We are caught up in the vortex of events and there are no fixed or

reliable points. The world cannot be taken back to some ultimate foundation. Rather it is subject to, as Nietzsche once called it, a 'sovereign becoming').

Here Modernity is interpreted essentially as an attack on New Right feelgood culture: New Right rootedness contrasts with an absence of rootedness and fixed points in Modernity. Figal quotes Nietzsche's critique of the notion of progress which the latter sees as no more than an attempt to present the changes that go with Modernity as meaningful. The idea of progress suggests than humankind is the expression of a 'development towards something better or stronger or higher'. For Nietzsche this is a 'modern' and a 'wrong idea': it embraces change but misunderstands its nature. Change is robbed of its full potential when it is reduced to a development from bad to good. Despite its commitment to freedom and emancipation this progressive characterisation of Modernity is trapped in narrow modes of thought. For this reason Nietzsche dismisses the Enlightenment itself as 'a wrong idea'.[60]

The political consequences of cultural bonds are set out with great regularity but little consistency in New Right publications. Karlheinz Weißmann quotes from an article written in 1927 by the Conservative Revolutionary Friedrich Hielscher. To the East of Germany, says Hielscher, lie the lands of culture. This culture has deep roots and a permanence lacking in the West. Germany also possesses a great culture and is therefore a brother to these lands which sustain noble and powerful traditions.[61]

The more philosophical New Right sources tend to look to the traditional conservative opposition between German culture and Western civilisation, but at the level of political parties feelgood culture is associated with the West: the 2002 party programme of the Republikaner proclaims Germany as one of the 'great cultural nations' of the world, and this culture provides the Christian and Western foundations for state and society. Its principles shape our views on the family, marriage, protection of the unborn child, and they are the force behind the drive for freedom, democracy and social justice. This culture is endangered not by Modernity, as is argued by the intellectuals of the New Right, but rather by multi-culturalism.[62] From the publishing house owned by Gerhard Frey, leader of the DVU, the *National-Zeitung* argues that European cultures are based on a mixture of 'Germanic, Christian and Roman civilisation'.[63] The NPD sees nations as the guardians of cultures, but sees multi-cultural societies as incapable of producing culture. At best they can have a civilisation which is based on purely material values.[64] The New Right contribution to the debate about the need for a so-called German *Leitkultur* (dominant culture), sparked off in October 2000 when Friedrich Merz, leader of the CDU/CSU parliamentary group in the Bundestag used the term 'dominant culture of Germany' to describe what values immigrants coming to Germany should subscribe to, is confused: one strand of New Right thought contributes a conventional sense of an external threat from other cultures,[65] yet this is scarcely compatible with Botho Strauß's reflection on an elitist 'Leitkultur' that goes back to the poet Stefan George, is located in a secret zone far removed from the politics of the day, and is useless for purposes of political mobilisation: 'The only Germany that is fit to provide a dominant culture would be the "secret Germany", not just George's secret Germany but one that is permanently hidden, and only to be found by the person who takes the path of poetic emigration. At any time and under any regime'.[66] With National Socialism in mind Strauß declares that Thomas Mann was the last writer to live in the tradition of the secret Germany: Mann lived within an unbroken tradition that extended from Hartmann von Aue in medieval times to Wagner and Schönberg in the modern period.[67] For Strauß this uncomplicated attachment to cultural tradition is now blocked by the memory of National Socialism, however, and in order to describe today's compromised attachment to German culture he uses the baroque allegory of the *Frau Welt* (World as Woman) who is beautiful when viewed from the front. Her back, however, is 'eaten away and writhing with snakes'.[68]

The New Right's need for cultural rootedness is matched by its need for fixed points in the sphere of politics. Karlheinz Weißmann draws directly on the work of Arnold Gehlen who had described the benefits of political institutions having a religious foundation. Although the link between religion and politics has now been broken, argues Weißmann, political institutions need to have more than a merely practical function, and on this point he quotes Gehlen enthusiastically:

'Das Wesentliche einer dauerhaften Institution ist ihre Überdeterminiertheit: sie muß nicht nur im nächsten, praktischen Sinne zweckmäßig und nützlich sein, sie muß auch Anknüpfungspunkt und Verhaltensunterstützung höherer Interessen sein, ja den anspruchsvollsten und edelsten Motivationen noch Daseinsrecht und Daseinschancen geben: dann erfüllt sie die tiefen vitalen, aber auch geistigen Bedürfnisse der Menschen nach Dauer, Gemeinsamkeit und Sicherheit – sie kann sogar etwas wie Glück erreichbar machen, wenn dieses darin besteht, im Über-Sich-Hinauswachsen nicht allein zu bleiben.'[69] ('The essential feature of a lasting institution is its overdetermined nature: it does not just have to be fit for purpose and useful in an immediate practical sense, it must also offer a connection to and support for our behaviour from higher interests, it must grant our most ambitious and noble motives the right to exist and the opportunity to prevail. If it does this it will meet people's profound physical and spiritual need for permanence, community and security – it can even make something like happiness achievable where this means growing beyond oneself and not remaining alone.').

Weißmann uses Gehlen's term 'unquestioning comfort' to suggest that such institutions can have a stabilising function and create a harmonious mentality.[70] This is the mentality Habermas seeks to capture with the concept of traditions beyond question in his critique of neo-conservatism, but Weißmann presents it here as an ideal rather than a reality. Weißmann argues that Gehlen's thinking could once more become relevant in the light of current trends: people are now talking about the 'end of individualism, and about the need to strengthen the community and convince the individual that he must work for that community'. He also detects a 'secret longing for drill' among young people, warnings against permissiveness and calls for an elite.[71]

In Weißmann's mobilisation of Gehlen we start to see what kind of society the New Right seeks to establish: self-criticism as a key component of public life should give way to self-assurance. The individual should take second place to the community, and this community should be organised as a disciplined hierarchy.

The call for a form of politics that will meet the most profound spiritual needs of humankind emerges as one of the chief characteristics of the New Right. Weißmann's enthusiasm for political institutions that have more than a purely practical purpose finds a parallel in Roland Bubik's enthusiasm for a blend of politics and religion. Bubik argues that the conservative does not resort to Utopian thinking in the search for new foundations. The liberal principle of freedom has destroyed all sources of authority, eliminated all bonds, and removed God from his throne. Emancipation has led only to a chilling isolation and chaos. In this situation a young conservatism seeks to reestablish bonds and to resume the 'search for transcendence', and Bubik has no doubt that the new foundation for this brand of conservatism throughout Europe is Christianity.[72]

Yet religion is far from being a stable foundation for the New Right. We have seen how Günter Rohrmoser regards people who vote for the Republikaner as the victims of Modernity.[73] The mainstream parties have lost their power to integrate citizens, and the old political methods and concepts no longer suffice. Writing in 1990, he quotes the SPD's Peter Glotz, on how his party lost political power after it had lost intellectual and cultural hegemony in the mid-1970s.[74] In a reference to the very development that Weißmann had noted in his study of Gehlen, Rohrmoser sees a religious renaissance which the CDU failed to harness. Yet even though Rohrmoser seems to advocate the reintroduction of religion into politics in order to address what he sees as the profound problems of modern society which conventional politics cannot deal with, he also seems to rule out the availability of a religious solution in his study of the rise of National Socialism when he describes the disintegration of traditional religion and the failure of the 'political substitute religions' of communism and National Socialism.[75] Rohrmoser is at once preoccupied with the mental unease that comes with Modernity and unable to provide a solution that has not already been discredited. As we shall see, this tension is at the heart of New Right thinking.

A further ambiguity of the feelgood culture is illustrated by Marcel Reding in his discussion of tradition. He can start his reflections on the subject with an endorsement of the beneficial interaction between tradition and culture: 'Just as personal disposition and habits shape the lives and destiny of individuals, so too do institutions and traditions shape the life and culture of society. Culture determines how a society lives, and tradition determines that culture'.[76] Reding's premodern reflections, reminiscent of de Benoist's take on tradition and continuity, give way, however, to an awareness that tradition can be either a 'treasure-house of tried and tested wisdom' or, quoting Marx and Engels, a 'nightmare in the minds of the living' and a 'collection of nonsense'.[77] The sense that the feelgood culture that was meant to provide the contents of or foundation for politics is no longer intact is regularly conveyed in the pages of *Junge Freiheit*: 'A true culture has a sense of its own worth. This can no longer be said about us since the nihilistic destruction of values is well advanced and has brought about a deficit that future generations are unlikely ever to make good'.[78] What has been lost is a specifically German culture which was once not open to criticism but which gave way to a Western pluralist culture after 1945.[79]

The New Right wish for a feelgood culture to provide the basis for politics is thus not readily fulfilled. Culture is under threat from Modernity, and the reinforcement of politics through religious culture is called into question by New Right figures themselves. These problems are relatively minor, however, when compared with the profound pessimism that pervades New Right culture and renders politics irrelevant. Botho Strauß, whose *Anschwellender Bocksgesang* was the key essay in the New Right volume *Die selbstbewußte Nation*, writes of the precariousness of human existence as the 'alarming adventure of an encounter with oneself' in his volume of philosophical reflections, *Beginnlosigkeit* (No Beginning), which appeared just one year before *Anschwellender Bocksgesang*. Strauß describes how the very delicate chemical balance at work in the body between chaos and ossification, form and formlessness allows us to create our image of the world, but the balance may be lost at any moment.[80]

Conservative Revolution

This sense of the fragility and precariousness of existence can be traced in the thought of leading figures of the Conservative Revolutionary precursors of the New Right: the First World War hero, writer, and political journalist Ernst Jünger, much written about and revered by the New Right, explains bouts of depression by saying that he senses the terrible significance behind all events:

Ich fühle mit unzweifelhafter Klarheit, daß irgendein fremder Sinn, eine furchtbare Bedeutung hinter allem Geschehen lauert.

Das habe ich schon manchmal gewußt auf dem Grunde toller Räusche oder in würgenden Träumen, ich habe es nur im wogenden Leben wieder vergessen. Über solche Dinge pflegt man zu lachen, wenn man frisch und gesund im Lichte schreitet; treten sie an uns heran, so zersplittert im Nu alle Erkenntnis wie Glas und wie der Traum einer Nacht. Jeder hat Ähnliches erlebt, aber er vergißt es, weil er es vergessen muß.[81]

(I feel with total clarity that some alien meaning, some terrible significance lurks behind all events. I have on occasion come to know this through wild intoxication or in choking dreams, but I have forgotten it again in the great surge of life. We tend to laugh off such things as we step out in the daylight, fit and healthy; when they come close to us, our certainties shatter in an instant like glass or like a night's dream. All of us have experienced something similar, but we forget it because we have to forget it).

Strauß registers a 'crisis of consciousness' which must shake us to the core. This effect reaches right into language, for Mechtersheimer one of the defining features of a *Volk*. Strauß does not reflect on language as the basis for a community but is taken up instead with the language of public communication which he describes as worn out; it cannot be the instrument by which the crisis may be mastered. The main figure in *Beginnlosigkeit* explains how there is hardly a sentence or expression in newspapers or journals that does not reveal just how exhausted a whole way of thinking has become. This exhausted form of communication has become apparent at the very time when old certainties are being challenged and it is time to rethink everything.[82]

This mentality is reminiscent of the insight into chaos which was one of the major themes of the Conservative Revolution. Ernst Jünger commented on Alfred Kubin's picture 'Der Krieg' (War) that it showed 'the master of the sword and the slaughterman', and he concluded: 'Ultimately the nightmare gains supremacy: dread, the anxiety of living dominate everything,[83] and a related image in a poem by Jünger in response to Kubin's picture 'Der Mensch' (Man) is quoted by the New Right author Heimo Schwilk in his Jünger biography:

Traum, hindurchglüht, wird Vision, Krystall,
Urfrage Sein zu Wahnsinn, Katarakt:

Aufrechter Mensch; geschleudert in das All,
Orkan im Haar, bleich, einsam, nackt.

Ausschnitt endloser Kurve dämmert Welt,
Absturz in Dunkel, transzendenter Schwung,
Aufschrei das Leben, jäh aus Nichts geschnellt,
Ein Rampenlicht zu irrem Zirkussprung.[84]
(Dream, glowing, becomes vision, crystal
Archetypal question as being turns to insanity, cataract:
Upright man; cast into the universe,
In his hair a tempest, pale, alone, naked.

Section of infinite curve, world dawns,
Plunge into darkness, transcendent swing,
Life cries out, suddenly propelled from nothingness,
A footlight for a crazy circus leap).

This mentality at the cultural heart of the New Right seems to find not only its inspiration but also a kind of resolution in the literature of the Conservative Revolution: the figure Tronck in Ernst Jünger's war novel *Sturm* seeks discipline as a way out of laming introspection. Jünger describes how Tronck's appearance is a mixture of constraint and freedom, and it is a revelation of his inner self. There is something of the priest or officer about him, strict and uniformed, yet this was shot through with a certain artistic lightness. Jünger concludes that a man dresses in this way because he longs for form and wishes to subject himself to the rules and regulations of a particular social group although he is intellectually superior to the group.[85]

Botho Strauß registers with initial disapproval a parallel thought process for his own time, criticising what he calls 'the central metaphors of mankind' as 'makeshift belts and restraints by means of which man attempts to hold his disintegrating form together'.[86] The tension between form and formlessness is played out in the individual, and Strauß reminds the reader of Gottfried Benn's solution in his portrayal of the mentality of the expressionist poet whose innermost wish is to see harmony and form prevail over excess and formlessness:

'Zucht will er, da er der Zersprengteste war; und keiner von ihnen, ob Maler, Musiker, Dichter, wird den Schluß jener Mythe anders

wünschen, als daß Dionysos endet und ruht zu Füßen des klaren delphischen Gottes'. Das war der Verrat. Er geschah indessen nicht aus Opportunismus, sondern aus tiefster Sehnsucht nach der Linie.[87]
('He seeks discipline because he is the most fragmented person; and nobody, whether artist, musician, or poet, wants the myth to end in any way except with Dionysos finishing and resting at the feet of the clear Delphic god'. That was a betrayal, yet it was done not out of opportunism but out of a profound longing for form).

The Dionysian urge to cross boundaries is held in check by the Delphic principle of avoiding excess, and the perception of chaos and the experience of the disintegration of the individual produce a desire for order.[88] Strauß takes up the idea as a strategy for living. Erecting a barrier against existential chaos takes the form of a conscious decision to set limits and preserve taboos:

Die Alten hielten Begrenzungen heilig. Wenn man bedenkt, wie selbstverständlich, wie 'kostenlos' das Tabu schützte und welche mühevollen Umwege die Aufgeklärten nun gehen müssen, um nach der verheerenden Tabuzertrümmerung, die Natur und Seele gleichzeitig betraf, dem gewalttätigen Verfügen wieder Sperr- und Schutzzonen entgegenzurichten.[89]
(The ancients held limitations sacred. Just consider how taboos gave protection at so little cost and what great lengths enlightened people now have to go to in order to erect barriers and protected zones against violent exercise of power after the devastating demolition of taboos that struck at nature and the soul).

What is the connection between this awareness of chaos and a strategy for keeping chaos in check on the one hand and the political thinking of the New Right on the other? If the original hope was that culture would provide a solid foundation or the contents for politics, Botho Strauß must make the political figures of the New Right think again. The cultural position outlined above is characterised by 'grief', and Strauß emphasises that one cannot base politics on such a position: 'Grief, mankind's most honest feeling, will never produce a manifesto, or a suggestion for reshaping the world, or a doctrine or prophesy'.[90] In *Die Fehler des Kopisten* (The Copyist's Mistakes) Strauß paints a picture of society that is worn out. One can only expect to see it bleed to death. And as for politics, he cannot see anything good on any side or in any group, nor even the prospect of anything good; in politics there are only moral and strategic deals on offer.[91] His life in his country retreat outside Berlin becomes a symbol of the distance between the writer and a society he cannot influence.

Other New Right figures take a similarly pessimistic line. Quoting Heidegger's famous image for existence, the writer Hartmut Lange declares:

> Wer aus nichtigem Grund in diese Welt geworfen ist und eben diese Nichtigkeit als Grund selbst zu übernehmen und wie eine Schuld abzuarbeiten hat, wie sollte der noch von Parteiprogrammen oder sonstigen politisch motivierten Hilfsversprechen zu beeindrucken sein? [...] 'Dasein heißt – Hineingehaltenheit in das Nichts' – vor diesem Satz besteht keine nationalistische Parole mehr, aber auch keine Sehnsucht nach einer verlorengegangenen völkischen Identität.[92]
>
> (How could anyone who is propelled out of the void into this world, having to accept the void itself as a foundation and work it off like some kind of guilt, be impressed by party programmes or any other kind of politically motivated promises of help? [...] 'Existence means being held out into nothingness' – no nationalist slogan or yearning for some long lost identity based on race can stand up to this declaration).

Critics regard the 'culturalisation of politics', ie the replacement of the traditional right-wing concept of race by the concept of culture, and the presentation of culture as the basis of a German identity as one of the key features of the New Right. On this point Hajo Funke argues that in the New Right's ethnocentric definition of culture the Old Right paradigm lives on. Culture is an authoritarian source of meanings for the whole German people. Culture is ethnic and homogeneous, and one is part of this culture through the myths of one's origins, language and history. New Right culture, comments Funke, is a means of marking nations off from each other, and it is a counter to 'civilisation'. In this latter role it wards off the isolation of individualism and the fear of the chaos created by Modernity. Cultural identity is made into the foundation of an ethnically homogeneous and hierarchical society.[93]

This is in fact a description of what the New Right is trying, but largely failing, to achieve: culture is meant to convey the substance of a shared and homogeneous national identity based on ethnic roots, history and language, and for the party political wing of the movement this 'substance' feeds straight into political programmes. Yet 'culturalisation of politics' turns out to be a very uncomfortable and costly process. For it brings with it not only functionality but also dysfunctionality, as Zygmunt Baumann uses the terms. When New Right intellectuals turn their attention to culture they do so in a highly critical way, concluding not only that stereotypical cultural images of Germany have little meaning, but also that these images cannot be mobilised for political purposes. For this reason it is difficult to see the New Right as the model for more mainstream politicians who seize on the unproblematic version of a German culture: Schönbohm's notion of a national identity rooted in culture, history and language takes little account of the trouble the New Right has with all these concepts.

Moreover New Right intellectuals demonstrate a cultural pessimism that politics can do little or nothing to alleviate. Culture itself is the medium for reflecting on and probing the depths of chaos rather than a source of reassuring values. Karlheinz Weißmann thus refers to Ernst Jünger's friend Alfred Kubin as 'the graphic artist who dwelled in the abyss of the human soul and was regarded by Jünger as a kindred spirit'.[94]

Yet there is not just a simple tension in the New Right between cultural pessimism and political action. There is also a process at work which is meant to resolve this tension. Whereas Hartmut Lange may invoke Heidegger's images of precarious human existence at one point as proof of the irrelevance of political action, Pierre Krebs uses them elsewhere to explain the need for such action. For Krebs Heidegger's ultimate questions of existence are decidedly political, and he sees them most effectively posed by Oswald Spengler in the 1930s. These ultimate questions are to do with threats to the white race. Krebs thus blends culture and politics when he confirms Heidegger's view that we have reached midnight, a period when we are losing our spirituality and our spiritual powers; we are rejecting all questions about our ultimate purpose, yet these questions about our roots and our identity are precisely the questions that we must bring to the fore. Questions of this kind are not new, declares Krebs. Oswald Spengler was asking one such question half a century ago: 'Is there today any member of the white race who can sense what is going on on this earth, anyone who can sense the magnitude of the danger which hangs over and threatens this mass of races?'[95]

Karlheinz Weißmann illustrates a similar fusing of culture and politics when he draws a parallel between a philosophical loss of meaning and a loss of direction in society. He cites Joachim Fest's idea of a 'metaphysical deficit' which could undermine modern European and American societies.[96] And Weißmann sees in Ernst Jünger's work the possibility of compensating for the rise of nihilism by expanding nationalist politics: nationalism was for Jünger a philosophy in the full sense of the word, argues Weißmann. He regarded nationalism as the inevitable consequence of the nihilistic situation Modernity had got itself into when it shattered its own promises. If people could no longer believe in the religion of progress, and if the ways of life that preceded Modernity cannot be retrieved there remains only the option of moving forwards.[97]

Weißmann suggests a causal connection in the mind of a key figure of the Conservative Revolution between a perception of chaos, of a fundamental loss of meaning and the striving for absolute political values. Hartmut Lange makes the same connection when he writes of the individual's 'experience of existential homelessness'[98] and goes on to present such values as a counterweight:

Die Idee einer Volksgemeinschaft, einer Nationalkultur, das Bedürfnis nach Familie, Heimat, Kameradschaft, meinetwegen auch nach staatspolitischer Geborgenheit, werden um so kostbarer, je eindringlicher wir wissen, daß dies alles gegen unsere grundlos geworfene Existenz errungen werden muß und nicht gegen einen rassischen oder sozialpolitischen Feind, den wir nur allzugern und allzurasch auf die andere Seite der Barrikade setzen.[99]
(The idea of a community of the people, a national culture, the need for family, home, comradeship, even political security are all the more precious if we have a very acute sense that every one

of these things has to be achieved against an existence that has no foundation and no fixed points, and not against some racial or socio-political enemy that we are all too keen and quick to place on the other side of the barricade).

Lange thus alternates between cultural pessimism and political commitment, and in the above extract he seems to suggest that the two are linked in precisely the way Weißmann suggests they were for Jünger, with the awareness of existential chaos strengthening political commitment. Importantly, however, he marks himself off from the sentiments expressed in the programme of the Republikaner: whereas they had seen the main threat to culture as the external one of multi-culturalism, for Lange locating the enemy in terms of racial difference is a nonsense: the threat is rather the internal one of philosophical loss of meaning.

The New Right's perception of meaninglessness and meaning is prefigured in the writings of the Conservative Revolution, and it is Günter Figal who takes the analysis of Ernst Jünger's work one step further in order to suggest that it contains the resolution to the problem. Figal correctly identifies as a recurrent feature of Jünger's work his perception of loss of meaning and his tendency to rediscover meaning in the typical experience. Figal quotes Jünger's famous words from *Das abenteuerliche Herz* (The Adventurous Heart) on how the typical experience is the meaningful experience:

'Dann aber weiß ich auch, daß mein Grunderlebnis, das, was eben durch den lebendigen Vorgang sich zum Ausdruck bringt, das für meine Generation typische Erlebnis ist, eine an das Zeitmotiv gebundene Variation oder eine, vielleicht absonderliche, Spezies, die doch keineswegs aus dem Rahmen der Gattungskennzeichen fällt. Aus diesem Bewußtsein heraus meine ich auch, wenn ich mich mit mir beschäftige, nicht eigentlich mich, sondern das, was dieser Erscheinung zugrunde liegt und was somit in seinem gültigsten und dem Zufall entzogensten Sinne auch jeder andere für sich in Anspruch nehmen darf'.[100]
('And I also know that my basic experience, what finds expression through life's events, is the typical experience of my generation, a variation on the motif of the times, an exotic species perhaps, but one that still displays the characteristics of the

genus. In this knowledge I feel that when I write about myself everyone else can connect not with me personally but with what lies at the heart of my being and what is therefore most valid and least random').

Figal explains that Jünger is uncovering a basic feature of his century, and attempting to gain mastery over it. This basic feature is, according to Figal, 'poverty of experience', a concept Figal traces back to Walter Benjamin. In his 1933 essay "Erfahrung und Armut" (Experience and Poverty) Benjamin had written that experience had undergone a devaluation, and it had done so in the minds of the very generation that from 1914 to 1918 had lived through one of the most powerful experiences in world history. What this generation had experienced, however, could not be comprehended or judged within any existing and trusted framework. Poverty of experience therefore means the loss of continuity and experience that could be retold.[101] Figal comments on how this loss finds expression in Jünger's *Das abenteuerliche Herz*: poverty is not the useful one of having a clean slate with which to start anew. Rather, it is the loss of established and secure options for living, the disconcerting loss of certainty.[102] Jünger manages to overcome the loss of meaning provoked by the experience of the First World War, argues Figal, by stressing that whatever experience he had was typical. Yet a glance at Jünger's accounts of the war in fact shows him to be plagued by doubts about its meaning – doubts which are never finally banished and which Figal's analysis does not take into account. Jünger's typical experience is the product of a reworking of the reality in order to make the shock of modern warfare more tolerable. Yet since his unease is never finally laid to rest Jünger can also use the idea of the typical to convey the breakdown of conventional frameworks of understanding. In his war book, *Der Kampf als inneres Erlebnis* (Struggle as inner Experience), he uses the type to suggest that his understanding of reality is in fact a misunderstanding. Beneath the stylised existence of the hero lurks a chaotic and meaningless reality: space dissolves into infinity, and he perceives himself as an atom, tossed about by malicious forces. He is overcome with weariness and wishes he were dead. He is a 'lansquenet, a knight-errant, a Don Quixote, who has broken many a lance and whose illusions dissolve into mocking laughter'.[103]

If New Right intellectuals turn to Jünger for an adequate response to the shock of Modernity, they can find at most an uncertain one. Although reassurance is expected and, in the case of Figal, found in Jünger's work, Jünger himself is neither reassured not reassuring. His images of the type are either conscious reworkings of scenes in which he is the isolated individual or else they point to a superficial grasp of a profoundly disturbing reality.

Restoring culture

A further strand of New Right thinking on culture draws on the long established opposition in German intellectual history between culture and civilisation, and it sees cultural decline as inevitable and irreversible. As we shall see, it is very different from New Right thinking on a feelgood culture, and it is an implicit criticism of those who seek to restore or preserve traditional cultural forms. The clash is symptomatic of the problem the New Right has in setting out not just a political programme but also its broad philosophical beliefs.

The starting point for this second strand of New Right thinking on culture is not far removed from the kind of thinking that went into the feelgood culture. Writing in *Junge Freiheit* Baal Müller goes back to Nietzsche's definition of culture which Rohrmoser quotes. But he moves from there to Oswald Spengler's view of culture and civilisation as stages of one life: for Spengler culture is the totality of the ways of being of humankind which has its home in a particular location during its youth and in its prime, whereas civilisation is the inevitable old age of every culture.[104] The consequence of this 'natural' interpretation of culture is the irreversibility of its decline: if cultural disintegration is 'natural', argues Müller, it makes no sense to look to history in an effort to revive it. Müller proceeds to his criticism of restorationist conservatism by dismissing the all-too-easy antithesis of an intact world in the past and a crisis-ridden, rootless present. Anyone who refuses to accept the 'genetic connection' between culture and civilisation is in danger of resorting to wholly inadequate conspiracy theories about Jews, Freemasons or socialists to explain the decline of the former and the rise of the latter. By adopting Spengler's model of the life phases of a culture as his own, Müller is rejecting external explanations of cultural decline and driving home his point that there can be no restoration: 'The fact that civilisation's annihilation of culture is itself a result of cultural development rules out any nostalgic longing for past culture and any attempt at a restoration'.[105] Ultimately Müller's reading of Spengler gives a temporal dimension to the model of the dual function of culture put forward by Bauman: functionality gives way to dysfunctionality.

The second strand of New Right thought on culture draws the conclusions from the first. One must acknowledge that there can be no return to a lost age of cultural harmony and that the culture one produces not only registers decline but is also part of it. Heimo Schwilk thus detected the theme of leave-taking in the work of Botho Strauß even before he had written 'Anschwellender Bocksgesang': Strauß's gift for detail enables him to present the eternal human condition through snapshots, and he does this 'with a melancholy gesture of farewell'.[106] This echoes Strauß's own thoughts on the 'right-wing imagination':

> Anders als die linke, Heilsgeschichte parodierende Phantasie malt sich die rechte kein künftiges Weltreich aus, bedarf keiner Utopie, sondern sucht den Wiederanschluß an die lange Zeit, die unbewegte, ist ihrem Wesen nach Tiefenerinnerung und insofern eine religiöse oder protopolitische Initiation. Sie ist immer und existentiell eine Phantasie des Verlustes und nicht der (irdischen) Verheißung.[107]
>
> (Unlike the left-wing imagination with its parody of salvation, the right-wing imagination does not set out any goal in the shape of a future world empire. It does not require a Utopia but rather seeks to reconnect with the long unaltered past. It is essentially a profound remembering and to that extent a religious or protopolitical initation. It is always and irrevocably an imagination bound up with loss and not with (earthly) promises).

Jürgen Habermas writes of the neo-conservative need for affirmation that characterises a disenchanted Modernity and that has to be satisfied by a process of reenchantment. This reenchantment is meant to be achieved by, among other things, inspirational literature.[108] Yet the literature most closely associated with the New Right is far from being consistently inspirational: it frequently confirms the loss of the absolute values it was supposed to revive. Botho Strauß writes approvingly of 'remythologising the text', of reverence for the work of art, but he seems to know also that this 'revolt against the modern world' is a lost cause in the face of 'parasitic' academic literary analysis and journalism which he refers to as the 'mentality of the secondary'.[109] He provides an example of literature registering loss when he describes a particular shepherd whom he sees near his home. He comments that people who live in the area have no sense of the general significance of the shepherd figure as a hero in literature. The shepherd Strauß sees lives cut off from his eternal model, cut off from his tradition, and in his restricted existence in the here and now he is 'more gruesomely alone' than the shepherd figure of legends ever was.[110] The writer of literature cannot make the link to the inspirational tradition, but only register the disconcerting isolation of modern man.

Literature is not a separate and protected sphere where absolute truths can be preserved. Rather, as Schwilk himself argues, it is part of a random and relative postmodern world, offering any truth that sells.[111] Jochen Schaare thus reduces modern and post-modern artistic movements to mere fashion, writing that we have been facing massive disruptions for over a century, as can be seen in the avant-garde movements such as Surrealism, Futurism, Expressionism, Dadaism, and Cubism. In the postmodern era the latest fashions spiral up for a brief moment, only to sink back into the underworld. All these fashions feel committed to the principle of progress, wishing to clear out the old and destroy traditional forms of representation so that the new can break through. Schaare comments that this mentality is totally at odds with earlier times when preservation and perfection of traditional art forms was the aim of all aesthetic endeavour. The work of remembering and repeating defined art, not striding forwards and emancipating oneself from the past.[112]

The New Right project of providing itself with a cultural dimension as a solid foundation for new political thinking has not gone according to plan. What emerges is a volatile mixture of politics and philosophy. The recurrent stance embedded in New Right thinking is based on a cultural pessimism which can at one point dismiss politics as irrelevant but at another view politics as a potential source of meaning. The writer Rüdiger Safranski seems to sum up the difficulty for the New Right as he registers a hollowing out of traditional religious and artistic values which leaves an existential void. For Safranski the attempted solution takes the form of the creation of values and meaning, but it seems bound to fail: what he sees is the will to believe in something, whether one is talking about aesthetics or ethics. But this will is broken since it has been exposed to the Enlightenment. It is delicate and looks more like 'the will to will than the will itself'.[113]

Critics have argued that the 'hallmark of the New Right is its belief that the present world system is not only decadent, but that it will eventually give way to a new type of civilization based on healthy mythic forces'. The New Right thus sees contemporary history as an 'interregnum'.[114] This perspective is also set out by the New Right itself in Armin Mohler's study of the Conservative Revolution: in the course of the 19th century the blend of Christianity and Antiquity that once formed the core of Western beliefs lost its substance and significance, argues Mohler, and a new order is not yet in sight. We therefore live in an 'interregnum'.[115] Yet the New Right cultural awareness that there can only be decline ultimately undermines any notion that in the long term the West is on its way to a new type of civilisation. Mohler himself seems to have some insight into the difficulty of creating a new order when he explains that the Conservative Revolution itself is characterised by the interregnum even as it tries to overcome it.[116] Alain de Benoist also takes up the idea of living in an interregnum when he writes that 'the present is a pivotal period – a turning point or an "interregnum", characterized by a major crisis: the end of modernity'.[117] De Benoist's comment reflects the more positive (albeit long-term) perspective that is a feature of the more directly political thinkers' writings: the interregnum can be followed by his 'relentlessly reemerging nationalisms' which show no trace of the pessimism underlying much of the German New Right's cultural thinking. The cross-cultural comparison also highlights the easier relationship that the French New Right has with nationalism. For the German New Right nationalism is a key value, but, as we shall see in our later analysis, it is also a troublesome one in the light of the Nazi past.

Multi-culturalism and German identity

The tension between culture and politics that we have seen at the heart of New Right thinking also shows itself in the issue of multi-culturalism. This issue is sometimes presented by observers as one on which there is a New Right consensus,[118] yet the reality is more complex: whereas politicians and some political journalists externalise the problems of German identity by blaming them on the legacy of National Socialism and on immigration, the intellectuals tend to chart an internal process of dissolution which has its roots in their attitude to the processes and progress of Modernity.

The external threat

Günter Rohrmoser objects to the process of *Vergangenheitsbewältigung* (mastering the Nazi past) which he sees as bound up with the notion that Germany took a different path from all other nations and that all of German history is therefore suspect. He argues that Germany is required to accept that National Socialism marked the end of its history and that a transformation of Germany into a multi-cultural society would be the most effective way of solving the German question.[119] Karlheinz Weißmann claims that most Germans want limits set on immigration and resent official policy. Occasionally, he writes, anger tips over into violence against foreigners while the media persist with an illusory xenophilia. Unlike in the rest of Europe, in Germany any vote against the growing influx of non-Germans can be made suspect by pointing to 'Auschwitz'. The decidedly friendly attitude towards foreigners is a kind of atonement for Nazi crimes, argues Weißmann, and although one can understand the psychology behind this behaviour, Germans should not be blinded to the fact that turning it into policy must end in disaster.[120]

New Right authors insist that any decline in the number of Germans cannot be made good by immigration. At a Summer Academy talk at the Institut für Staatspolitik in the year 2000 Stefan Maninger warned of a collapse in the number of the indigenous population of Germany and a fall in the birthrate that would quickly become irreversible. If the shortfall were to be made up with foreigners Germany would witness ethnic conflicts of the kind seen in other countries. Maninger also warned of problems of cultural incompatibility and the danger of newly arriving groups having a 'bridgehead mentality'.[121] Immigration is regarded as a major external threat to German identity. Trade unions protest against xenophobia even as a 'reserve army' of foreigners is competing with their members for the same jobs, declares *Junge Freiheit*, and encouraging immigration from Third World countries is leading to the dissolution of European peoples.[122] *Junge Freiheit* quotes the Italian journalist Oriana Fallaci's notorious critique of immigration into Italy as a threat to its culture:

'Ich meine, daß unsere kulturelle Identität keine Immigrationswelle verkraften kann, mit der Menschen hereinströmen, die auf die eine oder andere Weise unsere Lebenswelt verändern wollen. Unsere Prinzipien, unserer Werte. Ich meine, daß bei uns kein Platz ist für Muezzins, Minarette, den verfluchten Tschador und die noch verfluchtere Burkah. Und auch wenn welcher da wäre, würde ich ihnen diesen Menschen nicht geben.'[123]
('I believe that our cultural identity cannot take a wave of immigration, allowing people to pour in who in one way or another wish to change the world we live in. Our principles, our values. I believe there is no room here for muezzins, minarets, the accursed chador and the even more accursed burkah. And even if there were room, I would not give it to these people').

Cultural integrity is here portrayed as intact but under threat, and according to *Junge Freiheit* Germany needs a Fallaci of its own to protect its values, culture and national identity.[124] The retired CDU Berlin senator and one-time mayor of Berlin, Heinrich Lummer, takes up the point in *Junge Freiheit* when he argues that if Turkey became a member of the European Union, its culture would eventually destroy 'European identity'.[125] Turks living in Germany are being encouraged to form a 'state within a state', warns Rolf Stolz.[126] For Pierre Krebs cosmopolitanism is nothing less than universal genocide.[127] Krebs laments a loss of cultural heritage and tradition, and he links this loss to immigration and 'multi-racial society'. He calls for people to unite in their various European identities against a 'universal mixed culture'. By mixing races, cultures and philosophies, he argues, the egalitarian principle goes against the basic right to be different.[128] Guillaume Faye, a leading figure of the French New Right and one-time ally of de Benoist, condemns racism but works with the concept of homogeneity within a society which categorises multi-racial society as undesirable: the strength of the bond between people depends on the relative 'ethnocultural homogeneity' of the Europeans.[129]

The New Right generally steers clear of open racism in favour of what it calls ethnopluralism, yet it does see any mixing of races leading only to problems. This is the case with de Benoist who is at pains to out point that race is at the heart of history, culture and a shared destiny. Where races live together the result can be discrimination, segregation, loss of culture, and criminality.[130] New Right organisations and individuals who subscribe to the notion of an external threat pursue their thinking to the conclusion that immigrants should leave Germany. The Thule Seminar sees multiculturalism as a form of disintegration and looks for support from Europeans who are aware of their identity and who have recognised the dangers to their 'biocultural' future. The 'system' promotes a multi-racial society of ethnosuicidal nations, and what is needed is an ethnocultural rebirth of Europe. The mission of the Thule Seminar is to promote a 'European biocultural consciousness'.[131] Pierre Krebs asserts that multi-racial societies inevitably experience an eruption of aggression, and the only way to guarantee the identity of the host country and the survival of immigrants is for them to return to the land of their ancestors.[132]

It is a standard feature of the New Right presentation of foreigners coming to Germany that the incoming group possesses a strong and intact culture. This culture may be attacked as Fellaci attacks Islam, but it can also be admired for its supposed underlying discipline, a characteristic regarded as lost to Western culture. In a speech to the right-wing organisation Synergon Deutschland Martin Schwarz declares that if Europeans were to adopt the principles of Islam their nations would flourish: a positive attitude to sexuality and to children, an ordered but not puritanical sex life which takes place in private and not in homosexual processions through town centres, rejection of drugs, and providing role-models for children.[133]

Internal collapse

The attitudes outlined above are based on the notion of an external threat to German identity. Yet these are not the only attitudes in evidence in New Right thinking. Peter Meier-Bergfeld takes a similar view to Schwarz's when he refers to Western individualistic culture being displaced by cultures that are less individualistic. Yet Meier-Bergfeld sees an internal process of decline at work in Western societies and a solution that has little to do with immigration: Western culture is destroying itself, and he quotes approvingly from Meinhard Miegel and Stefanie Wahl's *Das Ende des Individualismus* (The End of Individualism) which sees salvation in a reassertion of the supremacy of the collective over the individual: 'The individual would be placed on the same level as the community, not above it, and where there was a conflict the individual's interests would be subordinated to those of the community. The rights of the individual would have to be reduced and those of the community would have to increase'.[134]

Whereas Krebs and de Benoist see external forces behind a loss of cultural identity, other New Right authors take a philosophical approach which locates the origins of decline within German society itself and, more broadly, within Modernity. Hartmut Lange stresses the 'individual's experience of existential homelessness',[135] and he goes on to advocate as a counter to this experience the standard New Right values of community, nation and family. As we have seen in our discussion of New Right culture, however, he is acutely aware that what threatens these values is the lack of fixed points in a chaotic world, not some artificially constructed enmity based on race or politics.

Lange is not alone in his view. Botho Strauß argues that public morality is marked by hypocrisy since it always took every opportunity to pour scorn on military values, the Church, tradition and authority, and it should therefore not be surprised if these concepts have no substance in times of need.[136] For Strauß cultural identity is not undermined by the influence of immigration but by the internal progression of a liberal agenda. Martin Schwarz takes a similar line when he addresses the issue of crime among foreigners: committed Muslims, he argues, see all crime as an affront to the divine order and are therefore unlikely to engage in criminality. The aim of integration, however, is to 'disconnect people from their higher principles and fool Turkish and Arab immigrants into loving the French or German constitution'. Young people get involved in crime because the system they are encouraged to adopt has no divine roots and is therefore not taken seriously.[137] Here we see a very different take on foreigners, with the problem lying in a decline of the old order, and Schwarz is drawing the conclusions from Gehlen's thoughts on the need for political institutions to have a religious foundation. Schwarz elaborates when he goes on to suggest that humankind is subjected to the same process:

> Wir leben in einer Zeit des Chaos und der Auflösung. Wollen wir diese Zeit bestehen, dürfen wir uns nicht einreden, das Hauptziel unserer Aktivitäten müsse in der Frontstellung zu jenen stehen, die in diesem Zersetzungsprozeß der alten Ordnung ebenfalls herumgewirbelt und entwurzelt werden. So geraten wir nur weiter in den Strudel. Wir müssen aber unsere spirituelle Integrität bewahren, welche diese auch sei, neue Koalitionen bilden, aber nicht Religionskriege vom Zaun brechen! Es gibt keine islamische Weltverschwörung zum Sturz des Abendlandes![138]
> (We live in a time of chaos and disintegration. If we wish to survive we must not convince ourselves that our main aim is to confront those people who are also being uprooted and tossed around as the old order disintegrates. If we do, we shall only sink deeper into the vortex. Instead we must retain our spiritual integrity, whatever form this may take, and build new coalitions, not start new wars of religion! There is no Islamic conspiracy to bring down the West!).

Schwarz's imagery draws on the familiar New Right terms used to describe a chaotic existence lurking beneath the feelgood culture. Rootedness and order give way to an uprooted existence in which people are subjected to forces they cannot control. This kind of thinking is in evidence at the social and the psychological level, and there is a tendency for the sense of social dislocation to lead into an existential unease. This tendency makes it difficult for New Right thinkers to retain the focus on foreigners as the source of Germany's problems. In Günter Rohrmoser's interpretation of Nietzsche's view of culture we see the origins of cultural chaos extending back into the 19th century as the result of the rise of cultural pluralism. At this point he is at odds with Guillaume Faye whose 'pluricultural society' is the product of a mixing of the races: quoting Nietzsche's under-standing of culture as 'above all else the unity of style in all the vital utterances of a people',[139] Rohrmoser argues that Nietzsche found the precise opposite of this unity in the bourgeois culture of his day: unity of culture dissolved into a plurality of styles, and Nietzsche spoke of a 'chaos of styles'.[140] Rohrmoser is here describing Nietzsche's account of the emergence of a cultural pluralism within the German bourgeoisie of the 19th century. Significantly, however, Rohrmoser goes on to convert this internal process towards cultural diversity into an external one: Nietzsche's account becomes the starting point for Rohrmoser's explanation of social disintegration in his own time as the result of the influence of foreigners in Germany: society is falling apart into a plurality of ways of life, and this can present a serious danger for democracy, primarily when people no longer speak the same language and cannot discuss new problems as they arise. People find themselves more and more in different linguistic worlds, and the result is a general cacophony.[141]

A similar conversion is at work in the thinking of Hans-Dietrich Sander who concludes in *Staatsbriefe* that German culture no longer exists. Today's Germans have lost all contact with their own classical arts and philosophy, and they have abandoned their customs and habits. This seems at first to be due to a Spenglerian decline from culture into civilisation, but Sander switches to the view that foreign influence after the Second World War is to blame for the loss. Germans must realise that their 'reeducation' after the war was not designed to integrate them into the community of Western states but rather to do away with the German nation.[142]

We gain a further insight into the mentality of the New Right when Rohrmoser makes a connection between Modernity and racism. He sees the 'tragedy of German conservatism' since the French Revolution in the fact that its main impulse was a fear of modernisation. Modernisation threatened everything that had developed over time and everything that conservatives regarded as worth preserving. In Hegel's terms they were afraid of the 'Fury of Disappearance'. Rohrmoser sees this fear as an essential factor in any explanation of fascism in Germany and Europe. Turning to his own time he argues that if the progressive and anti-fascist camps wish to win their fight against conservatism, nationalism and racism they will have to take this fear away from people to whom Modernity means the disappearance of everything close to their hearts.[143]

Other intellectuals associated with the New Right stick more resolutely to a sense of social disintegration that has its roots in the changes brought about by Modernity. Günter Figal's interpretation of Nietzsche demonstrates the contrast. Figal argues that where

Nietzsche doubts the validity of traditional habits of thought and concepts he is a supporter of Modernity; where he criticises his own time and turns to the past for inspiration, however, he is a supporter of tradition. Where he is both at the same time he shows the difficulty his epoch has in asserting 'the validity of the old in the period of Modernity'. What Nietzsche is left with is a summoning up of the old, natural world and the more or less open admission that he is not part of this world since it is impossible to escape from the decadence of his own time. Moreover, one thing that makes Nietzsche an exemplary modern thinker is the absence of a fully developed and consistent theory in his work.[144]

New Right wavering between internal and external explanations of a mounting threat to German identity reflects a complex attitude towards issues of race and multi-culturalism. There is however a tendency for the two explanations to merge when the feeling of losing everything that is familiar generates a nationalistic mentality intent on recapturing the familiar in the shape of a rehomogenised Germany. When asked whether a multi-cultural society is an option for Germany Günter Rohrmoser's answer shows how complexity gives way to a simple opposition: 'Of all the problems we discuss publicly one of the key issues which will decide the whole ideological and political development of the Federal Republic is the choice between a multi-cultural society and a society built on the idea of national identity'. Rohrmoser wants the issue to feature in an election campaign, and he has no doubt which way the German people would choose.[145]

3
A Cultural Interpretation of National Socialism

Living in the era of fascism

The New Right presents its rejection of National Socialism as one of the major defining characteristics of the movement: *Europa vorn* points out that there is no room in modern Germany's ideological baggage for the Hitler cult and nostalgia for National Socialism.[1] It is certainly the case that many of the typical features of extreme right-wing propaganda in which the link with National Socialism has not been explicitly severed – such as Holocaust denial and anti-Semitism – are generally absent from New Right publications,[2] and the programmes of the political parties associated with the New Right go out of their way to underline their commitment to democracy. Hitherto observers have tended to focus on individual statements by New Right authors and to detect a relativisation of National Socialism. Such is the critical view of *Ich war dabei* (I was there), for example, Franz Schönhuber's best-selling autobiographical account of his years in the Waffen-SS, published in 1981 and leading to his dismissal from Bavarian State television.[3] Relativisation of National Socialism is clearly an important trend in New Right thinking and it is one we shall pursue, yet considering the New Right's views on National Socialism and fascism as a political and cultural whole reveals a further matter for analysis. As we shall see, a recurrent pattern in New Right thinking presents humankind with a stark choice between chaos and order, and this is coupled with the conviction that we are still living in the fascist era. This broad cultural context of New Right thinking must lead critics to look beyond the New Right's basic assertion that is has distanced itself from National Socialism.

Keeping a clear distance from National Socialism is difficult for the New Right because of its understanding of that movement's original impulse. The Polish-born Israeli historian Zeev Sternhell has attracted the attention of the New Right for his theories on the origins of and prospects for fascism. Armin Mohler notes that Sternhell does not use the word fascism as a term of abuse.[4] Karlheinz Weißmann recounts a lecture Sternhell gave in Munich in which he told his audience that one must come down on the side of the Enlightenment, rational discourse, the ideals of the French Revolution, and the isolation of the individual in a meaningless world. Sternhell, says Weißmann, does not consider the epoch of fascism to have ended, but Weißmann argues that the danger cannot be countered through any return to a simple belief in progress since Sternhell himself has shown that criticism of the optimistic assumptions of the Enlightenment is entirely justified. For Weißmann Sternhell has also shown how fascism dismissed naïve liberal expectations of the future, but for political reasons he has now changed his mind about the value of these expectations. Sternhell sees in the present the same symptoms of decay that existed in the closing decades of the 19th century, and he has therefore added to his historical research a warning from a 'concerned citizen' against a resurgence of fascism and a plea to support the ideals of the Enlightenment even though he has already shown how Enlightenment thinking on mankind is not convincing.[5]

Sternhell's account of the circumstances in which fascism can thrive is strikingly similar to the New Right's expression of cultural despair we have already noted. Sternhell writes that in a world that is falling to pieces fascism can easily appear as the heroic will to tame the forces of nature, the economy and society.[6] In Weißmann's reading of Sternhell we see the construction of a model for living which offers just two options: on the one hand a commitment to a fascist spirit which strives for mastery over all aspects of existence and the restoration of order; on the other a commitment to reason which knows no community, only isolation. Weißmann's comment on the first option suggests a sympathy with the fascist will and a sense that it has a role to play in the future: it is a 'misled and misleading will, but it is a historical force of incredible significance for the development of this and possibly the next century'.[7] Weißmann thus takes up the idea that fascism may have a role to play in the future, but unlike Sternhell, he does not attach any kind of health warning to this possibility. In Weißmann's construction we catch a glimpse of the New Right mentality which deals in the stark opposites of order and chaos, community and isolation, and he conveys the thought that these stark opposites may be the forces that will shape our future.

For Weißmann the fascist will was led astray by the practice of National Socialism, and New Right authors refer to Sternhell's view that fascist ideas were developed in France 20 years before they appeared anywhere else. The fact that fascism was never put into practice in France meant that it could remain in its pure theoretical form. Armin Mohler thus quotes Sternhell:

'Er (fascism) hat hier (in France) nie das Stadium der Theorie überschritten und blieb so von jenen Kompromissen verschont, die bei der offiziellen Ideologie eines Regimes unvermeidbar sind und diese stets auf irgendeine Weise verfälschen. So kann man hier den tieferen Sinn des Faschismus besser erkennen. Und da man hier die faschistische Ideologie in ihren Ursprüngen und in ihrer Inkubationszeit beobachten kann, werden auch die von ihr geprägten Mentalitäten und Verhaltensweisen deutlicher sichtbar.'[8] ('It (fascism) never got beyond the theoretical stage here (in France) and it was therefore spared those unavoidable compromises with the official ideologies of regimes which always somehow distort it. For this reason it is possible to discern more clearly the more profound meaning of fascism here. And since one can observe fascist ideology here in its origins and its incubation period, the attitudes and behaviours it produced also become clearer').

This thought is developed by Mohler, the Swiss national who had at one stage attempted unsuccessfully to join the Waffen-SS. Mohler illustrates the New Right tendency to separate what it regards as a pure version of fascism from the various attempts to put it into practice. He uncouples what he calls 'fascist style' from historical fascism, and on the basis of this distinction declares: 'I am a fascist'.[9] Similarly, Franz Schönhuber looks to Sternhell's work to stress the idealism of fascism and its distance from National Socialism. Schönhuber quotes from an interview given by Sternhell in 1983 when his book *Ni droite ni gauche. L'idéologie fasciste en France* first appeared:

'Der Faschist ist von einem Ideal der Modernität und der Jugend besessen: Er möchte einen neuen Menschen schaffen, der Liebhaber des Sportes und des Autosports ist, in einer neuen Stadt wohnt, die durch die futuristische Architektur wiederbelebt wurde. Er bewundert Le Corbusier, Marinetti, Gropius. Er liebt Motoren, Mechanik, Geschwindigkeit.'[10]
('The fascist is obsessed with an ideal of Modernity and youth: he wants to create a new man, a lover of sport and autosport, living in a new city that has been given new life by futuristic architecture. He is an admirer of Le Corbusier, Marinetti, Gropius. He loves motors, mechanical engineering and speed.')

Schönhuber comments that this sounds like a list of the leisure interests of today's young intellectuals, and he concludes that fascism and National Socialism are not the same thing.[11]

The New Right finds a model in fascism, but in a particular way which emerges from its difficulties with positive ideas. Mohler confirms the dilemma of the New Right when he highlights not the contents of fascism but its style:

Es wird hier nicht versucht, den Faschismus primär von seinen theoretischen Äußerungen her zu begreifen oder ihn (was nicht dasselbe ist) auf eine Theorie zu reduzieren. Im Bereich des Faschismus ist das Verhältnis zum Begriff nun einmal instrumental, indirekt, nachträglich. Voraus geht die Entscheidung für eine Gebärde, einen Rhythmus, kurz: einen 'Stil'. Gewiß kann sich dieser auch in Worten ausprägen – der Faschismus ist nicht stumm, im Gegenteil: er liebt die Worte, aber sie sind nicht dazu da, einen logischen Zusammenhang festzuhalten. Ihre Funktion ist vielmehr, eine bestimmte Tonlage zu setzen, ein Klima zu schaffen, Assoziationen hervorzurufen. Zusammengefaßt läßt sich sagen, daß Faschisten sich offensichtlich leicht mit Unstimmigkeiten der Theorie abfinden. Ihre Verständigung vollzieht sich auf direkterem Wege – eben über den 'Stil'.[12]

(I am not trying here to grasp fascism by means of its theories or to reduce it to a theory (which is not the same thing). As far as fascism is concerned the relationship to concepts is instrumental, indirect and supplementary. What is of primary concern is the commitment to a gesture, a rhythm, in brief: to a 'style'. Certainly this style can express itself in words – fascism is not silent; on the contrary, it loves words, but they are not there to establish logical connections. Rather, they set a particular tone, create an atmosphere, and evoke associations. In summary one can say that fascists can easily come to terms with theoretical contradictions. Their communication takes place in a more direct way – through 'style').

For Mohler, fascist style offers an appealing alternative to a coherent ideology. Asked whether fascism is 'in', he answers by stressing style over content: 'Young people are coming back to it. It is a fascist style that is attracting them. In my youth Mussolini's fascism fascinated me most of all'.[13] Leadership and hierarchy can take the place of programmes, as for example when Mohler is asked whether he admired Hitler: 'What do mean, admire? He certainly created real leadership. The cadres he shaped, they had real style'.[14] Mohler discovers many of the qualities of the fascist leader in Jörg Haider, leader of the Freiheitliche Partei Österreichs from 1986 to 2000: 'he has the confidence to speak out and enjoys confronting the ruling party bigwigs. He is skilful, dynamic, confident'.[15] Mohler's emphasis on Haider's personal qualities is echoed throughout the New Right. Without Haider, a reader of *Junge Freiheit* argues in the letters page, the FPÖ would not have been successful. This is true of all the 'patriotic' parties in Europe: their success or failure depends on just one person whose charisma is more important than a party programme. On the left socialists, communists and social democrats all have the same basic ideas, whereas the right is lightyears away from such consensus.[16]

The New Right interpretation of fascism directly echoes the Conservative Revolutionary understanding of the movement at a time when the Conservative Revolution had tried and failed in a series of public debates to produce a programme that would bring together the key forces of nationalism and socialism. As a result of this failure fascism was represented as a movement that rightly placed action and character above political programmes. In 1927 Wilhelm Kleinau wrote that nothing is more damaging than the parties' delusion that they had possession of the great and eternal truths about life once they had neatly packed their theories into a suitcase. Fascism possessed so much more than a programme: it possessed the will to act, a firm stance and character.[17]

For the Conservative Revolution Benito Mussolini took on particular significance as the great model of a leader without a programme: in 1933 Oswald Spengler asserted that although fascist ideology would not survive, Mussolini would certainly continue as leader since he was ruthless towards his party and showed the courage to take leave of all ideology.[18] Following this tradition for the New Right, Günter Maschke sees the successful politician as an artist who is not concerned with political programmes. Maschke refers to Mussolini's figure of the politician-artist who emerges at times of crisis and radical change. He at once pours scorn on political programmes as 'life-preserving illusions' or 'myths' and exploits them: 'The myth that is chosen at any given time is only important as a way of mobilising fighters and impressing the masses'.[19]

The New Right view of society facing a choice between order and chaos underpins its interpretation of totalitarianism: a plurality of truths created anxiety and made people susceptible to those movements which claimed to be in possession of the one and only truth. Thus Rüdiger Safranski writes that it was fear of freedom in modern pluralist societies that made people more susceptible to the temptation of totalitarianism. The very plurality of competing truths had a worrying effect. As a result fundamentalists latched onto one truth or another, and Europe's 20th century became the era of ideologies, totalitarianism, nationalism and fundamentalism.[20]

Despite the New Right attempts to separate fascist theory from National Socialist practice the two do merge when it comes to understanding their appeal. Karlheinz Weißmann argues that voters were attracted to Hitler's vision of a new Germany free from its conquerors and united in a national community. The NSDAP had the character of a religious movement of awakening and a national youth movement.[21] Religiosity is central to Günter Rohrmoser's interpretation of National Socialism: for Rohrmoser it is only possible to eradicate whole groups of people in a society in which Christianity has ceased to have any influence.[22] National Socialism and fascism are features of 'post-Christian religious history', and they must be understood as an attempt to fill the vacuum of religious meaning left in the wake of the Enlightenment. With the end of Christianity and the pushing back of the Church as an institution religious needs, longings and forces became amorphous and without roots. Hitler managed to channel these longings and forces. As was the case with Weißmann and Mohler's interpretation of National Socialism, this means for Rohrmoser that we are still living under the conditions that enabled National Socialism to thrive:

> Sicherlich wird es den Nationalsozialismus in seiner geschichtlichen Form nie wieder geben, aber wer weiß, ob wir nicht im post-christlichen Zeitalter des 21. Jahrhunderts noch Erfahrungen machen werden, die zeigen, daß der Nationalsozialismus vielleicht nur das grausame Vorspiel, aber noch nicht das Endspiel gewesen ist.[23]
> (Certainly National Socialism will never exist again in its historical form, but who knows whether, in the post-Christian era of the 21st century, we shall not experience things which will demonstrate that National Socialism was just the brutal overture and not yet the finale).

Fascism's 'deepest impulse' was to overcome the unbearable decadence of a post-Christian society in which the Conservative Revolution had taken the work of Nietzsche to explain its abandonment of any linear, progressive notion of history. We are currently living in the age of decadence that Nietzsche had foreseen.[24]

Rüdiger Safranski quotes Goebbels: 'Where is the man who will chase this petty-minded rabble out of the temple of the nation with his whip!' and comments that for Goebbels Hitler was the man with the whip. For Goebbels National Socialism is the 'catechism of a new political faith amid the despair of a godless world that is falling apart',[25] and it could bring 'redemption'. Safranski sets out his understanding of Goebbels's mind:

> Goebbels will erlöst werden von seiner Verzweiflung, seinen trüben Sinnlosigkeitsgefühlen, seiner sozialen Misere, seinen Verlassenheitsängsten. Er möchte wieder lieben können und geliebt sein. Die 'Hoffnung auf Zuhause' soll sich endlich

erfüllen. Aus der zerrissenen, von keiner gemeinsamen Idee zusammengehaltenen Gesellschaft soll eine Gemeinschaft werden, in der man sich geborgen fühlen kann.[26] (Goebbels desires to be redeemed from his despair, his dark feelings of meaninglessness, his social misery, his fear of abandonment. He would like to be able to love again and be loved. His hope of 'finding his home' must finally be fulfilled. Society which is torn apart and has no shared idea to hold it together should turn into a community where one can feel secure).

This interpretation of the appeal of National Socialism is not restricted to the New Right. Richard Herzinger summarises the CDU's understanding of National Socialism in very similar terms, with Nazi rule seen as a symptom of nihilisitic Modernity following on from a total collapse of values and man's abandonment of God and religion. Herzinger characterises as 'Christian-existentialist postwar conservatism' this interpretation of the rise of the Nazis and the later conservative claim to represent human dignity by valuing family, Church and State.[27] This similarity cannot be read as an example of the much discussed 'erosion of the barrier' between the extreme right and mainstream conservatism, however, since it has to be weighed against the additional items we have noted in New Right thinking: that there is a stark choice to be made between chaos and order, that we are still living in a fascist era, that the door is still open for a supposedly pure form of fascism to reassert itself, and that one should not automatically view this possibility with alarm. It is at this deeper cultural level that the New Right displays patterns of thought which undermine its frequent assertions of its distance from National Socialism. What we have seen to be a New Right fondness for Gehlen's institutions that give a sense of permanence, security and a form of existence beyond question can spill over for many New Right authors into an enthusiasm for fascism's promise of bringing absolute order to a chaotic world.

Relativising National Socialism

Writing in the mid-eighties Jürgen Habermas argued that until that time the Federal Republic had a simple view of itself: 'After Auschwitz our national self-consciousness can be derived only from the better traditions in our history, a history that is not unexamined but instead appropriated critically. The context of our national life, which once permitted incomparable injury to the substance of human solidarity, can be continued and further developed only in the light of the traditions that stand up to the scrutiny of a gaze educated by the moral catastrophe, a gaze that is, in a word, suspicious'.[28] Habermas goes on to argue that the consensus on this point has now been terminated by the right because there is concern about the result of this simple view: 'An appropriation of tradition that takes a critical view does not ... promote naïve trust in the morality of conditions to which one is merely habituated; it does not facilitate identification with unexamined models'.[29] For the right, he argues, historiography is meant to provide for those uprooted by modernisation through a 'compensatory "creation of meaning"' which requires that the status of the Nazi period be relativised.[30] This relativisation is clearly at work in the New Right's interpretation of National Socialism.

The first recurrent feature of New Right interpretations of National Socialism is the idea that Germans were unaware of Hitler's real aims and that their support for him had nothing to do with anti-Semitism or military aggression. Günter Rohrmoser claims that while Hitler was in power he never disclosed his real aims to the German people. Those Germans who supported him did not support Hitler as we know him today. Hitler deceived them about his real aims, neither announcing in 1933 a programme for annihilating the Jews nor talking about an imperialistic war of conquest. Rather, in his speech of 1 February 1933 he spoke to the German people about family, honour and loyalty, nation and fatherland, and the solid foundations of the German people's morality and faith. Hitler claimed to respect Christianity as the basis of all morality and the family as the basic unit of nation and state. Some years later at Nuremberg he presented himself to the German people as the guarantor of peace. Rohrmoser concludes that the Germans could take any politician who spoke in such terms for 'an entirely normal conservative'.[31]

Karlheinz Weißmann's *Rückruf in die Geschichte* devotes large sections to the various allied plans for Germany which emerged towards the end of the war. He sets out the thinking of those who considered all Germans either as guilty and willing perpetrators of

Nazi crimes or else as morally compromised for failing to resist Hitler. He quotes from the American historian Louis Nizer's book *What to do with Germany?* which appeared in 1944 and which claimed that the German soul had a deep-rooted defect. Weißmann also quotes Robert Vansittart who was appointed Chief Diplomatic Adviser to the British Government in 1937 and who argued that the German people stood behind Hitler. National Socialism was a movement of the whole people and the war was a war of the whole people. Weißmann comments that Vansittart's views helped legitimise the concept of a war of annihilation against the civilian population of Germany in the minds of some British generals and to ensure that German resistance to Hitler was not taken seriously in Britain or the USA.[32] Weißmann concludes that even if one regards the occasionally expressed intention of wiping out Germany's elite or whole sections of the population as plans that were never taken seriously, the fact remains that if the Morgenthau Plan had been put into effect, it would have not only led to the permanent division of Germany, it would also have meant a considerable number of people starving to death.[33]

Weißmann thus adds to the New Right picture of National Socialism the notion that any suggestion that the Germans supported Hitler clears the way for their persecution. Weißmann also helps set the scene for the view that there is a continuity between Germany's wartime enemies with their plans for a defeated Germany and those Germans attacked in *Die selbstbewußte Nation* who supposedly identify National Socialism with all of Germany and thereby engage in the spiritual destruction of the nation. Ulrich Schacht demonstrates how Weißmann's presentation of allied plans for the destruction of Germany has a function in today's Germany:

> Muß man wirklich daran erinnern, daß es ausgerechnet Deutsche jüdischer Herkunft, die im Exil überlebt hatten, waren, die in jenem Jahr 1945 zu Papier brachten, was die wohlfeilen Anti-Faschisten und Deutsch-Suizidalen von heute nicht ums Verrecken in ihre Hirne lassen wollen: Daß der Nationalsozialismus eben *nicht* die Vollendung, sondern vielmehr den 'Zusammenbruch aller deutschen Traditionen darstellt'; daß es gerade *nicht* 'irgendeine deutsche Tradition als solche' gewesen ist, die den 'Nazismus herbeigefuhrt hat, sondern die Verletzung aller Traditionen' (Hannah Arendt).[34]

(Do we really have to remind people that it was Germans of Jewish extraction who had survived in exile and who wrote in 1945 what today's cheap antifascists and German suicide merchants won't acknowledge at any price: that National Socialism was actually not the culmination but rather the 'collapse of all German traditions'; that it was not 'German traditions as such' that brought about Nazism, but the 'violation of all traditions' (Hannah Arendt)).

New Right authors also portray the German people as the victims of National Socialism and of the war. The author and film-maker Wolfgang Venohr calls the British bombing of Germany a 'holocaust', but his account of the effect of the bombing is at odds with the New Right view that the Germans did not support Hitler: 'With their air attacks, the Allies achieved only one thing: they welded the Germans and Hitler together'.[35]

A further typical New Right strategy is to portray the German soldiers in the Second World War as heroic and this heroism as an end in itself. Armin Mohler thus defines the war 'not in the National Socialist sense of a war of liberation fought by an encircled people' but as struggle for its own sake.[36] In *Junge Freiheit* the virtues of the German soldiers are removed from their historical context and presented as laudable in their own right. Wolfgang Venohr thus describes the situation of the soldiers of the Wehrmacht, 'deep inside Russian territory and facing a military disaster on a Napoleonic scale'.[37] He turns to the memoirs of a German flying officer to describe the conditions at the front: in the vast snowy wastes the ordinary German soldiers dug in although their equipment was completely inadequate for winter and they had hardly any tanks left, and they brought the Soviet counter-offensive to a halt. Their descendants cannot remotely imagine what they suffered and what they achieved on the Eastern Front, and their heroism was unequalled. There is nothing to compare with it in the history of any nation.[38]

The heroism of German soldiers in the Second World War is praised in just the same way as Conservative Revolutionaries such as Ernst Jünger, Franz Schauwecker und Werner Best had praised the soldiers of the First World War. In the case of the Conservative Revolutionaries the soldiers' personal qualities had to bring meaning to what they themselves realised may have been meaningless mechanised slaughter on a massive scale which ended in defeat. For the New Right the memory of the soldiers who fought in the Second World War can be rescued if it is detached from Nazi war aims. Venohr has no doubts on this point: German soldiers were not to be blamed for the fact that they were fighting in an unjust war. Ordinary soldiers have never been made responsible for the errors, aggressive acts or massacres of their leaders. German soldiers on the Eastern front were vastly outnumbered, and their achievement was 'nothing less than miraculous'.[39]

Yet Venohr drifts from his original position in which the war is considered in its own right when he describes the bolshevik offensive. The 'errors, aggressive acts or massacres' of the leadership seem to be justified after all in Venohr's eyes as he goes on to explain how the German soldiers rescued Germany from communism:

Gedenkt jemand in Deutschland unserer Soldaten, die damals, vor fünfzig Jahren, das Höchste, das sie hatten, die ihr Leben in die Schanze schlugen? Wenn die deutschen Landser damals stiften gegangen wären, dann hätten die bolschewistischen Armeen ein Jahr später, Ende 1942, an der deutschen Ostgrenze gestanden, und wieder ein Jahr später, Ende 1943, an der deutschen Westgrenze. In Bonn, Düsseldorf und Saarbrücken hätten sowjetische Stadtkommandanten regiert. Der Rheinländer Adenauer wäre nach 'Zoffjetrußland', nach Sibirien, transportiert worden; die West- und Süddeutschen hätten das zu schmecken bekommen, was die Ost- und Mitteldeutschen später allein auslöffeln mußten. Von einer 'Bundesrepublik' oder der 'EG', von deutscher Einheit und Freiheit wäre nie die Rede gewesen.[40]

(Does anybody in Germany commemorate our soldiers who risked their greatest possession, their lives, 50 years ago? If the German soldiers had cleared off then the Bolshevik armies would have been standing at Germany's eastern border one year later, at the end of 1942, and one year after that, at the end of 1943, at Germany's western border. In Bonn, Düsseldorf and Saarbrücken Soviet town commanders would have been in power. The Rheinlander Adenauer would have been transported to Soviet Russia, to Siberia; the West and South Germans would have had a taste of what the East and Central Germans had to endure later on their own. Nobody would have been talking about a 'Federal Republic' or the 'EC', or German unity and freedom).

Günter Rohrmoser also praises the qualities of the Wehrmacht for their own sake when he recommends reading the memoirs of British field marshals who readily admit the greatness of its achievements. They write that the Wehrmacht was the best, most courageous and effective army in the history of human warfare.[41]

However, the Wehrmacht is for Rohrmoser also the German institution that offered the strongest resistance to the spirit of Nazism.[42] This is the reason for the New Right's hostile response to the exhibition 'Vernichtungskrieg. Verbrechen der Wehrmacht 1941 bis 1944' (War of Annihilation. Crimes of the Wehrmacht 1941 to 1944). The exhibition, mounted by the Hamburg Institute for Social Research, toured 33 German and Austrian towns between 1995 and 1999, at which point it was withdrawn after experts cast doubt on the accuracy of the descriptions of some of the photographic exhibits. A new exhibition on the subject was launched in November 2001 in Berlin. The New Right called the original exhibition 'a diffamatory hate show of the kind that is only possible in Germany',[43] and Erich Vad, a CSU specialist in foreign and security policy, asked what army ever remains blameless in war. The difference for Vad is that such an exhibition would be unthinkable elsewhere: despite any amount of empirical historical material such an exhibition with such a purpose would be unthinkable in Washington, Paris, London or Moscow. In those cities people honour their soldiers who fall in war, and history and memory are treated differently from the way they are treated in Germany.[44]

The problem of remembering the war is presented through New Right eyes by Brigitte Seebacher-Brandt. Collective memory of war reinforces other nations' identity, but this reinforcement is not available to the Germans. Indeed the memory of the Second World War is a force for national disintegration. By remembering and honouring their dead other nations find an inner unity that is timeless and more profound than any standardisation of life. 'Mort pour la patrie' is the inscription on memorials in every French village, and this expresses pride mixed with grief. 'But for what German fatherland were Jews wiped out, opposition eliminated, a war fought and the Army sacrificed?' What other nations take for granted Germans no longer take for granted. The general consensus is that there is no German Fatherland and there should never have been one'.[45]

In some 50 articles for *Junge Freiheit* contributors stressed the Wehrmacht's opposition to Hitler and Hitler's mistrust of the Wehrmacht,[46] and in an interview with *Junge Freiheit* a colonel proposed a day of remembrance for the men who planned and carried out the bomb plot of 20 July 1944. These men, he argued, were the fathers of the tradition honoured by the Bundeswehr.[47] Relativising the memory of National Socialism also means exporting it. Günter Rohrmoser argues that it was not the Germans who invented the idea that race is a significant factor in shaping history. Rather it is the brainchild of Gobineau, a Frenchman. Racism, he concludes, is not a German but a French invention.[48] Moreover, imperialism based on racism was a British invention.[49] He also traces Hitler's Social Darwinism back to the ancient Greeks. In an obvious reference to the *Historikerstreit* (historians' dispute) of the mid-1980s Rohrmoser concludes that National Socialism was not unique: the Social Darwinist component of Hitler's philosophy of power is ancient, and what we rightly find repulsive about National Socialism is not unique. It has deep roots in Western European tradition and it was alive in the 19th century.[50]

Political figures associated with the New Right further relativise National Socialism by suggesting that it has little to do with present-day Germany. Franz Schönhuber thus argues that the guilt associated with National Socialism can be worked off over time and that one can draw a line under the Nazi past by demonstrating that there was nothing unique about it:

Trotz aller angepriesenen und verordneten Potenzmittel ist Deutschland lendenlahm geworden, nicht nur physisch vergreist, sondern auch politisch verblödet. Alzheimer ad portas. Das von Nietzsche erwähnte 'präparierte Herdentier' wird am Nasenring der Medien immer näher an die Zelle des nationalen Masochismus herangeführt. Der Mensch, der stets gebückt durch die Weltgeschichte schlurfen muß, verliert seine Selbstachtung und erkrankt an Rückenmarkverkrümmung. Wo liegen die Heilungsmöglichkeiten? Vor allem in der dem Zeitgeist widersprechenden Feststellung: Die NS-Zeit ist inzwischen Geschichte. Die Untaten des NS-Staates gehören zu unserer Historie genauso wie die Ausrottungspolitik gegenüber den Indianern zur amerikanischen, die Greueltaten der Kolonialzeit zur englischen und die blutigen, stalinistischen Säuberungen zur russischen.[51]
(Despite all the recommended and prescribed potency cures Germany has become weak, not just physically aged but also

politically demented. Alzheimer's is waiting at the door. What Nietzsche referred to as the 'herd animal for dissection' is led by the nose ring of the media ever closer to the cell of national masochism. Anyone who always has to shuffle bent over through world history loses his self-esteem and grows ill with curvature of the spine. Where are the remedies? Primarily in the point that is at odds with the spirit of the times: that the Nazi period is now history. The atrocities of the Nazi state are part of our history, just as the policy of wiping out the Indians is part of American history, the outrages of the colonial period are part of English history, and the bloody Stalinist purges part of Russian history).

Set against the New Right's systematic relativisation of National Socialism, however, is the uncomfortable voice of its most prominent figure from the cultural sphere, Botho Strauß. Strauß raises National Socialist crimes to the existential level and thus puts them beyond any kind of *Vergangenheitsbewältigung*:

> Die Verbrechen der Nazis sind so gewaltig, daß sie nicht durch moralische Scham oder andere bürgerliche Empfindungen zu kompensieren sind. Sie stellen den Deutschen in die Erschütterung und belassen ihn dort, unter dem tremendum; ganz gleich wohin er sein Zittern und Zetern wenden mag, eine über das Menschenmaß hinausgehende Schuld wird nicht von ein, zwei Generationen einfach 'abgearbeitet.' Es handelt sich um ein Verhängnis in sakraler Dimension des Wortes.[52]
> (The crimes of the Nazis are so massive that they cannot be made good through a show of moral shame or other bourgeois sentiments. They place Germans in a state of shock and leave them there, under the tremendous burden. It makes no difference what Germans do with their trembling and wailing, a guilt that transcends all human measure is not simply to be 'worked off' by one or two generations. It is the Germans' fate in the sacred meaning of the word).

On the basis of this comment Strauß has been accused of seeing all reactions to National Socialism as equal: justifying it, denying it, ignoring it thus turn out to be as valid or invalid as remembering it for some public moral purpose.[53] But, seen against the broader background of cultural pessimism in the thinking of Strauß and other New Right intellectuals, this accusation misses the mark. Strauß's interpretation flows from this cultural pessimism, and it is no mere passing thought. He returns to it in *Die Fehler des Kopisten* where he writes that for five or six years the Germans had been intoxicated with their community. Their punishment for this intoxication is to examine for a thousand years how this could have happened: part of Germany's damned past is the eternal nature of its damnation.[54] Strauß the intellectual puts forward a view that offers no solace, and is impossible to reconcile with that of Schönhuber, who is looking to score points in the political arena.

One final New Right strategy for dealing with the Nazi past is to argue for it to be forgotten for the sake of the present. Günter Rohrmoser develops the strategy in his consideration of why there was no debate in West Germany about fascism in the first 20 years after the war. His answer: because it would have been impossible to construct a democracy after 1945 with such a debate going on in the background. One could not put a large section of the population in the dock and expect their support in building a democracy even as one was 'discriminating against them'.[55] Taking this line of thought even further Rohrmoser argued that the GDR declared that any responsibility for National Socialism had been eliminated with the establishment of a socialist state. Rohrmoser seems to show a degree of admiration for this stance when he declares that the GDR would have collapsed much sooner if it had not successfully ruled out any discussion about the Nazi past.[56]

The psychology of this attitude towards history which wants nothing to do with Habermas's 'critical appropriation' is illuminated by Peter Meier-Bergfeld, correspondent for *Rheinische Merkur* in Austria and contributor to *Die selbstbewußte Nation*. Meier-Bergfeld writes of the 'permanent retrospective on the Third Reich that is running in the cinema of Germany'. He argues that this preoccupation with the Nazi past renders Germany 'incapable of having a present or a future', and he quotes Nietzsche on how a certain level of insomnia, of rumination, of historical awareness can damage a living being and ultimately destroy it, whether that being is a person, a nation or a culture.[57] Instead of presenting an intellectually coherent answer to the question of how to deal with the Nazi past, Meier-Bergfeld contents himself with a complaint about the debilitating effects of the act of remembering. Here again, the cultural dimension of the New Right sheds light on a mentality which is unable to bear uncertainty. If a simple faith in an unchallenged past is not to be had, then this past should not be discussed. Nietzschean vitalism provides the either-or construction: reflection loses out to self-assertive 'life'. In Schönhuber's terms, a national sickness must be cured.

The mentality which is ill at ease in a self-questioning culture reveals itself in the New Right rejection of what it sees as an obsessive guilt complex in German public life. Wolfgang Saur writes in *Junge Freiheit* that teaching about the Holocaust in schools goes hand in hand with a 'nihilistic dismantling of the self'.[58] Joschka Fischer's declaration in an interview with Bernard-Henry Lévy that the memory of Auschwitz was the only possible foundation of the new Berlin Republic[59] prompts Saur to quote Michael Kleeberg's comment that a state that is founded on Auschwitz can only have one possible fate: to disappear.[60] Günter Rohrmoser argues that after 1945 very little attention was given to National Socialism, but as historical distance increased, the Nazi past became an almost obsessive feature of all political debate.[61]

Critics of the New Right argue that its limited success is due not least to the continuing debate about National Socialism and its significance for the democratic political culture of the Federal Republic,[62] and that German confidence is not undermined but strengthened by remembering the Nazi past. In the broader arena of public debate those behind the Holocaust memorial in Berlin, dedicated to the Jewish victims of Nazi terror, declare that only a confident and democratic Germany is capable of erecting a monument in honour of the murdered Jews of Europe. It is also a warning to future generations to learn from history, and its location in the centre of Berlin where the new government quarter has been established is a sign that the memory of National Socialism forms part of the core of the Federal Republic's identity.[63]

For the New Right, however, the Holocaust memorial is 'the last testament of the generation of 68'. Before they retire they want to deal Germany a blow that will shake it to its core.[64] *Junge Freiheit* quotes Rudolf Augstein's view that the memorial is aimed against the newly emerging Germany in Berlin and the sovereignty that Germany had taken so long to restore.[65] Those who approved its construction were intent on impressing Germany's neighbours. Only through relentless propaganda, by keeping alive a sense of shame and guilt can a climate be created that makes Germans the submissive followers of foreign powers.[66]

The 'Other Germany'

If one New Right strategy for dealing with Nazism is to relativise it, another is to direct attention towards what are presented as alternative German traditions. Ulrich Schacht quotes from *Galeerentagebuch* (Galley Diary) by Imre Kertész, a Jewish survivor of Auschwitz and Buchenwald from Budapest, who declares he almost feels sorry for being part of the basic guilt that Germans are confronted with as they live out their lives in spiritual misery.[67] Schacht also reminds us how Thomas Mann felt after 1945, 'despite having been deeply offended by Germany under the swastika'.[68] Thomas Mann refused to identify Nazism with the whole of German history:

'ich glaube an Deutschlands Zukunft, wie verzweifelt auch immer seine Gegenwart sich ausnehmen, wie hoffnungslos die Zerstörung erscheinen möge. Man höre doch auf, vom Ende der deutschen Geschichte zu reden! Deutschland ist nicht identisch mit der kurzen und finsteren geschichtlichen Episode, die Hitlers Namen trägt'.[69]
('I believe in Germany's future, however desperate its present may look, however hopeless the destruction may appear. People should stop talking about the end of German history! Germany is not the same as the short, dark historical episode that bears Hitler's name').

New Right authors find support for these views on the left. Karlheinz Weißmann quotes the communist Alexander Abusch upon his return to Germany from exile in Mexico: 'Because Hitler was able to come to power in Germany, the German name became the most hated in the whole world at the end of the Second World War. But Hitler's end in blood and disgrace amid the ruins of Germany is not the end of the German nation, however low it fell'.[70] Weißmann comments on how Abusch distinguishes between the German people and the Nazi leadership, and he concludes that the German left argued from a patriotic position, presenting itself as the representative of 'the better Germany' and giving defeated Germany a way out: Germans could see themselves as misled.[71]

The New Right also stresses that the Nazi era was only a brief period in German history. Wolfgang Venohr quotes Peter Graf Yorck von Wartenburg, a conspirator in the July 1944 bomb plot to assassinate Hitler. Shortly before he was executed he wrote that his actions were not guided by any personal ambition or desire for power, but by his feelings for his fatherland, his concern for the Germany that had grown over the preceding two thousand years.[72] This reference to a long German history is developed by Karlheinz Weißmann who argues that German history should not be reduced to 'twelve years'. Instead the nation should take stock of its entire history, including the phases in which it can take pride and satisfaction.[73]

For the New Right the alternative German traditions seem to be embodied by the Conservative Revolution and the aristocratic and military resistance to Hitler. The New Right also turns to these groups for inspiration about the positive values it might espouse once it has set itself off from the Old Right and dismissed mainstream conservatism as part of the liberal consensus. New Right interest in the Conservative Revolution means that intellectuals such as Carl Schmitt, Martin Heidegger, Ernst Jünger, Oswald Spengler are today experiencing a comeback as the innovative thinkers behind the movement, and Friedrich Nietzsche is revered as a source of inspiration for the Conservative Revolution and the New Right alike. Yet these models are far from straightforward.

Observers suggest that the New Right and the Conservative Revolution have similar political positions and strategies,[74] and the New Right itself sees the Conservative Revolution as a source of values. Karlheinz Weißmann quotes the prominent Conservative Revolutionary, Edgar Julius Jung, on the 'Conservative Revolutionary principle' that metaphysically rooted values provide the basis of all communities and that the urge to preserve these values is a conservative one.[75] Given the trouble the Conservative Revolution had in setting out what it stood for, it would be more accurate to say that both movements share a desire for absolute values. In the case of the Conservative Revolution this mentality is set out in Hugo von Hofmannsthal's essay of 1927, 'Das Schrifttum als geistiger Raum der Nation' (Writing as the spiritual Location of the

Nation), in which he sees the major characteristic of the Conservative Revolution as a search for bonds, wholeness and unity that is replacing the search for freedom.[76] Understanding the Conservative Revolution as a movement engaged in searching for rather than finding absolute values may help explain the openly critical account from Angelika Willig, a regular contributor to *Junge Freiheit*, of the New Right's preoccupation with the major figures of the Conservative Revolution in its search for usable political positions. In 1998 Willig wrote that she had spent five years trying to put down on paper something of use on the political theories of the right. Despite studying philosophy, reading Nietzsche, Heidegger, Jünger and Carl Schmitt, however, she was left empty-handed. She concluded that sometimes one just had to turn around in order to make progress, and one time to do so is when one is on the wrong track.[77]

Two further and equally problematic functions of the Conservative Revolution for the New Right are its supposed theoretical purity and anti-Nazi stance. Armin Mohler's long-term project after 1945 was to portray the Conservative Revolution as a distinctive intellectual movement which was distorted by the Nazis and which, in its pure form, had a role to play as a model for Germany's future. Mohler presents the Conservative Revolution as theory, and National Socialism as practice, and he asks to what extent a theory can be made responsible for a practice which varied from it.[78]

However, the New Right's presentation of the Conservative Revolution as non-Nazi or even anti-Nazi does not stand up to close scrutiny. Typically the New Right takes political statements by Conservative Revolutionaries as proof of the distance between thinkers like Oswald Spengler and the Nazis. In the New Right journal *Etappe* Frank Como sees Spengler as a model because he distanced himself more and more from National Socialism, turning away in disappointment at its lack of a sense of reality.[79] Similarly Günter Rohrmoser calls Oswald Spengler's *Jahre der Entscheidung* (Years of Decision), which appeared in 1933, 'the first fundamental critique of National Socialism'.[80] But there is a difference between political statements – Spengler did indeed turn away from the Nazis in his political statements, and basic philosophical beliefs which were not abandoned in 1933. Like the New Right, the Conservative Revolution operated not only on the level of political statements but also at the level of broader philosophical reflections on the nature of humankind. At the level of political statements Spengler could mock National Socialism as 'the organisation of the unemployed by the workshy',[81] but *Jahre der Entscheidung* contains no fundamental philosophical objections to the Nazis. An examination of the Nazi reception of this work actually shows general enthusiasm, with the Nazis philosophers not understanding why Spengler would not line up with them.[82] His basic position, which he did not alter when the Nazis came to power, was that in politics only success or failure counts: in an amoral world moral objections are irrelevant.

Similarly, Ernst Jünger began to voice his doubts about National Socialism as early as 1926, yet his views on the emergence of a new elite which would combine primitive man's will with the technical expertise required of the modern warrior, on politics as essentially beyond questions of morality, and on political issues not being judged by moral standards – all views which Jünger later came to see at the heart of Nazi thinking – persist into the thirties. This response to the Nazis at two levels is common among Conservative Revolutionaries, and it undermines the absolute distinction made by the New Right between the Conservative Revolution and National Socialism.[83] It also undermines the New Right idea that those involved in the July 1944 bomb plot represented some other German tradition since they are explicitly portrayed by the New Right as having taken their political lead from the Conservative Revolution. Wolfgang Venohr thus writes that two of the conspirators, Caesar Freiherr von Hofacker and Fritz-Dietlof Graf von der Schulenberg, came from the Conservative Revolution school of thought, and writers such as Oswald Spengler, Moeller van den Bruck, Ernst Jünger, Ernst Niekisch, and Reinhold Schneider were their political mentors.[84]

Research has also pointed to the involvement of Conservative Revolutionary individuals and groups with Nazism. Some figures were absorbed into the Party: the new nationalist Werner Best, who had written on legal aspects of the First World War, was able to put his ideas of natural justice and the 'absolute state' into practice when he became an SS officer and a key figure in the development of the Gestapo.[85] Nazi Party documents indicate a wide variety of responses to Nazi overtures, with many Conservative Revolutionaries joining the Party when it came to power. Albrecht Erich Günther, for example, editor of *Deutsches Volkstum* and of a 1932 book on what nationalists expected of National Socialism,[86] became a Party member in 1933 and was a member of the Reich German Press Association.[87] Wilhelm Stapel rejected attempts in 1933 to recruit him into the Party, but he did apply to join the Reich Association of German Writers in December 1933, signing a declaration that he would always support German writing in line with national government policy.[88]

Within the Conservative Revolutionary movement Edgar Jung expressed the sentiments of some, though certainly not all, when he took the credit for the electoral successes of the NSDAP in 1932, claiming that the intellectual preconditions for the German Revolution were created outside National Socialism, and he and intellectuals like him 'paved the way for the German people to vote for National Socialist candidates'.[89]

It is important to note that many of these compromising aspects of the Conservative Revolution are alluded to by New Right thinkers themselves. On the one hand Karlheinz Weißmann writes about Friedrich Hielscher whose 'resistance group' was meant to occupy key positions in the Nazi regime in order to undermine it, and he points out that Edgar Jung was killed by the Nazis in 1934. Similarly, Dieter Stein explains that *Junge Freiheit* sets out to refute the accusation that the whole of the German right was involved with the Nazis. Rather, the right presented a constructive critique of parliament and democracy that warned of the consequences of the Nazi dictatorship. Ultimately it was followers of the Conservative Revolution who opposed the criminal regime of the Nazis.[90] On the other hand, Weißmann also notes that one of Hielscher's group, Wolfram Sievers, ordered medical experiments on concentration camp inmates and was executed in 1948. Weißmann also cites historians who have called Hielscher's resistance into question, and he gives an account of an interview he conducted with Hielscher during which he felt a considerable tension.[91]

Whereas Armin Mohler sticks rigidly to the theory versus practice distinction between the Conservative Revolution and National Socialism, Günter Rohrmoser argues that the Conservative Revolution played a key role in facilitating a Nazi cultural revolution. Without the intellectual superstructure of Conservative Revolutionary theories National Socialism would never have been able to develop its cultural revolutionary force.[92] Rohrmoser considers the theoreticians of the Conservative Revolution, together with large sections of the educated middle class, to have shared Hitler's idea of a nationalism based on race.[93] Günter Rohrmoser may call Spengler's *Jahre der Entscheidung*, 'the first fundamental critique of National Socialism' and quote what Spengler is supposed to have said after meeting with Hitler in the early 1920s: 'the man is too stupid, he doesn't understand anything', yet Rohrmoser also concedes that the Nazis' success among the bourgeois intelligentsia would probably not have been as great as it was without Spengler's influence.[94] Looking to the future, Rohrmoser's answer to the question whether conservatism should be defined as Armin Mohler demands, namely in line with the Conservative Revolution, is a further indication of that movement's disputed status for the New Right: 'No. All that is a thing of the past'.[95] Also from within the New Right, Henning Eichberg gives a surprisingly detached account of Armin Mohler's post-war writings on the Conservative Revolution, describing the term as Mohler used it in the 1950s as 'a concept for rehabilitating and justifying in the period straight after the war'.[96]

In his book of essays on 'ideas, thinkers and prospects' for the right, Karlheinz Weißmann offers a study of Ewald von Kleist-Schmenzin, the aristocrat whose country estate was the venue for meetings of the conservative opposition to Hitler in 1944 and who was arrested by the Gestapo and executed shortly before the war ended. Weißmann clearly admires von Kleist-Schmenzin's 'instinctive aversion' to Hitler and sees him as the embodiment of the 'Prussian spirit'.[97] Weißmann quotes Johannes Gross's assessment that the resistance to Hitler founded on morality was conservative and aristocratic in character. It was an uprising in the name of freedom and decency.[98] Weißmann goes on to deal with the circle around Goerdeler and his 'restorationist solutions', and with Stauffenberg and Tresckow who favoured 'Prussian Socialism'. Any expectation that a study of these leading figures of the moral resistance to Hitler could help map out the shape of future right-wing politics starts to look improbable, however, when Weißmann goes on to describe von Kleist-Schmenzin's absolute resistance to his estate workers' attempts to unionise, his distance from his 'underlings' and his 'well-intended patriarchy'.[99] Indeed, Weißmann himself characterises von Kleist-Schmenzin as someone who wanted to turn back the clock and restore the old order. He was a 'lone reactionary' whose views hardly went beyond the attitudes of 19th century conservative thinkers.[100] We have already noted the New Right's wish for rootedness and absolute values beyond question, and ultimately it is the presence of these fixed points in von Kleist-Schmenzin's life that explains Weißmann's fascination for a person whose particular political attitudes Weißmann himself regards as an irrelevance for the present. Thus Weißmann enthusiastically quotes von Kleist-Schmenzin on the meaning of conservatism:

'Konservatismus ist etwas Unbedingtes, das kein Kompromiß zuläßt. Denn er ist eine Weltanschauung, also eine Gesamtschau aller Dinge von einem festen Standpunkte aus. Da er nur religiös zu begründen ist, so ist dieser feste Punkt in Gott, und von dort aus ist die Aufgabe des Menschen zu begreifen, nämlich Gottes Willen zu erkennen und zu tun.'[101] ('Conservatism is something absolute that admits no compromise. For it is a *Weltanschauung*, a comprehensive way of looking at the world from a firm standpoint. Since it can only have a religious foundation the fixed point is God, and from here Man's task can be understood, to recognise and do God's will.').

Stauffenberg, Goerdeler and Tresckow are also made to do service at one point as representatives of the other Germany,[102] but their political ideas are dismissed elsewhere by the New Right as outmoded. In the journal *Criticón* Harald Holz suggests a 'mental experiment' of introducing a 'Day of National Honour' to be celebrated each year on 20 July. But he adds immediately that he is not thinking of any particular socio-political plans such as the corporative state put forward by the groups involved in the attempt on Hitler's life. Rather he is thinking of their commitment to rescuing Germany's honour in the eyes of the whole world, even at the cost of their own lives.[103] The limitations of this other Germany are formulated more forcefully by the New Right author Rainer Zitelmann who supposes that the political views of men such as von Hassell, Goerdeler or Stauffenberg would today be regarded not just as 'right-wing' but as 'extreme right-wing'.[104] For the New Right the 'ideas of 20 July 1944' cannot provide the substance of any kind of alternative vision for Germany.

Nevertheless there is clearly a lingering respect and deference towards these men and their rigid beliefs. Wolfgang Venohr quotes admiringly from a secret oath sworn by the brothers Berthold and Claus von Stauffenberg in the event of their persecution by the Nazis or in the event of any occupation of Germany by a foreign power. In this oath we see prefigured the mentality of the New Right itself: the sense of German traditions under threat, a German destiny and a leading role for Germany, the rejection of the alien principle of equality and the wish to see a social structure based on hierarchy, the need for a sense of rootedness, community and discipline, and the willingness to use military force to protect this order:

'Wir wissen im Deutschen die Kräfte, die ihn berufen, die Gemeinschaft der abendländlischen Völker zu schönerem Leben zu führen. Wir bekennen uns im Geist und in der Tat zu den großen Überlieferungen unseres Volkes, das durch die Verschmelzung hellenscher und christlicher Ursprünge in germanischem Wesen das abendländische Menschentum schuf. Wir wollen eine Neue Ordnung, die alle Deutschen zu Trägern des Staates macht und ihnen Recht und Gerechtigkeit verbürgt, verachten aber die Gleichheitslüge und fordern die Anerkennung der naturgegebenen Ränge. Wir wollen ein Volk, das in der Erde der Heimat verwurzelt den natürlichen Mächten nahebliebt, das im Wirken in den gegebenen Lebenskreisen sein Glück und sein Genüge findet und in freiem Stolze die niederen Triebe des Neides und der Mißgunst überwindet. Wir wollen Führende, die aus allen Schichten des Volkes wachsend, verbunden den göttlichen Mächten, durch großen Sinn, Zucht und Opfer den anderen vorangehen. Wir verbinden uns zu einer neuen Gemeinschaft, die durch Haltung und Tat der Neuen Ordnung dient und den künftigen Führern die Kämpfer bildet, derer sie bedürfen.'[105]

('We recognise in Germans the forces which make them destined to lead the community of Western peoples to a better life. We declare our allegiance in mind and deed to the great traditions of our people which created Western humanity through the merging of Hellenic and Christian roots in a Germanic essence. We want a New Order that makes all Germans upholders of the State and guarantees them right and justice, but we despise the lie of equality and demand that natural differences of rank be recognised. We want a people that has its roots in the earth of home and that remains close to the forces of nature, that finds its happiness and contentment in working in its given surroundings and that overcomes the low impulses of envy and malevolence in freedom and pride. We want leaders who come from all strata of the people, close to the divine powers, guided by great sense, discipline and sacrifice. We join together in a new community that will serve the New Order through its attitudes and deeds and that will provide the leaders of the future with the warriors they need').

Wolfgang Venohr's biography of Stauffenberg displays many of the structural features we have noted in the New Right's cultural interpretation of National Socialism. His admiration for his subject is clear from the first page where he wishes that he could have been born 15 years earlier so that he could have accompanied Stauffenberg on the 20th of July as his adjutant and protected him with his own life.[106] Venohr describes how the young Stauffenberg came under the influence of the poet Stefan George. George in turn is slotted into a supposedly non-Nazi tradition: whereas the 1938 Brockhaus proclaims him to be the 'prophet of the dawn of the Third Reich', Venohr dismisses the thought of any spiritual link between George and the Nazis. The poet was neither of the right nor of the left, but rather the precursor of the Conservative Revolution, and this was his great appeal to the Stauffenberg brothers.[107] In seeking to explain Claus von Stauffenberg's decision to have a military career Venohr sees George as a key influence since it was George who urged his followers to serve and to take responsibility. Stauffenberg had also read Ernst Jünger's first war book, *In Stahlgewittern* (In Storms of Steel, 1920) in which the young lieutenant had described how the idea of the fatherland had attained a purer form in the filth and misery of battle.[108] Stauffenberg's association with the other Germany is also portrayed as his link with the majority of Germans. Asking why Stauffenberg was not repelled by Nazi anti-Semitism as he rose through the ranks from 1933 onwards, Venohr answers that Hitler had played down his anti-Semitism between 1928 and 1933 and even declared that he had nothing against 'decent' Jews. Like most Germans, Stauffenberg 'had no reason to take Nazi racism seriously', and, like most Germans, he was wrong.[109] While it is true that there are similarities between the Conservative Revolution and the New Right in the area of political attitudes, it is also clear that both movements are notable for their lack of clarity in this very area. However, at the deeper level there are parallel structures of political and cultural thought, and there are also parallel responses to the problems contained within this body of thought: both movements need absolute values at a time when traditional religious, political and moral values have been called into question. We see a New Right that is hindered in its search for absolute values by what Habermas calls the devaluation of an exemplary past: exemplary periods in the past that the present might have been able to use without hesitation for their guidance have faded into insignificance. Just as the New Right was unable to block out a cultural awareness of Modernity, it is an awareness of the effects of Modernity that prevents the New Right from finding its historical equivalent of institutions that let the individual live in 'unquestioning comfort'. At their most self-critical, New Right intellectuals appreciate this problem, but it is hard to live with. For this reason finding models but seeing through them is one of the recurrent patterns of New Right thought. Günter Rohrmoser shows an acute awareness of the problem in his discussion of Nietzsche's essay *Vom Nutzen und Nachteil der Historie für das Leben* (On the Advantages and Disadvantages of History for Life). Rohrmoser argues that in modern society tradition and science are at odds with each other. Tradition loses out to science because tradition cannot provide a rational basis for anything. It has lost all authority in modern society.[110]

Martin Greiffenhagen sees a 'conservative dilemma' arising from this kind of self-questioning, and among Conservative Revolutionaries this prompts a shift towards activism.[111] Our next chapter examines how the New Right deals with its own conservative dilemma.

4
Values and Programmes

Nationalism: a simple commitment?

One might suppose that despite the confusion over culture, multi-culturalism and National Socialism, at least the nation and nationalism would be beyond question in New Right thought. Certainly an assertive nationalism is a consistent feature of New Right political philosophy. Pierre Krebs offers one of the most aggressive portrayals of the renewed sense of nation which followed the demise of Marxism in the East and German unification and which now challenges the liberal order of the West. Krebs sees the revolution that swept away Marxism in the East as still having some way to go. It will reach beyond political unification and seek a more profound reconnection with German history. It will search out the 'essence of what is German' and the sacred things that today's politicians, from whatever party, would let sink into oblivion. Through this revolution the founding myth of the people will burst forth, the myth of Germans' origins, the source of what makes Germans special and different. Representatives of a chaotic one-world ideology, from liberals to Marxists are hostile to German unification because it is based on a law of identity that undermines cosmopolitan nonsense about all people being equal.[1]

After unification Krebs sees the need for a healing process: Germany is a sick nation, and this sickness is spiritual. It has been 'reeducated', and all it has left is the prospect of maximising its material consumption. Its Germanic myths have been converted into apparitions inspiring fear. Germany must recover its 'Nietzschean health' by regaining its values and ideals, its intellectual sovereignty, its spiritual roots and its sense of history. His Thule Seminar is helping to bring about Germany's 'cultural rebirth'.[2] Nationalism is a key element in the psychology of the New Right. Karlheinz Weißmann points to the 'inner dimension' of the debate about the nation: quoting Max Weber he argues that even in Germany the national is regaining its 'specific pathos'. There is no discernible alternative to the nation, no other modern form of political community that satisfies the human need for clarity.[3] De Benoist advances a similarly simple psychological proposition: that it is good and necessary for all people to take pride in their predecessors, their country and the achievements of their race.[4] He puts the case for nationalism in a way that highlights the inhibitions of most German authors of the New Right but underlines the psychological value of a clear and simple commitment:

> Es bedarf heute eines Rahmens zur Selbstentfaltung und Selbstbehauptung. Das Vaterland ist das Territorium eines Volkes und das Land seiner Väter. Das Volk ist kein abstrakter Begriff, das Vaterland ist keine philosophische Schule. Es handelt sich um konkrete Realitäten.[5]
> (We need a framework within which we can develop and assert ourselves. The fatherland is the territory of a people and the land of its fathers. The people is not an abstract concept, and the fatherland is not a school of philosophical thought. These things are concrete and real).

The German New Right achieves a degree of clarity about the particular brand of nationalism it embraces by expressing itself indirectly: the journal *Nation und Europa* quotes Oswald Spengler, on the shortcomings of the people in the nationalist formula and the need for strong leadership if the people are to fulfil their destiny:

> Ein Volk ist das, was man aus ihm macht. Fur sich allein ist jedes Volk unfähig, die Bedingungen zu erfüllen, welche die Weltlage seit Jahrhunderten stellt, wenn es sich durchsetzen oder auch nur behaupten will. Sein Schicksal hängt aber nicht von Ansichten ab, sondern von Menschen, also nicht von Theorien oder Beschlüssen darüber, wie dies oder jenes sein soll, sondern von Persönlichkeiten, die das tun und tun können, was getan werden

muß. Ein leitender Typus ist notwendig, der die schöpferischen Eigenschaften des Volkes im Hinblick auf seine geschichtliche Lage zusammenfaßt und herausbildet.[6] (A people is what one makes of it. Left to its own devices a people is not able to meet the conditions that have been imposed by the world situation for centuries, if it wishes to prevail or merely to survive. Its fate does not depend on opinions but on individuals, not on theories or resolutions about how things ought to be, but on personalities who can and do carry out what has to be done. What is needed is a leader type who can focus and develop the creative qualities of a people with an eye to its historical situation).

With fewer inhibitions than most, Franz Schönhuber declared before the October 1998 elections that he would vote for the party that combined measured patriotism with radical social reform. On this point there should be no taboos or threat of prosecution against anyone studying models from Nazi Germany and fascist Italy to see if parts of them could be used in order to tackle the problem of unemployment in Germany today. Such a study would be entirely compatible with a rejection of fascist doctrine as a whole.[7]

The prospect of unification prompted the New Right journal *Wir selbst* to address the issue of German identity. Whereas the left traditionally saw identity as the product of the changing relationship between base and superstructure it is now starting to embrace the notion of regional identity. The Christian Democrats spout their empty phrases about a European identity that has superseded the sense of belonging to a nation. Both positions are attacked as a flight from the nation which, according to *Wir selbst*, offers ethnic and cultural bonds and a moral commitment that emerges from a rediscovery of German history, traditional continuities and ethical ties.[8] Even the 'national revolutionary' strand of New Right thought that is quick to point out that German unification is not in itself a resolution of the German question when one considers the threat to national identity posed by globalisation,[9] can embrace a feelgood nationalism. When asked what national revolutionary means in the 21st century the anonymous interviewee responds:

Es heißt zunächst einmal, auch weiterhin von der Nation als wirkungsmächtiger Größe auszugehen, von einem historischen Faktum, das als Schicksals-, Sprach-, Kultur- und damit

Identitätsgemeinschaft im besten Falle Vaterland und Mutterland zugleich ist und politischen Handlungs- wie kulturellen Orientierungsrahmen bieten kann.[10] (It means firstly continuing to place the nation at the centre of our thinking as an effective force, a historical fact that is at its best both fatherland and motherland, offering a community based on a shared destiny, language, culture and identity as well as a political framework for our actions and a cultural framework for our guidance).

Karlheinz Weißmann considers the definition of a nation offered by Ernest Renan: 'A nation is a great community, founded in the knowledge of the sacrifices one has made and those one is ready to make in the future; it assumes a shared history, but in the present it is held together by a hard fact: the general agreement and the clearly expressed wish to continue in this shared existence', and Weißmann concludes that by these criteria there can be no doubt that the Germans remained a nation throughout the period of their separation.[11] Unification is a great opportunity, with Germans no longer being the defeated people or having to take sides in a 'worldwide civil war', yet he also hints at the challenge of unification when he writes that Germans lack a compass to show them the way forward.[12]

Henning Eichberg sees German unification as a turning point and opportunity for the New Right. At first he describes Armin Mohler's post-war preoccupation with the Conservative Revolution not as a necessary step back from practical politics in order to achieve cultural hegemony but as a sign of isolation: the Conservative Revolution was an affair for academic study, for bibliographies and bibliophiles. It could do no political damage, but nor could it bring any political gains. It was not meant to provide the basis of a political movement in the present.[13] Yet he goes on to contrast this post-war interest in the Conservative Revolution with the 'new significance' the movement has gained since the collapse of the Soviet state. The conservative right has lost its convenient communist enemy, the left has lost its alternative to capitalism, and hopes of a triumph of American-style liberalism have given way to fears of a clash of civilisations. In the resultant political vacuum and confusion the paradoxical concept of a Conservative Revolution is the appropriate model for the future: even if there is no longer any coherent political direction from the right or the left, and even if there are no intact values on offer, at least the paradoxical formula of the Conservative Revolution can provide a philosophical context. The concept also has the advantage of embracing nationalism which has unexpectedly become so relevant now.[14]

These New Right reflections on nationalism underline the principles of clarity, commitment, leadership and an assertive attitude towards Germany's past, and even Eichberg's portrayal of a more chaotic time points to nationalism as a potential constant. Academic studies of the New Right generally focus on these principles in order to characterise the movement, seeing a simple commitment to nationalism as an essential ingredient of New Right thought.[15] Kurt Lenk argues that motifs such as the *Volk* and the *Reich* are the foundation of the New Right view of the world, providing meaning and identity as hard facts.[16] Hajo Funke detects something of the cause and effect behind New Right nationalism when he describes how it is a reaction to vague feelings of impotence, and a rejection of Modernity and moral decline. Against these feelings the *Volk*, the state and the nation offer an order which is greater than the individual.[17]

This reading of the New Right harks back to Habermas's interpretation of neo-conservatism as requiring 'affirmative pasts'. Yet, as we have seen, Habermas notes elsewhere that the more academic expressions of neo-conservative thought are committed to critique. This commitment tends to work against the aim of creating affirmative pasts and is more likely to play a role in what Bauman refers to as the permanent struggle for order. In the analysis that follows we shall see how strident New Right nationalism is like the feelgood culture. Beneath it runs a deeper current of doubt about the viability and relevance of nationalism. An examination of conflicting New Right attitudes reveals an acute awareness that nationalism is a compromised value.

In the context of research on the Conservative Revolutionary Tat-Kreis (Action Group) Klaus Fritzsche has stressed that the group's political philosophy is not to be viewed as a 'timeless arsenal of ideas'. It is important to appreciate the 'element of process' underlying these ideas, that is, the way in which attitudes develop in response to change in the outside world.[18] This dynamic approach based on processes will prove useful for our understanding of the New Right's attitudes towards nationalism: as we shall see, consideration of the cultural dimension of the New Right reveals the process at work that Funke puts forward as a theoretical proposition: an unstable nationalist commitment emerges as the product of the need for fixed beliefs in a chaotic world.

Externalisation and internalisation

The bond with the nation can on occasion be portrayed as having survived all attempts to replace it. Karlheinz Weißmann takes the collapse of communism as proof of the durability of nationalism and the fragility of all ideologies which seek to transcend it: the great upheavals of recent years have proven that nations have not been overtaken by history. They are not relics of tribalism or some piece of dangerous folklore, nor are they values that one can take up or swap for others at will. The bond with the nation is an existential one, and dreams of world citizenship or of a united Europe have lost all substance.[19]

Yet this assertion has to do battle with a very different reality described by the political journalist Johannes Gross and which Weißmann himself acknowledges:

Im Jahre 1986 schrieb Johannes Gross in seinem Notizbuch: 'Kein Mensch weiß, wozu es noch Deutschland, wozu es noch Deutsche gibt. Niedrigste Geburtenrate der Welt. Kein Gottvertrauen, kein Selbstvertrauen. Die tonangebende Generation könnte die letzte sein, wenn es nicht schon eine neue gäbe.' Gross bezog seine Feststellung auf die tief lebensfeindlichen Züge hinter der optimistischen Fassade der alten Bundesrepublik, diese Mischung aus Überheblichkeit und Minderwertigkeitsgefühl, Sentimentalität und Krämergeist, den Unwillen gegenüber aller Selbstverständlichkeit, den Mangel an innerem Gleichgewicht. Solche Impressionen sind keines Beweises fähig. Sie teilen sich bloß demjenigen mit, der ein Auge dafür hat. Der psychische Zustand der Nachkriegsdeutschen hatte seine Ursache darin, daß sie sich offen oder insgeheim als das 'von der Geschichte widerlegte Volk' betrachteten.[20]
(In 1986 Johannes Gross wrote in his notebook: 'Nobody knows what the point of Germany or of Germans is today: Lowest

birthrate in the world: No belief in God or themselves. The current elite generation could be the last if there were not already a new one'. Gross backs up his assertion with the profoundly life-denying features behind the optimistic façade of the old Federal Republic, this mix of arrogance and feelings of inferiority, sentimentality and narrowmindedness, indignation over things that should be taken for granted, lack of inner balance. Such impressions do not need to be proven. They are obvious to anyone with half an eye. The psychological condition of Germans after the war is rooted in the fact that they regard themselves openly or in private as a 'people that has been proven wrong by history').

This tension between a confident nation and a people lacking in confidence is typical of New Right thinking. For Günter Rohrmoser it is a 'historical reality' that no people or society can exist without a national consciousness, and the cultural pessimism of the New Right surfaces when he suggests a parallel with religion, quoting the political philosopher Hermann Lübbe on religion as the rational response of humankind to its vulnerability to absolute contingency.[21]

The tension over the issue of the nation is demonstrated in the very different diagnoses of the problem offered by Pierre Krebs and Karlheinz Weißmann. For Krebs the obstacle to Germany reasserting itself on the world stage is the external one of Western allies imposing a reeducation on Germany that caused it to break with its intellectual traditions. German unification swept away this external obstacle and cleared the path for reconnecting with Germany's traditional identity: 'In the land of Nietzsche and Wagner, Bach and Kant, Clausewitz and Thomas Münzer a single word could fan the red glow of history back to life, smash to pieces half a century of dictatorial 'reeducation' that thought it could displace this word from the mind of a whole people without encountering any resistance'.[22]

The word is Germany, and Krebs goes on to associate it with the rebirth of organic communities and the defeat of a mechanistic and collectivist social order.[23] Krebs's vision of an unbroken German tradition being able to reassert itself once the external constraints of Western and Eastern domination have been removed contrasts with Weißmann's assessment. When Weißmann attributes the psychological condition of the German people to the feeling that they have been proven wrong by history he is explaining Germany's lack of confidence in terms of a military defeat which was also a spiritual defeat. The German national consciousness had been bound up with a search for its own path between western liberalism and eastern collectivism, and this search had ended in failure. Weißmann quotes the poet Gottfried Benn's wartime diaries on his 'wishes for Germany':

'Wünsche für Deutschland: neue Begriffsbestimung für Held und Ehre. Ausmerzung jeder Person, die innerhalb der nächsten hundert Jahre Preußentum oder das Reich sagt. Geschichte als Verwaltung mittleren Beamten des gehobenen Dienstes überlassen, aber als Richtung und Prinzip einer europäischen Exekutive öffentlich unterstellen. Die Kinder vom sechsten bis sechzehnten Jahr nach Wahl der Eltern in der Schweiz, in England, Frankreich, Amerika, Dänemark, auf Staatskosten erziehen'.[24]

('Wishes for Germany: new understanding of heroism and honour. Elimination of anyone who utters the words Prussia or Reich in the next one hundred years. History as an administrative matter to be left in the hands of clerical grade civil servants, but its direction and principles to be placed publicly in the hands of a European executive. Children to be educated at State expense from the age of six to sixteen in line with parents' wishes, in Switzerland, England, France, America, Denmark').

This profound challenge to German identity posed by military and spiritual defeat is a major theme for the New Right. We have already seen that the calls to draw a line under the Nazi past for the sake of Germany's future are only one strand in a much more complex pattern of New Right responses to National Socialism. Now it becomes apparent that when Schacht speaks out against Germany's anti-fascists and 'suicide merchants' and Saur regards teaching about the Holocaust in German schools as going hand-in-hand with a 'nihilistic dismantling of the self' they are not just attacking their political enemies on the left;[25] they are also confronting a form of self-doubt within the New Right itself. When the New Right turns its attention to Germany's future and its identity it is equally preoccupied with the Nazi past as an insurmountable obstacle. Moreover, this obstacle is not externally imposed but rather internally generated by Germans themselves: Weißmann writes that Germans' massive doubts about their national identity were the direct consequence of their loss of history and perhaps the greatest spiritual defeat in 1945. Division and modernisation played a part, but nowhere else in Europe was there such a high degree of disorientation. Germans seemed to lack the will to be a nation.[26]

Weißmann's account of a Germany that felt the need to break with its own history, and of a 'loss of history' is in stark contrast to Krebs's expectation of a reassertion of German historical traditions. For Weißmann German unification exposes the opposite trend. He quotes from 'A United Germany. The New Superpower', a 1990 issue of *Newsweek* that highlighted the opportunity unification had given the Germans: after 45 years of doing penance for the Third Reich they could dispense with the national reflex of self-denial and be German once more.[27] Weißmann comments that the Germans learn more slowly than the American author supposes and that the plausible expectation that they would return to normality and take on a responsible role in Europe and the rest of the world has not been realised: 'the nation is having trouble finding its feet'.[28] Whereas Weißmann seems to register this point with a degree of resignation, other New Right voices show a more combative tone: Günter Maschke argues that since unification German servility towards other countries has grown. Germany is intent on showing how harmless it can be, and nationalist sentiment is on the wane. Maschke criticises Germany's failure to participate directly in the Gulf War and he explains Germany's inability to act on the stage of world politics in terms of Germany's efforts to deal with the Nazi past. Maschke concludes that there will be no German politics until these efforts are 'wiped out'.[29]

Nationalism as a spent force

Just as bothersome as the New Right's awareness of the disturbed relationship of Germans to the nation is its insight that nationalism as a concept has had its day. What is generally presented as a left-wing hostility towards nationalism can be regularly detected within the ranks of the New Right itself. Rainer Zitelmann presents this hostility in the conventional form when he attacks the German left for being ever ready to accuse Germans of xenophobia, anti-Semitism and fascism.[30] Yet this conventional right-wing explanation of anti-nationalism has to withstand internal criticism of nationalism. If Armin Mohler imported Alain de Benoist's ideas in order to prompt the German New Right to work out a coherent set of positions for itself, the message de Benoist brings with him is a challenging one. Whereas de Benoist had been happy enough in the mid-eighties to see the nation and the 'fatherland' as the ultimate realities, by the time he starts thinking about globalisation in the new millennium he has radically rethought the role of the nation: the fall of the Berlin Wall marked the start of the post-modern era, in which all political remains of Modernity have been rendered obsolete. This obsolescence embraced not only the competition between parties but also the nation state, an entity that is too big to respond to the everyday concerns of its citizens and too small to counter world-scale threats. In the face of globalisation there is a temptation to emphasise one's own identity, notes de Benoist, yet if one says 'I am a Frenchman' or 'I am a German', one needs to explain what this means. Identity is not static but dynamic, and it cannot be limited to a more or less idealised past. Identity is no longer natural, and in the post-modern period there are no absolute foundations upon which it might rest. With a clear dig at what once passed for innovative New Right thinking he dismisses the notion that one can escape globalisation by clinging to ethnocentric notions of identity as a 'bunker mentality'. It is also a mistake to attempt to stop history in its tracks. Right-wing movements have spent the previous century fighting battles that were lost from the start. There is no point in moaning about the present and mourning for the past.[31]

De Benoist's harsh judgement on so many items of faith, not just of traditional conservatism but also of the New Right, is not merely echoed but anticipated within the German New Right itself. Writing in *Wir selbst* 10 years after German unification, Richard Schröder, who led the SPD-Fraktion in the short-lived GDR parliament after the *Wende*, quotes approvingly from a speech given in 1995 by the Federal President Roman Herzog, that the nation state is becoming too small to tackle the big issues and too big to tackle the small ones.[32] Moreover, German unification is presented not as a source of pride and strengthened national identity but rather as a stimulus to reflection on the consequences of war. Germans can only understand the burden of unification if their memory stretches back further than their own lives. The costs of unification are the delayed costs of the war. Unification thus brings a heightened awareness of Germany's past. It also creates a rift between East and West Germans, with East Germans being made to feel that they are the recipients of aid, or that they came off second-best when the socialist economic and social system was established in the GDR and when the GDR eventually went bankrupt. When Schröder does identify something that binds East and West Germans together it is their responsibility for Germany's reputation abroad, and he expresses his rage at the stupidity of those Germans who damage this reputation by committing acts of violence against foreigners as they declare their pride in being German.[33] This exploration of the contents of German national identity in the pages of what is admittedly one of the more ideologically adventurous New Right journals is notable for the problems it raises rather than for any positive values that might give shape to the German nation a decade after unification.

The 1995 volume of essays, *Wir 89er*, authored by the younger generation of the New Right, raises more problems for nationalism: its contributors have little time for a German identity based on the nation as a fixed point, supposedly providing absolute political bonds. Whereas Alfred Mechtersheimer, representative of the older generation of the New Right, had argued that the nation satisfied the basic human need to belong, *Wir 89er* presents a very different view:

Alle Versuche der Neuen Rechten, eine nationale Identifikation zu schaffen, müssen fehlschlagen, denn die Nation existiert nur als Mythos – sie ist ein diffuses Gefühl: Weder irgendwelche Grenzen können die Nation konstruieren (man denke an die Deutschen außerhalb Deutschlands) noch die Kultur (sie ist primär regional; denkt man andererseits an die Sprache, geht sie über alle Grenzen hinaus) und genetische Differenzen schon gleich gar nicht (diese sind fließend, sie zu katalogisieren ist Unfug). Da nicht einmal mehr ein Mythos von der Nation besteht, ist ihr Begriff heute durch eine leere Menge definiert. Wer in unseren Tagen noch von der Nation redet, spricht von einem geschichtlichen Phänomen, das vergangen ist.[34] (All attempts by the New Right to create a national identity are bound to fail because the nation only exists as a myth – it is a vague feeling: no particular borders can construct the nation (just think of the Germans outside Germany), nor can culture (which is mainly regional; on the other hand, if one thinks of language, that transcends all borders), and genetic differences can be ruled out from the start (they are ever-changing and it is a nonsense to catalogue them). Since not even a myth of the nation still exists, the concept today is defined by a vacuum. Anyone who still talks about the nation these days is talking about a historical phenomenon that has had its day).

Here the nation is presented as something that is already permanently lost. Similarly, whereas Ansgar Graw calls for the rediscovery of values and religious and emotional ties which encourage self-sacrifice, a sense of state and nation,[35] we have seen Botho Strauß making it clear that as far as he is concerned such values have already been irretrievably lost: public morality has tolerated or even encouraged a contempt for the military, for the Church, for tradition and authority, and people should not be surprised if these words have no substance in times of crisis.[36] For Strauß the *Volk* no longer represents a supreme value. Today the German *Volk*'s specific character has been lost to an Americanised mentality.[37] As we have already seen, this pessimism is confirmed in *Anschwellender Bocksgesang* where Strauß insists that the right-wing imagination is not to do with promises of a better life but with loss.[38] It has been argued of the New Right's predecessor, the Conservative Revolution, that it understood that what it would conserve is already lost and hence had to be created anew.[39] In the case of the New Right such a mentality is present in the work of Pierre Krebs with his hope for a rebirth of organic communities, yet the more reflective voices of the New Right seem not to be able to get beyond loss.

Gunnar Sohn uses his journal *Criticón* to take one branch of German conservatism to task for its adherence to the idea of an organic community. He sees the contemporary preoccupation with the Conservative Revolution as a sign of a renewed interest in the idea of losing oneself in the shared destiny of the nation: many leading conservatives do not embrace the ideal of a society made up of responsible and independent individuals but rather the ideal of a natural or historical community. Sohn criticises this philosophy for its lack of interest in securing individual freedom through institutions and rules, and for its eagerness to see the individual being totally absorbed into the community of the nation.[40] Sohn's disapproval of such sentiments becomes apparent when he describes a German preference for community over society as symptomatic of a distaste for any institutions that could restrict abuses of power. In a 'community of the mind' there is no room for checks and balances. The idea of an 'Inner Reich', the fondness for vague emotions and the tendency to other-worldliness encourage Germans to turn away from the West and the 'ideas of 1789', and to nurture instead a disastrous belief in a special German cultural mission. Sohn sums up the mentality he describes as the wrong conservative traditions in Germany.[41]

The relevance of Sohn's critique of these traditions not just to conservatism but also to New Right thinking itself becomes apparent just a year after he expresses his concerns. In 1994 Tilman Krause contributed an essay to *Die selbstbewußte Nation*[42] in which he notes that forty years after the war the 'better Germany' has won out: the country is a stable and reliable partner of the West. Nobody can deny that leaving behind Germany's 'dark old ways' was beneficial, yet these dark ways cannot be suppressed for ever since what is suppressed has a habit of resurfacing with destructive force. It is time, Krause argues, for Germans to set aside their timidity and political correctness and stand by the complex of introversion and other-worldliness which is part of their make-up and which is hard to reconcile with the Western belief in progress and reason. Krause agrees that Thomas Mann had called upon his countrymen to align themselves with Western traditions in his 1930 *Appell an die Vernunft* (Appeal to Reason) but he had not renounced German introversion. Krause sees this tradition reemerging in Botho Strauß's work which is an invocation of a prerational culture represented in the past by poets such as Klopstock, Hölderlin, Stefan George, Theodor Däubler and Rilke. Krause likens the literary world's reception of Strauß's work to the teacher raising his finger in disapproval, and he sees criticism of East German notions of community after unification as further instances of the raised finger. He calls upon Germans to have the confidence to reassert their proper cultural heritage. Sohn and Krause show how two of the supposedly most innovative and thoughtful New Right forums can take diametrically opposing views on the key issue of German national identity. Sohn may regard the 'renaissance of the Conservative Revolution' as a sign of a renaissance of nationalist thinking, yet, as so often turns out to be the case, the Conservative Revolution is actually an ambiguous model. Rather than having adopted the nation as a value beyond question, many Conservative Revolutionaries actually saw traditional nationalism, in much the same way as many New Right thinkers, as a thing of the past. In the years of the Weimar Republic the Conservative Revolution was preoccupied with establishing a 'new nationalism' that would break with the Wilhelmine state and all restorationist tendencies, and find new ways of meeting the challenge of organised labour by embracing the 'front-line socialism' of the First World War. Writing in 1933, Edgar Jung, adviser and ghostwriter to Franz von Papen, dismisses the idea that true conservatives are intent on stopping the wheel of history,[43] and other new nationalists of the Conservative Revolution mock traditional conservatism for its restorationist outlook and for failing to come to terms with such key features of the present as technology, the city and the proletariat.[44]

New Right authors are not unaware of this debate within the Conservative Revolution: Heimo Schwilk calls Ernst Jünger a 'prophet of globalisation' for predicting as early as 1960 the end of the nation state. We gain a further insight into the New Right mentality when Schwilk draws a parallel between Jünger's account of soldiers in the First World War trying to find a way of asserting themselves against mechanised warfare and citizens today trying to find a way of asserting themselves against the effects of globalisation.[45] Schwilk describes how Jünger foresaw globalisation in his writings on technology. In war, technology had reduced the volunteer to a nameless 'worker-soldier', fighting in a situation where material superiority, not an individual's courage was the deciding factor. Schwilk understands the dilemma Jünger faced as he tried to give heroic status to the individual combatant. On the one hand the massive destructive force of mechanised warfare can make the soldier who masters it appear all the more heroic. Yet Schwilk also notes the other fact of war that makes up Jünger's dilemma: the reduction of the soldier to a specialised unit whom the State may crush as it pursues its own goals. Schwilk sees this dual face of war reflected in the inner turmoil of Sturm, the main character in Jünger's novel of the same title.

We see at work here a similar psychological structure between the Conservative Revolutionary need for meaning in the face of impersonal mechanised warfare and the New Right need for a fixed point in the face of the impersonal forces of globalisation. Given the New Right's doubts about nationalism, the structural similarity extends into the troubling state of mind in which meaning gives way to its opposite: just as Jünger's construction of meaning in the shape of front-line socialism and the heroic soldier who was ultimately the master of the technology of war could break down into images of the isolated individual dying a meaningless death, New Right nationalism is an unstable foundation that can crumble in the face of moral doubts about the appropriateness of any nationalist revival in Germany, and in the face of doubts about the relevance of the nation in the era of globalisation. The parallel is underscored when Schwilk characterises Jünger's work as an account of how the mechanisation of man turned Europe into a desert, and how the most remote village in the Congo sees the films that will lay down the values of the future; the sexes will no longer meet in squares to the background of drums but in fashionable dance halls. Schwilk sees this as Jünger's anticipation of the 'tendency towards cultural globalisation' which will destroy cultural identity.[46]

Nationalism as process

The disconcerting elements of the New Right's internal debate on the status of the nation need to be worked into something that can be a source of reassurance. Despite all the reservations about nationalism a nationalist position does emerge through the philosophical work of the New Right. The element of process, of cause and effect underlying New Right nationalism, becomes apparent in this philosophical work, and it helps us to understand the New Right mentality.

One constant in this mentality is the need for fixed points. In our discussion of New Right culture we saw how Karlheinz Weißmann found in Ernst Jünger's work the possibility of compensating for the rise of nihilism by expanding nationalism into an absolute value. In his co-edited volume of essays in honour of Ernst Jünger's one hundredth birthday the philosopher Günter Figal fills in the theoretical details of the processes at work as the New Right faces up to the problem of a loss of meaning. Figal's essay on Nietzsche exactly meshes with the process by which Weißmann sees nationalism coming to the fore: 'Nihilism is, according to Nietzsche, a "pathological transitional condition" in which one cannot actually live but in which one nevertheless tries to do so'.[47] One feature of nihilism is the realisation that the area occupied by exhausted and abandoned values is growing. Values do not simply disappear; rather they lose their credibility. One cannot continue to hold onto them, but their continued presence makes one all the more aware of them.[48] This situation produces the passive and the active nihilist. The passive nihilist cannot believe in traditional sources of meaning such as duty or morality and can only conclude that everything has equal value or lack of value, whereas the active nihilist has the power to give himself a goal or a set of beliefs.[49] Figal points out the problem with giving oneself goals or beliefs, however, in a way that is reminiscent of the New Right's awareness that nationalism is a thing of the past. Nationalism may emerge from nihilism as a new value, yet it is already tainted. Figal concludes that giving oneself values or beliefs is not without its problems: the very thing that one sets up as a fixed point in order to escape from what has allegedly already had its day is often drawn from traditional sources.[50]

The culture of the New Right displays an acute awareness of a precarious existence with no foundation. One response is to dismiss politics as an irrelevance; another is to follow the line of the 'active nihilist' and turn to an inflated nationalism as a source of meaning. This latter response becomes apparent when we consider the political and philosophical thinking of the New Right as a whole.

The positive political value of nationalism has to be associated with form and collective identity, since it has to counter a profound awareness of loss of meaning and direction. Matthias Bath gives expression to this view of nationalism as a response to a loss of direction and identity in the pages of *Junge Freiheit*, arguing that the mainstream centre parties are no more than the political representatives of globalisation, deregulation and monopolisation of the economy and public life. The solution is to be found in the energy of one's own 'Volk' and nation. This means looking to the political right which is at the moment, however, insignificant.[51] Roland Bubik registers how communities are breaking down into the mere sum of individual elements in the period of advanced liberalism. The family, religion and the nation are all being undermined, and the Islamic daughter of an immigrant family can only despise her German classmates who seem to make fun of their own Christian religion. Bubik calls for a 'conscious act of will' to create an idea of the nation that would be powerful enough to carry people with it and generate a new community and identity for those who call themselves German now and for the future generations of descendants of immigrants.[52] In these examples we see how the New Right perceives the nation as a minority interest in the hands of the extreme right, or else as a value that is already lost and needs to be recreated.

The anonymous national revolutionary interviewee in *Wir selbst* who could insist that the nation was a historical fact that continued to provide the foundations of a shared linguistic and cultural identity also conveys the sense of nationalism emerging as a stage in a process. His assertion of an intact national identity is called into question when he goes on to explain that the political sphere must be expanded to become part of a far greater project that will remove the artificial barriers between politics, culture, everyday life, science and philosophy. At the heart of this project is national identity. The nation must be 'reconstructed' in order to help shape a vision of a new form of existence. Significantly the writer turns to the National Revolutionaries of the 1930s for his inspiration, for they too realised the need for such a project, and Ernst Jünger is the prime example of a thinker with a 'transpolitical vision'. We see here how the nation shifts from intact foundation to something that needs to be constructed or reconstructed, and the reference to Jünger and the broader definition of politics takes us back to a nationalism that fills an existential void.[53]

If Figal noted the problem that creating values could in fact be a matter of drawing on past values, Franco Volpi, writing in the same volume, raises a further concern which latches onto the doubts about nationalism that we see in the political pronouncements of the New Right. He starts by mapping out the territory of nihilism:

myths, religion, and political ideologies have all been drained of meaning, and in this nihilistic world virtue and morality, good and evil, right and wrong no longer seem necessary. Yet the total lack of fixed points gives rise to a profound unease as we even distance our-selves from the ideal of reason in the post-modern era. As we seek to 'reactivate' absolute fixed points such as myth, art, religion or pol-itics in order to restore order to the world we cannot prevent the emergence of the ghosts of irrationalism, anarchy and chaos.[54]

New Right nationalism has to be seen as the product of a process in which the phases are the projection of a simple nationalist commitment, a sense that nationalism is not being held back by external constraints but by internal doubts, an awareness that nationalism may be a thing of the past, a need for fixed points which can be met by elevating nationalism to the status of an absolute value, and an unsilenced set of concerns about such absolute values being accompanied by irrationalist tendencies and the very opposite of order. Given this process, there can be no simple nationalist commitment, only a complex and reflective one which must by its very reflectiveness undermine the wish for values beyond question.

Unacceptable alternatives

We have seen how the New Right's profound cultural pessimism can lead to a scorn for the whole business of politics, yet we have also seen evidence of the opposite tendency: to endow political institutions with particular significance and expect them to play a stabilising role against a background of existential unease, to see politics as the potential locus of values beyond question, and to project these values as a counter to the spread of nihilism. Simultaneously holding unrealistically low and high expectations of politics thus emerges as one of the defining characteristics of the New Right, and understanding the depth of cultural despair and the expectations of the required solution helps to explain why the New Right rejects mainstream politics as inadequate.

The New Right reserves its particular scorn for *Verfassungs-patriotismus*, a commitment to the principles of the Basic Law which is dismissed as a 'cold project'. Ansgar Graw elaborates on what the New Right associates with *Verfassungspatriotismus*: it is the whole set of liberal values that is interpreted not as a positive set of freedoms but as a loss of community and order. Freedom is over-extended in the name of freedom, and the result is total isolation. More democracy, Enlightenment and emancipation mean the loss of identity, transcendence, and bonds. Faced with the trauma of the Third Reich and the shock of Auschwitz, the nation is consigned to the rubbish heap of history. In place of tradition and history committed teachers, journalists, social workers and clerics offer modernisation and Utopias, but any belief in these disappeared with actually existing socialism. What is left are emptiness and values that one can take or leave: human rights which are declared to be universal, together with the principles of the constitution. The political principles of a free society are generally welcomed, but they do not inspire anyone.[55]

Graw's characterisation of liberalism gives a good insight into the New Right mentality. The need for absolute bonds is a recurrent feature of New Right thinking, and these bonds are not to be found in a political order intent on extending the range of personal freedoms. Moreover the liberal order is lumped together with socialism which, as a result of the disintegration of the Eastern bloc, has lost all credibility. At the most profound level lurks Modernity which provokes only anxiety in the New Right mind. This anxiety is not specific to the German New Right: Alain de Benoist and Charles Champetier attack the 'ideology of progress' that promises an ever improving world but is in a deep crisis:

> The future appears unpredictable, no longer offering hope, and terrifying almost everyone. Each generation confronts a world different from the one its fathers knew. Combined with accelerated transformations of lifestyles and living contexts, this enduring newness predicated on discrediting the fathers and old experiences, produces not happiness but misery.[56]

This French attack on progress mirrors that of the German New Right, and it undermines Graw's suggestion that misery could be relieved if the nation were available to the Germans as a fixed point.

Karlheinz Weißmann nevertheless presents the nation as a fixed point with his criticism of civil society. For Weißmann civil society treats Man as an entirely rational being and not a being with roots in historical tradition. By contrast the binding force of the nation provides a sense of community.[57] This sentiment is also encountered in the mainstream conservative parties, however, and does not of itself constitute an exclusively New Right way of thinking. Wolfgang Schäuble, CDU-CSU parliamentary leader in 1994, made the same point in the same language:

> Wir brauchen eine Balance zwischen den Individualinteressen und der Gemeinschaft. Als Bindeglied für die Gemeinschaft reicht das rationale Bekenntnis zu gemeinsamen Verfassungs- werten nicht. Weil viele Entscheidungen eben mehr aus der Emotion als aus dem Intellekt begründet sind, brauchen wir ein emotionales Bindeglied: das ist eben das Wissen um die Grundlagen der Gemeinschaft, der Zusammengehörigkeit – man kann das dann Vaterland oder Nation oder gemeinsame Geschichte nennen.[58]
> (We need a balance between the interests of the individual and the community. As a binding force for the community a rational commitment to the shared values of the constitution is not enough. Since many decisions are founded more in the emotions than in the intellect we need an emotional bond, and that is a sense of the foundations of our community and a sense of belonging together – one can call this the fatherland or the nation or our shared history).

The more radical New Right aversion to liberalism is articulated by Pierre Krebs who also comes up with an alternative. Krebs harks back to Ferdinand Tönnies's categories when he detects the gradual disappearance of *Gemeinschaft* (community) in favour of *Gesellschaft* (society). The latter is a random and artificial collection of organisa- tions based on promises and contracts instead of the organically developed bonds which would guarantee values that are greater than the individual. World-weariness, materialistic nihilism, des- truction of the environment, consumerism, the waning of political will, the levelling of hierarchical structures, the crisis of the soul, the nonsense of dogmatic egalitarianism, the suppression of aristocratic values in every sphere of life are all signs of a terrible decadence. In their place Krebs calls for a national socialism.[59] Krebs's mixture of political, psychological and philosophical categories to create an impression that the totality of human existence is at stake, and his call for a national socialism, are the characteristics that mark the New Right off from the more narrowly defined sense of loss expressed within mainstream conservatism.

Krebs's all-embracing diagnosis of existence is echoed by Eberhard Straub who writes of the fear of the isolated individual, the meaningless of his existence, and the filling up of the empty soul with social trivia. These features of modern existence he ultimately attributes to democratisation since the individual is left to his own devices under liberalism. Together with democracy, liberalism removes the individual from all communities.[60] The typical language and attitudes of the New Right expressed here remind the reader of the movement's cultural pessimism which can easily tip over into the view that politics has nothing to offer humankind in the face of existential chaos. The process by which nationalism comes to be a fixed point of New Right beliefs nevertheless reasserts itself, and Paul Berlin illustrates this process when he reflects on order and chaos in nature and society: in nature, he argues, there are certain rules that govern everything and make life possible. Without them there would be only chaos. Switching to politics he asserts that liberalism is today in the process of dismantling all acknowledged principles for a functioning community. Liberalism is becoming distorted, and it is expanding like a tumour, developing metastases in all areas of life. When all laws and morality lose their validity there is the danger of chaos, as in nature without rules. All forms and structures shows signs of falling apart, the community can only look forward to a descent into chaos. Violence and counter-violence will escalate.[61]

Here nature and society are depicted as subject to the same laws. The imagery is reminiscent of Botho Strauß's view of existence which is maintained by a delicate chemical balance and is one step away from slipping into chaos. Unlike Strauß, however, with his sense of 'grief' which cannot be the basis of a political position, Paul Berlin suggests the solution may be political by tying the problem tightly to liberalism.

A return to Christianity?

The New Right is preoccupied with the search for meaning and an attachment to something greater than the individual. De Benoist attacks the State for having nothing to say on these matters: it offers no grand vision of the future even though once people's basic needs have been met they fervently wish to be part of some purpose greater than themselves. It is only such a purpose that can lend meaning to their lives, yet the State provides no meaning.[62] The German New Right takes this thought further when Günter Rohrmoser describes bourgeois culture as a culture without absolutes. Nietzsche had described such a culture as in need of 'eternalising forces', which Rohrmoser interprets as spiritual forces that are not subject to change and that proclaim an enduring truth.[63] Like de Benoist Rohrmoser accuses the political parties – more particularly the CDU and CSU – of failing to meet the expectations of conservatives: a spiritual turnaround had been promised but not delivered, and as a result conservatives stayed away from elections.[64]

Against the background of high expectations of politics it is not surprising that religion emerges as one possible source of eternal values which can be folded into politics and lend meaning to the lives of individuals. Klaus Motschmann writes in *Criticón* about the Charter of Basic Rights being produced as the basis for a European Constitution. He complains that there is no 'transcendent bond' of any kind in the Charter. The word God does not occur in the preamble or in the individual articles. Merely guaranteeing religious freedom falls a long way short of what is needed, he argues: it neither conceals the absence of a proper reference to God, nor does it ensure that the rich heritage of the West will be the 'foundation of the European house'. Motschmann quotes the Conservative Revolutionary August Winnig who wrote in 1938:

'Was Europa geworden ist, ist es unter dem Kreuz geworden. Das Kreuz steht über Europa als das Zeichen, in dem es allein leben kann. Entweicht Europa dem Kreuz, so hört es auf, Europa zu sein. Wir wissen nicht, was dann aus Europa würde; wahrscheinlich ein Gemenge von Völkern und Staaten ohne verbindende Idee, ohne gemeinsame Werte, eine Gesellschaft, aus der jedes Bewußtsein eines gemeinsamen Auftrages und einer höheren Verantwortlichkeit gewichen wäre. Das ist der Abgrund, an dessen Rande Europa dahinschwankt.'[65]

('What Europe has become, it has become under the cross. The cross stands over Europe as the only sign in which it can live. If

Europe abandons the cross, it will cease to be Europe. We do not know what would then become of Europe; probably a jumble of peoples and states with no binding idea, with no shared values, a society from which any notion of a common task and a higher responsibility has faded. That is the abyss on the edge of which Europe totters').

The quotation underlines the search for a higher purpose and a sense of belonging that characterised much Conservative Revolutionary writing, and it also further explains the New Right's keen interest in that movement. Yet religion does not go unchallenged as an absolute value. Botho Strauß regards religion as a thing of the past. He registers the atheism all around him and concludes that 'the power of religions is nearing its end'.[66] When other religions arise, the liberal response is not to build a bulwark against them but to give them as much space as possible. The aim here is to enable the atheistic forces of disintegration that have already gripped Christianity to attack these other religions. Here again we see how the intellectuals associated with the New Right have little to offer in the way of a cultural foundation for a political programme. Their cultural impact is in fact more in line with that critical and challenging function ascribed to culture in the period of Modernity.

Günter Rohrmoser may agree with Nietzsche that bourgeois culture needs eternalising forces, yet he has trouble discovering these in religion. He argues that all forms of conservatism that spill over into irrationalism have learnt from Nietzsche that one cannot use Christianity for political purposes. Any appeal to Christianity is merely an ideology designed to preserve the status quo.[67] Yet Rohrmoser's frank assessment of what happens when politicians seek to instrumentalise religion ultimately gives way to the notion that religion can provide the contents of conservatism. In the same book in which he sees no positive role for religion in politics he examines what he refers to as the extremely embarrassing position in which genuine conservatism finds itself. In the Federal Republic there is nothing it can identify with. What Rohrmoser is looking for is a force to counter the spread of a 'technological nihilism'. Whereas Armin Mohler wants some kind of alliance with technocrats Rohrmoser contradicts his own previously stated position when he appears to find this force in Christianity, arguing that if German conservatism does not take up Christian traditions and attitudes it will never get beyond mere reaction.[68] Here we see Rohrmoser casting around for values and opting for a revival of religious beliefs even if Christianity has already been declared dead. Rohrmoser's position is contradictory but it does provide a further illustration of the process at work which is already familiar from the New Right's contradictory position on nationalism. Reinstating religion after it has been devalued parallels the idea of reviving and expanding nationalism in the age of nihilism even though nationalism has already been dismissed as a defunct value or as ineffective in the age of globalisation. The intense discussions about religion, says Rohrmoser, are a result of what he calls the crisis of Modernity.[69]

The need for fixed points overrides any appreciation of the questionable value of nationalism and Christianity, and Rohrmoser's reflections give us a valuable insight into cause and effect at work. In his study of the rise of National Socialism he writes:

Es gibt heute keine geschichtlichen Anknüpfungspunkte, Ursprünge und Traditionen mehr, die man noch unter den Bedingungen der fortgeschrittenen Moderne restituieren oder bewahren könnte. Es gibt heute eigentlich keine substantielle Kraft mehr, mit der sich ein politischer Konservatismus noch identifizieren könnte. Die fortgeschrittene Moderne hat sich der alten Mächte – Staat, Kirche, Beamtentum, Soldatentum, Bauerntum, und auch Preußentum – entledigt. Vergleichbares gilt auch für den sozialistischen Gedanken. Es ist 1989 nicht nur der reale Sozialismus zusammengebrochen, sondern auch die sozialistische Idee. Der libertäre Liberalismus und Kapitalismus hat sowohl über den Sozialismus, wie über den klassischen Konservatismus einen grandiosen Sieg errungen. Wir sind heute an dem Punkt angelangt, an dem sowohl die progressive Utopie, wie der konservative Bewahrungsgedanke geschichtlich dementiert worden sind und an dem sich sowohl die konservativen wie progressiven Theorietraditionen und politischen Konstellationen erschöpft haben. Beide Formationen sind durch den Triumph der Moderne widerlegt worden.[70]

(Today there are no historical anchors, origins or traditions that could be restored or preserved under the conditions of advanced

Modernity. Today there are actually no forces of substance with which a political conservatism could identify. Advanced Modernity has discarded the old forces – the State, the Church, the civil service, the military, peasantry and Prussia too. Something similar has happened to socialism. It was not just actually existing socialism that collapsed in 1989, but also the idea of socialism. Libertarian liberalism and capitalism have celebrated a grandiose victory over socialism and over classical conservatism alike. We have reached the point where progressive Utopia and conservative ideas of preservation have been discounted and where both conservative and progressive theoretical traditions and political constellations have exhausted themselves. Both formations have been disproved by the triumph of Modernity).

This is an interesting piece of counter-thinking to the simple assertion that right-wing values can be reasserted after the collapse of socialism. In fact Rohrmoser see this collapse as no more than a catching-up exercise with conservatism whose values have already been dismantled. Rohrmoser believes that decadence and alienation may yet again turn out to be a problem, and he suggests that the answer will be found not in fascism, National Socialism or the Conservative Revolution, but in God. Underlining the process of converting defunct values into the foundation for the future, Rohrmoser writes that we shall one day have to address the question of whether the person who asks about God is indeed a relic from the past or riding in the vanguard of progress.[71]

Post-politics and the rediscovery of nature

Within the New Right we have seen how Botho Strauß figures both as a political critic and as a critic who cannot put his faith in political remedies. Writing in *Junge Freiheit* Michael Wiesberg presents Strauß as the political critic who, with the publication of *Die Fehler des Kopisten* in 1997 'piles more wood onto the flames of his essay "Anschwellender Bocksgesang"'. These flames, comments Wiesberg, cannot be extinguished by the 'those critical pencil sharpeners who are in a permanent state of indignation' and who work in the newspaper offices of the Republic. Wiesberg stresses Strauß's political criticism when he quotes his view of the mood in West Germany in the mid-eighties as run down by democracy, amorphous, and lacking energy, rage and purpose.[72] This political criticism is undoubtedly present in Strauß's thinking, yet in his work we also see a variation on his disregard for politics, and the variation is echoed in the work of others associated with the New Right. It is what has been described as post-political thinking, and it is bound up with an interest in nature. In *Die Fehler des Kopisten* Strauß seems to find an absolute value in nature. He describes how a flock of birds forms into a single flying body with a shared sense of direction. Nature contains a profound reality that has not been eroded by society. Nature is also a value because it is connected to the past. Gardens today, comments Strauß, are hardly any different from the gardens of his grandfather's day. Strauß himself will hand on to others what was once handed to him, and he stands for 'what once was and nothing else'. In this the countryside contrasts with the city and its fleeting contacts. In the city he is alert; outside the city this alertness gives way to trust, and he derives great pleasure from watching his son grow up in the country: he is profoundly satisfied to see his son running along a path, to be the creator of his memories of the house and its garden, of meadows and forests that surround the house, of the open land his son sees before him while he is still not aware of the world beyond and while this is his entire world.[73]

Strauß is clearly describing a retreat for a select few rather than any kind of workable programme for all Germans, and his description makes it clear that it is just a matter of time before even this retreat is compromised for his son. Yet this kind of thinking which seems to emerge once politics has been abandoned as worthless is not unusual among New Right intellectuals. As Wolfgang Bialas points out, it is a feature of *Die selbstbewußte Nation*. In particular Gerd Bergfleth's essay 'Erde und Heimat' (Earth and Home) illustrates the point and its political relevance, but also the attendant problems.[74] Bergfleth argues that the dominant ideology obliges Germans to be homeless, since 'a good German can only be a broken German who has been robbed of his people, fatherland and his nation, and thus of all his traditions'. A good German is meant to identify with asylum seekers who are also homeless. Instead of a homeland the Germans are meant to embrace a cosmopolitanism and a Utopia of total dislocation. Bergfleth hears a rumbling in the distance, however, and it is the rumbling of the people preparing for a revolt against this dislocation. Thus caught between left and right, Bergfleth proposes the watchword 'back to nature', since a *Reich* of freedom or a homeland will not take the form of a particular social model. Rather it will be a 'natural condition'. Bergfleth's line of thought illustrates the dilemma of the New Right. If the way to the Fatherland is blocked by its past associations, nature offers a way forward. Germans' search for eternal values, in Bergfleth's terminology a 'metaphysical home', ends in being 'bound to the earth' as 'brothers to the great forces of nature'.[75]

The post-political credentials of this position are called into question, however, when Bergfleth goes on to explain the natural connection not as universal but as bound to a particular location. The Earth can only become everybody's home symbolically through the attachment to a particular part of it. Not everybody will be able to experience this home since not all nations are able to carry out the tasks entrusted to them by the Earth. Germans have a special responsibility for the fate of the Earth, however, since they have a metaphysical link to it. They must therefore follow their special path which will lead away from the superficial Enlightenment and towards an understanding of myth. The anti-modern German tradition represented by Martin Heidegger and Ernst Jünger will do battle with Modernity and the ecological, economic and technological disaster it is heading for. A religion of the Earth must assert itself and reconnect humankind with the Earth.[76]

Bergfleth's musings on nature hardly seem to merit the term post-political once they focus on the specifically German aspect of the impending struggle for the Earth. If Germans are pushed off the nationalist path and onto the natural path, the natural path Bergfleth describes ultimately leads straight back to all those German traditions associated most closely with extreme forms of German nationalism. Post-political thinking is rapidly repoliticised.

If Strauß's view of nature as a value seems to offer a less objectionable vision, it is not without problems of its own, for Strauß has a strong sense not just that nature connects us with the past in a reassuring way but that it is slipping away from us and becoming part of the past, like the other values he misses. His interest in standing for 'what once was' and his portrayal of providing his son with future memories of nature within an enclosed space before he becomes aware of the world as a whole convey a sense of impending loss which is reminiscent of his view of what he refers to as right-wing values. This sense of loss is made explicit in *Die Fehler des Kopisten* where Strauß writes of the destruction of Nature which is therefore described as 'nature that has disappeared'. Man is a creator at odds with nature, and his history is one of creating artificiality. Returning to his garden image, but with a more pessimistic take on what he will find there, Strauß declares that there is not a single plant in it that is as God created it. Everything in the garden has been cultivated, worked on and refined.[77] Nature as a New Right value has to take its place beside other values which are dear to the right-wing imagination but which have been classified as belonging to the past.

These problems of post-political thinking are prefigured in the work of Arnold Gehlen, who is the focus of much New Right attention. Karlheinz Weißmann points out that Gehlen does not see humankind as close to nature, and anyone who seriously takes up the call 'back to nature' is heading for disaster. We need to create a danger-free environment in which to live, and this is located not in nature but in culture.[78]

Habermas draws the conclusion for neo-conservatism that sees a distance between man and nature when he comments that Gehlen emphasised the vulnerability of human nature. It is not fixed in instinct and therefore depends on the regulatory force of archaic quasi-natural institutions. From this perspective the dismantling of sacred institutions, the loss of authority on the part of the Church, the Military, and the State, as well as the erosion of the latter's sovereign substance, are signs of a pathological development.[79] Gehlen thus does not share the notion of human closeness to the Earth that Bergfleth takes to be a particularly German characteristic.

Rüdiger Safranski offers a variation on the theme of a return to nature when he describes Rousseau's view that human socialisation has torn man from his instinctive, unreflective, harmonious existence. Man must find a way out of this degenerate condition and discover the non-degenerate animal within himself. Unlike Weißmann on Gehlen, Safranski finds Rousseau's offer tempting: man can escape his miserable existence by finding a way back to himself. The door to this self stands open.[80] Safranski is tempted by the downgrading of the human capacity for reflection that goes with a reversion to an animal existence, and here we have an extreme rejection of human culture in its critical function. But

Safranski also has his problems with this apparently simple solution to the human condition. He quotes Kleist on his happiest moments being those in which he forgot himself. One cannot do this by merely deciding to, however, and all that is left is the longing for directness and a harmonious existence which does not seek to understand itself. This is the old dream of paradise from which we were expelled, comments Safranski. Eating from the tree of knowledge prevents us from attaining a preconscious state.[81] Reversion to nature is no simple task: the post-political path is blocked.

Instead of a New Right programme

Given the difficulty New Right thinkers have in retaining the integrity of the political concepts they advocate, it is not surprising that the movement has trouble putting forward a political programme. As we have noted, observers may emphasise certain aspects of New Right thought such as the 'Volk', the nation, the state, and a collectivist approach to politics in an attempt to clarify exactly what it does stand for, and they have suggested that the programmes of the Republikaner, DVU and NPD have an ideological core that is identical to that of the New Right.[82] Although they retain some elements of Old Right thinking such as playing down the crimes of the Nazi State, argues Gessenharter, these three parties, especially the Republikaner, are the party political incarnation of the New Right.[83] It has also been argued that the New Right has gone through a series of well defined phases from 'metapolitics' to direct political engagement. According to this model the first phase was that of the 'cultural struggle', with the aim of gaining cultural hegemony, and it dates back to the start of the seventies. This phase was given over to working out an ideology based on natural inequality, ethnopluralism, hierarchy, elitism, nationalism, anti-liberalism, and an authoritarian order. In the second phase, which started around 1982, the New Right saw itself as offering a right-wing corrective for a right-wing government. This was also the phase of the historians' dispute of 1986, the year in which the young generation of the New Right launched *Junge Freiheit*. The third phase is said to have started in 1989 with the collapse of socialism. This collapse and the subsequent unification of Germany gave the New Right a new confidence and self-assertiveness, and national identity became the main preoccupation.[84] As we have seen, however, this neat presentation of the New Right's thinking and its development as a movement is an over-systematisation which disregards the very different positions taken up by its prominent representatives and, most importantly, the tensions within the thinking of individuals.

How does this more complex and even contradictory thinking of New Right intellectuals relate to the ideological core of the three main right-wing parties? The party programmes stress patriotism and the need for Germany to be a confident nation. In some of their formulations they echo New Right thinking, particularly when it comes to their view of a multi-cultural society. The NPD programme uses the approach underlying the New Right concept of ethnopluralism – the idea that differences between peoples are to be celebrated and maintained by keeping peoples separate from each other – to explain its objections to multi-culturalism:

> Im Zusammenspiel von Großkapital, Regierung und Gewerkschaften wurden Millionen von Ausländern wie Sklaven der Neuzeit nach Deutschland geholt. Diese Politik wird durch eine menschen- und völkerverachtende Integration fortgesetzt. Ausländer und Deutsche werden gleichermaßen ihrer Heimat entfremdet und entwurzelt, ihnen droht der Verlust ihrer Identität, der bis zur Zerstörung der Familien führt. In zahlreichen Städten bilden sich Ausländerghettos, in denen die deutsche Restbevölkerung zur Minderheit im eigenen Land wird.[85]
>
> (Big capitalists, government and trade unions worked in league with each other to fetch millions of foreigners over to Germany like modern-day slaves. This policy was continued through integration which had no regard for people or nations. Foreigners and Germans were alienated and uprooted in equal measure from their homelands, and they are now threatened with a loss of identity that will end with the destruction of families. In countless cities foreigners' ghettos are forming in which the Germans who remain are the minority in their own country).

Such formulations are common in New Right thinking and they have displaced the overtly racist proclamations associated with the Old Right. Similarly, overt sympathy with National Socialism has given way to critical distance, with the new consensus stressing that the German present should not be lived in the shadow of the Nazi past. The Republikaner refer to the criminal actions of totalitarian states, rejecting National Socialism but putting it on a par with other regimes.[86] Similarly, the DVU regrets Nazi and communist injustice but rejects the idea that future generations of Germans should suffer discrimination for events in which they played no part,[87] and the NPD asserts that Germans are not a nation of criminals. The party programme calls for an end to a 'one-sided mastering of the past'.[88]

These items mark the limits of the usefulness of New Right thinking for the parties of the Right. Whereas New Right intellectuals continue their deliberations to the point where they conclude that nationalism has little relevance to the modern world, the political parties present nationalism as a cornerstone of their programmes. Whereas culture is troublesome for the intellectuals and the realm for exploring profoundly disturbing insights into the human condition, the parties know only of the feelgood culture. For the parties German culture may be under threat, but it is still intact and must be preserved; European culture and values are western and Christian, and they should provide the basis for the school curriculum. As a non-Christian state Turkey should not be allowed to join the European Union, and multi-cultural society cannot be accepted. The pessimistic messages of New Right intellectuals can have no place in the thinking of the political parties.

Analysts generally find it easier to pinpoint what the New Right rejects than what it supports: under this heading one can list democracy, equality, human rights, and the principles of political representation and sovereignty of the people.[89] Gessenharter adds liberalism to the list,[90] and Funke the West and parliament.[91] These rejections are certainly characteristic of the movement, but they do not add up to a programme. This is only partly because New Right intellectuals do not see themselves in the business of working out a programme. The clarity over what the New Right rejects and the lack of clarity over the details of what it embraces are also due to Germany's past. In this respect the French New Right has less trouble stating its position. In his study of the 'cultural revolution of the right' Alain de Benoist proclaims that the right approves of the variety and inequality in the world and the hierarchies generated by inequality, and it rejects the standardisation of the world through egalitarian ideology. Life is a struggle for nations and for individuals.[92] De Benoist is clearly at ease with this Social Darwinism, a point that Armin Mohler feels obliged to make in his foreword to de Benoist's text: young Frenchmen are starting from a better position than their German counterparts because they are more sure of their identity. Germany's defeat in 1945 and the consequences of this defeat weigh heavily on the generation of Germans who were not even born at the time of Hitler's death. This is a key difference for Mohler even thought he realises that the French right can also be labelled fascist.[93]

This comment from Mohler in the mid-eighties is still a challenge to the notion that in its supposed third, post-unification phase the New Right in Germany acquired a new self-assuredeness. *Die selbstbewußte Nation*, the New Right's post-unification reassessment of German identity, was clearly meant to reflect this new quality, yet, equally clearly, it failed: we have seen how its authors did not conclude that the Nazi past had been mastered by the notion that unification marked the end of Germany's post-war history. These authors have as much difficulty with German identity after unification as before, and this stands in the way of a programme. This is the background to Patrick Moreau's correct argument that the New Right has 'run out of intellectual steam, and has failed to provide a programme which could rally the various extremists'.[94]

Since a programme is not to be had, a strategy emerges. Although the New Right is unable to put forward a clear set of political positions there is a deeper and recurrent structure which unites its thinkers. A key part of this strategy is the cultivation of vagueness. Examples abound, and a particularly telling one is in the New Right reception of Carl Schmitt. Carl Schmitt is generally cited by observers as one of the key thinkers of the Conservative Revolution from whom the New Right takes its ideology. In particular the New Right is attracted by his view that a functioning democracy requires a high degree of homogeneity and the elimination of heterogeneity.[95] Those New Right figures directly involved in politics may turn to Schmitt as a systematic, persuasive thinker, but Carl Schmitt has a very different significance for New Right intellectuals. Armin Mohler examines in particular Carl Schmitt's reading of Georges Sorel on political myth. Nobody inquires into the truth behind political myth, writes Mohler, and Sorel saw in myth a collection of images that works as a totality at the intuitive level to shape the attitudes that can make things happen in the real world.[96] This is how Carl Schmitt saw Sorel, says Mohler, and he quotes from Schmitt's 1923 work, *Die geistesgeschichtliche Lage des heutigen Parlamentarismus* (The Intellectual Situation of Parliamentarianism Today), in which Schmitt gives the principles of freedom in the French Revolution and nationalism in the German Wars of Liberation of 1813 as examples of powerful myths that mobilised people.[97] Of the force of such myths Schmitt writes:

Nur im Mythus liegt das Kriterium dafür, ob ein Volk oder eine andere soziale Gruppe eine historische Mission hat und sein historischer Moment gekommen ist. Aus den Tiefen echter Lebensinstinkte, nicht aus einem Räsonnement oder einer Zweckmäßigkeitserwägung, entspringt der große Enthusiasmus, die große moralische Dezision und der große Mythus. In unmittelbarer Intuition schafft eine begeisterte Masse das mythische Bild, das ihre Energie vorwärts treibt und ihr sowohl die Kraft zum Martyrium wie den Mut zur Gewaltanwendung gibt. Nur so wird ein Volk oder eine Klasse zum Motor der Weltgeschichte.[98]

(Only in myth will it be decided whether a people or another social group has a historical mission and its historical time has arrived. From the depths of true vital instincts, not from reasoning or practical consideration springs the great enthusiasm, the great moral decision and the great myth. Through its simple intuition an inspired mass will create the mythical image that drives it on and gives it the strength for martyrdom and the courage to use force. It is only in this way that a people or a class becomes the driving force behind world history).

Here myth is aligned with vital instincts, enthusiasm and energy, and it has nothing to do with reason or practical considerations. Mohler's reading of Sorel interests fellow New Right author Karlheinz Weißmann who notes in particular that Mohler is impressed by the 'lack of clarity' in Schmitt's thinking, a characteristic that can be captured through descriptive rather than analytical language.[99] Gerwin Steinberger seizes upon Carl Schmitt's theory of decisionism – decisiveness as a quality in its own right – and sees it as the opposite to a political culture based on debate.[100] Cultivating vagueness when clarity would alienate potential allies was also a strategy among those Conservative Revolutionary figures who attempted to work out a programme in the mid-1920s that would bring together the key forces of nationalism and socialism. The essential dilemma of the Conservative Revolution in the Weimar period has been well summarised by Martin Greiffenhagen who sees a shift in the conservative theory of sacrifice at the end of the 19th century: instead of calling for sacrifice for the sake of generally recognised goals, conservative theory goes in search of values and institutions for which it is worth making a sacrifice. To the extent that existing religious, political and moral beliefs have been called into question, conservative interest shifts from the values for which sacrifices might be made to the act of sacrifice itself. On this point Greiffenhagen quotes Ernst Jünger's dictum: 'The greatest happiness known to man is to be sacrificed'.[101] From our consideration of the New Right's cultural pessimism and the attendant loss of absolute values the parallels are plain to see. Moreover, it was Carl Schmitt's concept of decisionism that Conservative Revolutionaries turned to for a way forward. In 1936 Ernst Niekisch wrote:

Es ist für diese Zeit [the years of the Weimar Republic] kennzeichnend, daß der 'Dezisionismus' an sich zum System ausgebaut wird. Man entscheidet sich nicht auf Grund gültiger Inhalte, sondern man macht erst aus einer Sache etwas, indem man sich für sie entscheidet. Die bürgerliche Welt ist sich ihrer Hohlheit und Entleertheit bewußt: sie erwartet, daß der, der sich für sie entscheidet, ihr zugleich neue Werte einbringt.[102]
(The characteristic thing about this whole period is that 'decisionism' is made into a system in its own right. Decisions are made not on the basis of compelling ideas which have substance to them, but an idea is made into something compelling by commitment to it. The bourgeois world is aware that it lacks substance and has become a void. It expects that whoever commits to it will also bring new values).

Conservative Revolutionaries go through distinct phases in their attitude towards political programmes. The switch away from a call for clarity over political aims towards anti-programmatic activism and the ideal of the strong leader is one of the major developments in their thought in the Weimar period: Ernst Jünger's words on self-sacrifice which Greiffenhagen quotes have their political parallel in his assertion in 1929 that programmes are not needed and that the young generation of nationalists must learn to march without flags.[103] In his memoirs Ernst Niekisch suggests firstly that the Conservative Revolution failed to overcome the left versus right split, and secondly that the result of this failure was a withdrawal from the problem.[104] The New Right, faced with its own failure to draw a line under National Socialism and make assertive nationalism acceptable to a wider section of the public, and faced with its failure even to agree on the value of nationalism, finds a model, albeit an uncomfortable one, for resolving ideological and philosophical problems in the thinking of the Conservative Revolution.

Part of the strategy of cultivating vagueness is a New Right devaluation of rational discussion, the next logical step once it has proved impossible to unite around a clear set of values or a political programme. Heimo Schwilk refers to Ernst Jünger's figure of the adolescent dreamer for whom the causal world of adults is not enough and who seeks more drastic bonds within an order that generates not the unique but the unambiguous experience of life. Schwilk explicitly refers to Jünger's 1932 work, *Der Arbeiter* (The Worker), often seen by Jünger's critics as a blueprint for the Nazi state.[105] In Jünger's work the unambiguous experience of life is bound up with sacrifice of the intellect. The Conservative Revolution is mobilised to hint at an authoritarian society which is the antithesis of an order based on rational debate.[106] Alain de Benoist takes the collapse of the Soviet Union as evidence of the limits of reason: egalitarian ideology may be blossoming, he argues, but it is also growing old, senile and foolish. It was originally based on the principles of the natural equality of all people, the omnipotence of reason, the purposefulness of the course of history and a belief in progress, but all these foundations have now crumbled.[107]

Just as the Conservative Revolutionaries had at one stage lamented the absence of a programme in the middle years of the Weimar Republic, the New Right is embarrassed by its lack of ideological coherence and theoretical models in the Federal Republic. It was the awareness of this gap that fuelled the debate about cultural hegemony in the first place, and it is the awareness that the gap has not been plugged that largely determines the rest of the political strategy of the New Right. If the systematic cultivation of vagueness is the first element of the strategy, the second is political purism: since no positive, non-fascist set of beliefs is at hand, and outright commitment to anti-democratic thinking is not an option, rejection of the existing system from a purist standpoint offers a way out. The New Right journal *Nation und Europa* regularly attacks liberalism as an exclusive and repressive system. Johanna Grund, one-time deputy leader of the Republikaner, regards the European Union's education policies as indoctrination and puts them on a par with Soviet propaganda.[108]

This apparent interest in a higher form of democracy sits uneasily with the third element of the New Right's strategy: appealing to an anti-democratic intellectual tradition. The intellectualisation of the New Right offers glimpses of an alternative, undemocratic social order. We have seen the New Right's admiration for Nietzsche's critique of democracy, and we have also seen how the New Right has to overlook Nietzsche's disdain for nationalism. Just as importantly, Nietzsche's whole method of enquiry is set to one side, a method which he himself described as perspectivism and which involves investigating an issue from many different, often contradictory, angles. Nietzsche had little time for absolute convictions of the kind the New Right so fervently desires, arguing that the need for a faith and for absolutes to affirm or reject was a sign of weakness. The pronouncements of the New Right are dominated by this need for certainty, by what observers refer to as 'binary coding': the solution to complex issues is reduced to a choice between the simple alternatives of chaos and order, liberalism and discipline, individualism and collectivism. If the New Right uses culture in an attempt to gain some intellectual standing and respectability, the culture it uses tends, by its complexity, to undermine the New Right's message. Moreover, it is clear that the New Right is itself unable to maintain a simple set of alternatives, embracing the one and dismissing the other. This was also true of the Conservative Revolutionaries whose attempts at a simple political stance were often at odds with the complex reality described in their own cultural writings.

The New Right's failure to unite around a programme encourages the emergence of the fourth element of its strategy which we have already seen in Armin Mohler's admiration of fascism and the New Right's admiration for Jörg Haider: emphasising style in politics. It has rightly been pointed out that the New Right is fascinated by the image of the politician who takes decisions not according to any agreed set of norms but arbitrarily.[109] De Benoist argues that a new aristocracy is needed, one with character and backbone rather than intelligence and brainpower. It should embody the values of the 'Volk'. The 'Volk' can be judged on its ability to bring forth such an aristocracy, and the aristocracy can be judged on its ability to make a reality those values which the people will instinctively recognise as their own.[110] The instinctive grasp of the values of the 'Volk' renders programmes and debate about their content superfluous.

Conclusion: From Exemplary Thinkers of Modernity to Living without Absolutes

Cultural Modernity

We have seen how Modernity provides the disturbing backdrop to much New Right thinking. It is invariably seen as a major cause of existential unease, of a lack of ultimate meaning and purpose, of social and political dissolution and chaos, and of psychological turmoil. Analysing the significance of Modernity deepens our understanding of the New Right by shedding light on the thought processes at work behind the movement's social and political commentary.

Modernity is associated with reason, the industrial age, and the rise of technology, all of which have supposedly undermined the fixed value systems which the New Right needs. Karlheinz Weißmann quotes Arnold Gehlen on the crisis of the industrial age which is total since the coordinates of our interpretation of the world have been called into question. One basic requirement for all people is a stable environment, and the 'technical culture' cannot provide this. We have no fixed points outside ourselves which could support our attitudes, commitments and beliefs.[1] Heimo Schwilk surveys what is on offer for an open-minded person who wants to educate himself though culture. This person is the 'Wilhelm Meister' of our time, and he will end his educational journey by reading about Zen. He will then conclude that what he has sampled is either 'post' and therefore too late to be of any use, or too modern and lacking in any binding force. The competing systems and theories, and the 'anything goes' attitude of Modernity 'corrupt one's ability to decide anything'.[2] For Schwilk culture is meant to provide an absolute set of values rather than a collection of conflicting ideas from which the consumer takes his pick. Culture that does not supply these values is arbitrary and has little value.

Jürgen Habermas sees this kind of thinking as the distinguishing feature of German neo-conservatism of the 1970s which accepts technical modernity and rejects cultural modernity.[3] Habermas's analysis of neo-conservatism addresses the issue that is always on the minds of the New Right: the nature and purposes of culture. Yet in his analysis of the neo-conservative mind the subversive threat of culture is externalised: neo-conservatives, he argues, present the explosive contents of cultural modernity as coming from the left and counter this threat by insisting on the value of tradition. This model is not an accurate reflection of the New Right mentality, however. Although Weißmann and Schwilk may appear to adhere to the model it is clear that New Right culture itself is part of Modernity that causes it such anxiety. There is more to its task than preserving the legacy of tradition in the face of an external cultural threat.

The New Right response to Modernity is complex. As we have seen, adhering to fixed positions based, for example, on a strong sense of tradition, is only one point in a process of New Right thinking. The intellectuals are aware that tradition is often lost forever, be it in the shape of the nation, the strong state, the church, religion, or language. This awareness leaves them in an untenable position, with no love for Modernity but also unconvinced by the upholders of tradition. If the politicians are more likely to be the upholders of 'compensatorily pacified modernity', the intellectuals find few sources of compensation and are given instead to a cultural pessimism. Where they do find a resolution, this is the outcome of the processes we have already seen at work beneath their unstable view of politics: at one point politics may be dismissed as superficial and irrelevant, at another it may seem capable of being expanded to provide meaning.

Günter Figal, the philosopher who so often pursues the dilemmas faced by the New Right, has traced this particular instability in the work of Rousseau and Nietzsche. On the one hand, he argues, both philosophers doubt the validity of traditional concepts in the modern period and line up with supporters of Modernity; on the other hand they are critics of their times who look to the past. In this role they are supporters of tradition. Figal dwells on the ambiguity of their positions, arguing that where they are supporters of Modernity and tradition at the same time Rousseau and Nietzsche illustrate the difficulty their times had in asserting the value of the old in the modern period. What Nietzsche seized upon from the past was the 'old natural world', even though he had to admit that he was not part of it since he could not escape the decadence of his own time.[4] Figal's reading of Rousseau and Nietzsche leads him to conclude that they are 'exemplary thinkers of Modernity'. They earn this title by failing to offer a thoroughly worked out and consistent theory of Modernity. Figal warms to his theme by asserting of their writings that the very fact that one does not find within them such a theory makes them modern. In their dramatically contradictory nature and their bold ambiguity they are documents of Modernity.[5] The relevance of contradiction, ambiguity and lack of theory for the New Right is not hard to detect. When the New Right both affirms and dismisses cultural and political tradition it is showing how it is beset with doubts about its own project in a way that transcends the kind of manipulation and mobilisation of a past which Habermas detects in neo-conservative thought.

National Socialism and the fear of Modernity

Fear of Modernity is also a feature of the New Right interpretation of the appeal of National Socialism. We have seen how Rohrmoser argues that anyone trying to understand the existence of conservatism in the modern world or fascism in Germany and Europe has to understand this fear. Conservatives did not share in the progressive camp's euphoria and hopes of Modernity.[6] We have also seen how he extends the argument into the present day when he declares that if the progressives and anti-fascists want to win their struggle against everything conservative, nationalistic or racist they will have to find a way of banishing people's fear of the forward march of Modernity which is wiping out everything they hold dear.[7] Here again we see the notion that we may still be living in the age of fascism, and we also see confirmation of the internal origins of racism in the thinking of the New Right which Hartmut Lange and Martin Schwarz had described. If Nietzsche is regarded as the philosopher who destroyed belief in progress and saw that life after the decline of Christianity was meaningless, then fascism followed as an attempt to restore meaning to the meaningless world of 'post-Christian nihilism'. In this world the choice of values is arbitrary and can have dire consequences: Rohrmoser argues that Hitler had the freedom to choose his values, and to act in accordance with them. Once one understands that the philosophical situation of a developed modern society implies absolute freedom about which values to espouse, one cannot prevent the choice of certain values, even if they have despicable consequences. Anyone agreeing with Nietzsche's fundamental critique of Christianity should realise what consequences follow.[8]

Modernity and the individual

At the level of individual psychology unease at Modernity also provides the backdrop to New Right thinking and provokes a typical response. The rapid disappearance of the familiar props of everyday life is the individual's personal experience of Modernity. As one might expect from the New Right's responses to other breakdowns of familiar structures and values, self-imposed external discipline and order are proposed as a way out of inner turmoil. Rüdiger Safranski explores how this was meant to work, but did not work for the writer Heinrich von Kleist, who ended up committing suicide. Kleist knew of the existential despair and chaos that contemporary figures such as Botho Strauß and Hartmut Lange describe. Safranski reports that Kleist had used reason to map out his life. This route map had provided him with his second external support against inner waverings, his first external support having been the military life. But Kleist's belief in reason was undermined when he read Kant. He abandoned external props and turned inwards, but at this point he realised that there was no 'inner reality' that might provide his life with a sense of direction. Outside himself he found only random distractions; within himself he found only dissolution and emptiness. These reflections on existence and on the military are reminiscent of Ernst Jünger's development of his character Tronck who seeks the discipline of the military life as a way out of crippling introspection. They are also reminiscent of Botho Strauß's 'make-shift belts and restraints by means of which man attempts to hold his disintegrating form together',[9] and Gottfried Benn's portrayal of the mentality of the expressionist poet who craves discipline in order to see harmony and form prevail over excess and formlessness. Yet the solutions on offer turn out to be inadequate for Kleist. All his values – be they justice, higher inevitability, the meaning of history, progress, salvation – turn out to be illusory.[10] Kleist is inspired by Rousseau at this point: he decides to settle in Switzerland in a search for natural bonds that will protect him from the meaningless and complicated actions of society: he will 'cultivate a field, plant a tree, father a child'. He wants to exist within a delimited area and become part of the natural rhythms of life.[11]

But, as Safranski, explains, he is drawn back into society by ambition.[12] What Safranski sees in Kleist's dream is reminiscent of what Botho Strauß had to say about the figure of the shepherd. Kleist finds out that there is no way back to a natural state, and Strauß knows from the start that the idyll is gone: the shepherd he sees has lost all connection with tradition.

Inadequate solutions?

In the preface to the 1974 edition of *The Politics of Cultural Despair* Fritz Stern writes of the attack on Modernity that has become a dominant theme of our culture. He describes the rebellion against the emptiness of a materialist age, against the hypocrisy of bourgeois life and the estrangement from nature, against the whole 'liberal capitalist system', and he describes the longing for a new communal existence, for a new faith, for wholeness. In seeking to explain the triumphs of irrationality that marked fascism he points to the need to take cultural, spiritual and psychic factors into account.[13] In the case of the New Right in Germany we have seen how a movement which is generally presented by observers as a loose but ideologically coherent set of unambiguous political attitudes is in fact a movement that can be better understood when treated as a political and cultural whole. This approach reveals a continuity with the attack on Modernity that Stern traces. Stern's cultural analysis is undertaken in order to shed light on the rise of fascism. When it comes to the New Right the cultural analysis is undertaken in order to shed light on a mentality that is potentially dangerous because it constructs an image of a society that is still living in the era of fascism, acutely aware of a loss of values beyond question and filled with a desire for absolute bonds. The danger lies not least in its instability: New Right cultural pessimism can lead either to a total rejection of politics as an inadequate response to the problems of human existence or, with the Conservative Revolution as a model, to an inflated version of politics that can overcome nihilism.

The problematic relationship between culture and politics, more specifically between culture and national identity, has been explored in sociological research that seems to anticipate the New Right dilemma of wanting to project an intact national identity based on culture even as the movement sees through the cultural concepts it mobilises. Stuart Hall points out that the anti-essentialist critique of ethnic, racial and national conceptions of cultural identity has not supplanted inadequate concepts with 'truer' ones. Rather it has put key concepts of identity 'under erasure', as Derrida uses the term, indicating on the one hand that they are no longer serviceable, but that on the other they have not been superseded and there are no other, entirely different concepts to replace them. There is nothing to do but to continue to think with them.[14]

Similarly, the related concept of identification can have the 'common-sense' meaning of recognition of some common origin or shared characteristics with another person or group. Yet it can also be regarded as 'a construction, a process never completed'. Identification is 'conditional, lodged in contingency', and the 'total merging' it suggests is a 'fantasy of incorporation'.[15] Cultural identity cannot be an 'unchanging 'oneness'; it is rather 'fragmented and fractured', constantly in the process of change and transformation. Hall concludes that identities are about questions of using the resources of history, language and culture in the process of becoming rather than being: not 'who we are' or 'where we came from', so much as what we might become.[16] One thinks of identity, argues Bauman in a similar vein, whenever one is not sure of where one belongs. 'Identity' is a name given to the escape sought from uncertainty.[17] This understanding of cultural identity is far removed from the feelgood culture apparent in one strand of New Right thinking, yet it is close to the uncertainty apparent in the thinking of the movement's cultural pessimists.

If New Right culture was meant to provide the foundation for politics, the foundation it provided turned out to be an unstable mix of feelgood factors and profound despair, touched by Modernity that it sought to exclude from its world view. Culture was not the resource politicians hoped for – one that would restore pre-modern bonds – but rather it was a disturbing force and a contested site. New Right politics at its most activist level – that of political programmes – can do little with this despair and tends to make use only of the feelgood culture which it projects as intact but endangered. New Right politics externalise this danger by attaching it to foreigners in Germany even as the cultural voice of the New Right sees immigration as irrelevant to what it interpreted as an internal disintegration of values.

The link between culture and politics has not turned out to be a superficial one, however, in which cultural complexity is discarded completely when values beyond question are required. This may be the case with the political parties and their notion of patriotism and their call to draw a line under the Nazi past, but in the middle ground of the New Right between philosophical thought and political programmes there is a widespread and unstable mixture of feelgood culture and cultural pessimism, disregard for politics and an expectation that politics will provide the absolute values that will overcome despair.

It is clear that the electoral achievements of the right-wing parties that see themselves as part of the New Right are modest. It is also clear that the New Right has had little success in its efforts to achieve cultural hegemony. We have heard the New Right's claim to newness, yet it is Henning Eichberg, himself a key figure of the New Right, who draws up the decidedly unimpressive balance sheet on the basis of the innovative potential he discerns in the pages of *Junge Freiheit*.

Eichberg's conclusion is largely correct. The New Right's claim to possess cultural depth and to have produced a new, non-Nazi ideology turns out to be unsustainable. At the heart of the New Right's attempts to spell out what is new lies a pattern of evasive manoeuvres: a purist attack on democracy; an appeal to the intellectual tradition of the Conservative Revolution which was by no means anti-Nazi and was itself incapable of resolving the very dilemma facing the New Right, or whose leading representatives had ideas which even the New Right cannot endorse; opting for politics based on irrational commitment instead of rational debate, on style instead of content. These evasive manoeuvres do not add up to a coherent and acceptable solution to the problem of how a newly united Germany might present itself to the outside world. They are at most a complex restatement of the problem.

Yet research into the cultural dimension of the New Right suggests that its significance lies not in its electoral or intellectual successes or failures. The internal contradictions and tensions we have noted indicate that it is a self-limiting movement in electoral and intellectual terms. Its significance resides rather in the recurrent patterns of thought it displays, for it is clear that these patterns are also in evidence outside the movement: Habermas detects an insistence on values beyond question as a characteristic of neo-conservatism, and his examples are drawn from the work of some of the most significant conservative theoreticians of the post-1945 period. This pattern can be traced back to a period that preceded the emergence of the New Right and further back to a period that preceded the rise of fascism. Moreover, the New Right itself acknowledges its Conservative Revolutionary predecessors in a way that erects no barriers against the kind of solutions they proposed to the problem of a lack of absolute bonds. These continuities with the past are matched by continuities with responses to Modernity outside the New Right. When Herzinger describes the unease towards a society without a moral centre he illustrates his point with the CDU's efforts at finding a solution in the form of a German 'dominant culture'.[18] The problem experienced and articulated by the New Right is not of concern just to a small group of thinkers. Rather it is the problem of open societies that have to learn to live without an unassailable and universally recognised ethnic, moral, cultural or religious core.[19]

Not least because of these continuities with the past and the present one needs to complement political categorisation of the New Right with an understanding of its patterns of thought and of the heavy psychological baggage that lies behind its political commitment. One also needs to consider a response. Stern traces the 'leap from despair to Utopia' in the work of Paul de Lagarde, Julius Langbehn and Moeller van den Bruck. For these men the major cause of despair was liberalism which they attacked as the principle premise of modern society: 'everything they dreaded seemed to spring from it: the bourgeois life, Manchesterism, materialism, parliament and the parties, the lack of political leadership'. Significantly Stern traces this dread into the personal psychology of the three men: they sensed in liberalism 'the source of all their inner sufferings'. Their one desire was for a 'new faith, a new community of believers, a world with fixed standards and no doubts, a new national religion that would bind all Germans together', but liberalism stood between them and the fulfilment of this desire.[20] This desire also characterises the cultural criticism of the New Right thinkers we have looked at, and liberalism is the enemy. We have also seen how liberalism has a political and a personal psychological dimension for the New Right: a 'metaphysical deficit', the concept seized upon by Weißmann. For Botho Strauß the history of liberalism is a process of shedding inhibitions and breaking taboos, and he regards any taboo as better than a destroyed taboo. Those who look out from the 'lost post' can see what the guardians of democracy cannot see: two thirds of the region they stand guard over has turned into a wasteland.[21]

To the extent that a response to the New Right has been set out at all, liberalism is at the heart of the response. Herzinger argues that Germany is now learning that the only reliable normative foundation of a free society is controlled, non-violent, discursive conflict. All attempts to restore some non-negotiable set of social values need to be countered with the principle that one can only rely on values that can be called into question. The values of a free democracy, however, are 'negative values' which set out no positive goals for the citizens of that society. The challenge of Modernity is to accept diversity, conflict, uncertainty as the norm in a free, pluralistic society.[22] This notion of living without absolutes and with uncertainty echoes Habermas's advocacy of a critically appropriated past. It also echoes Ulrich Beck's notion of reflexive Modernity: for Beck the 'seemingly dystopian outcome of rationalization' should not lead to pessimism. The effects of modernisation can be dealt with not through negation but through the radicalisation of rationalisation: modernisation must become reflective.[23] Herzinger insists that one cannot counter the danger of disintegrating into separate societies by appealing to some supposedly intact dominant culture. Instead one has to encourage citizens to commit to the laws of a secularised democratic society. Culture is more than ever before a variable entity, subject to constant change, subjective perceptions and not susceptible to definitive description.[24]

Living with uncertainty is also a strand in sociological analysis of the positive contribution of culture. Zygmunt Bauman, who had set out the functional and dysfunctional nature of culture, also discusses living with the ensuing ambiguity. In the modern era culture is pushed into opposition to society, but paradoxically this disharmony is precisely the harmony that Modernity requires. Bauman explores how there can be a peaceful coexistence between life and ambivalence.[25] Culture reveals the limitations of the order society creates. Culture's contribution to the struggle for order is to show that the struggle is permanent and that it will have no outcome, but culture also shows how to live with this lack of prospect. To this extent culture will also teach the value of moderation and tolerance.[26] Hermann Glaser looks to the Basic Law of the Federal Republic which, he argues, leaves no doubt that Germany is a 'Kulturstaat' (cultural state), even if this principle seems to have ever less to do with reality. Glaser sees it as one of the great achievements of the Enlightenment to have challenged all fundamentalist concepts of the truth, and it is an achievement of culture to give life a meaning and an identity in the midst of the relativism and aporia that follow from the destructive philosophy of doubt. Glaser finds the debate between Jürgen Habermas and Niklas Luhmann at the start of the seventies highly topical: whereas Luhmann had thought in terms of the smooth functioning of state and society as systems Habermas had called for values to be realised. In the desolation of a demystified world reason must help give a sense of direction.[27]

What these values might be in an open society is an open question. The list of candidates extends from civil society and activation,[28] involvement in the community,[29] direct participation of the young in political decision-making,[30] social justice,[31] and respect.[32] These are the values of a liberal democracy, and to the New Right this makes them part of the problem, as Heimo Schwilk's comments tend to confirm: all his Wilhelm Meister currently finds on offer is a so-called value community based on solidarity, responsibility, freedom, tolerance, achievement, and morality. These values, declares Schwilk, have been disappropriated, for how can one be responsible in an age when hard work, decency and solidarity can be misused by irresponsible boards of major companies?[33]

As we have come to expect, however, there are many contradictory voices within the New Right. One of them calls into question the desirability of the exalted expectations of politics that are widespread among New Right thinkers: German history has demonstrated to Rüdiger Safranski that it is dangerous to mix politics and metaphysics. The only politically useful philosophical ideas are those that deal with the preconditions for a peaceful and free society. Safranski looks for a modest form of politics that does not seek ultimate answers or meaning: what we need is a slimmed down form of politics that does not have any ambition to lend meaning to life, politics that is perhaps rather boring as a result, and ordinary, like our ordinary interests which politics should busy itself reconciling.[34]

Safranski's thoughts read more like those of a liberal critic of the New Right than the voice of the New Right itself: his call for expectations of politics not to be pitched too highly is at odds with Weißmann's need for an answer to perceptions of chaos and a fundamental loss of meaning, and the elevation of nationalism to the status of an absolute political value that can fill an existential void. Safranski's more sober approach may reflect a less radical view of politics, but it is undoubtedly also bound up with the realisation that one cannot revert to a premodern consciousness.

Notes

Introduction

1 See, for example, the websites of the New Right Thule-Seminar: http://www.thule-seminar.org; the Studienzentrum Weikersheim: http://www.studienzentrum-weikersheim.de; the Deutschland-Bewegung: http://www.deutschland-bewegung.de; the Institut für Staatspolitik: http://www.staatspolitik.de. Among the newspapers and journals *Junge Freiheit, Criticón, Nation und Europa, Staatsbriefe* all have their own websites. See bibliography for details.

2 *Der Spiegel*, no. 6, February 1993, pp. 133–8.

3 One example is the best-selling volume *Die selbstbewußte Nation. 'Anschwellender Bocksgesang' und andere Beiträge zu einer deutschen Debatte*, ed. by Heimo Schwilk and Ulrich Schacht (Berlin: Ullstein, 1994).

4 Kurt Lenk, 'Ideengeschichtliche Dispositionen rechtsextremen Denkens', *Aus Politik und Zeitgeschichte*, B 9-10 (1998), 13–19 (p. 14).

5 Horst von Buttlar, '"Neue Rechte" in Deutschland: Braune in Nadelstreifen', *Der Spiegel*, 10 October 2003.

6 See, for example, Wolfgang Gessenharter, *Kippt die Republik? Die Neue Rechte und ihre Unterstützung durch Politik und Medien* (Munich: Knaur, 1994), pp. 15–16; Bundesamt für Verfassungsschutz, *Rechtsextremismus in der Bundesrepublik Deutschland – Ein Lagebild* (Cologne: September 1996), p. 21.

7 Gessenharter, *Kippt die Republik?* pp. 13, 62.

8 See the report by Jörg Fischer and Frank Philip: 'Europa: Treffen von Haider, Lega Nord und Vlaams Blok', *Junge Freiheit*, 9 August 2002.

9 Armin Pfahl-Traughber: *'Konservative Revolution' und 'Neue Rechte'. Rechtextremistische Intellektuelle gegen den demokratischen Verfassungsstaat* (Opladen: Leske und Budrich, 1998), p. 224. Pfahl-Traughber puts potential support for the extreme right in Germany today at between 7 and 20%, in the Weimar Republic at between 20 and 40%. He also points out that the political cultures of both states are very different, with a strong preference for the 'Obrigkeitsstaat' (authoritarian state) in Weimar and liberalism in the Federal Republic. At the organisational level the New Right today does not have the political connections enjoyed by the Conservative Revolution. The political clubs of the Conservative Revolution counted senior civil servants, ministers, and businessmen among their members. (ibid.).

10 Wolfgang Gessenharter, *Kippt die Republik*. Pfahl-Traughber concludes that Gessenharter's title is hardly appropriate, rejecting his claim that the New Right has a strong influence on the media and politics. Uwe

Backes argues similarly: 'in sum when we talk about the "New Right" we seem to be dealing with a phenomenon whose significance is greatly exaggerated and which does not live up to expectations, either in terms of its intellectual originality or its effect on public life'. (Uwe Backes 'Rechtsextremismus in Deutschland. Ideologien, Organisationen und Strategien', *Aus Politik und Zeitgeschichte*, B 9-10 (1998), 27–35 (p. 33).

11 Kurt Sontheimer, 'Die Kontinuität antidemokratischen Denkens', in *Die Neue Rechte – eine Gefahr für die Demokratie?* ed. by Wolfgang Gessenharter and Thomas Pfeiffer (Wiesbaden: Verlag für Sozialwissenschaften, 2004), pp. 19–29.

12 Richard Herzinger, *Republik ohne Mitte* (Berlin: Siedler, 2001), p. 7.

13 Ibid., p. 32.

14 Ibid., p. 83.

Chapter 1   What is the New Right?

1 Lars Rensmann points to the consensus among most commentators on the anti-democratic nature of the New Right. Because New Right thinkers and politicians generally commit themselves to the principles of a constitutional democracy, however, some writers suggest that the movement does not qualify as anti-democratic but can be subsumed instead under the category of the 'radical right' (Lars Rensmann, 'Four Wings of the Intellectual New Right', unpublished manuscript, 2003, p. 3).

2 Wolfgang Gessenharter, *Kippt die Republik?* pp. 60–1. Benthin points to the line of research which suggests that neo-conservatism and the New Right are two separate groups which merge or cooperate (Rainer Benthin, *Die Neue Rechte in Deutschland und ihr Einfluß auf den politischen Diskurs der Gegenwart* (Frankfurt am Main: Lang, 1996), 28–9. The best known critic of neo-conservatism, Jürgen Habermas, cites many sources which precede the emergence of the New Right and which suggest neo-conservatism is the precursor of the New Right. See *The New Conservatism* (Cambridge: Polity Press, 1989), especially the essay 'Neoconservative Cultural Criticism in the United States and West Germany', pp. 22–47.

3 Bundesamt für Verfassungsschutz, *Rechtsextremismus in der Bundesrepublik Deutschland – Ein Lagebild*, p. 21. See also Eckhard Jesse's survey of the literature attempting to define the New Right: 'Fließende Grenzen zum Rechtsextremismus? Zur Debatte über Brückenspektren, Grauzonen, Vernetzungen und Scharniere am rechten Rand – Mythos und Realität', in *Rechtsextremismus: Ergebnisse und Perspektiven der Forschung*, ed. by Jürgen W. Falter, Hans-Gerd Jaschke, and Jürgen R. Winkler (Opladen: Westdeutscher Verlag, 1996), pp. 514–29.

4 See, for example, Hans-Gerd Jaschke, 'Nationalismus und Ethnopluralismus. Zum Wiederaufleben von Ideen der "Konservativen Revolution"', *Aus Politik und Zeitgeschichte*, B 3-4 (1993), 3–10.

5   Ibid., p. 7.
6   Gessenharter, *Kippt die Republik*, pp. 60–1.
7   Quoted by Gessenharter, *Kippt die Republik*, p. 194.
8   Gessenharter, pp. 15–16.
9   Ibid. p. 14. Pfahl-Traughber rightly points out, however, that the characteristics Gessenharter detects in the New Right are features of virtually all extreme right-wing movements and therefore do not offer a specific enough definition (Armin Pfahl-Traughber: *'Konservative Revolution' und 'Neue Rechte'*, pp. 157–8).
10 Karlheinz Weißmann, *Alles was recht(s) ist: Ideen, Köpfe und Perspektiven der politischen Rechten* (Graz, Stuttgart: Leopold Stocker Verlag, 2000), p. 11.
11 Michael Hageböck, 'Endzeit', in *Wir 89er*, ed. by Roland Bubik (Frankfurt am Main, Berlin: Ullstein, 1995), pp. 145–62 (pp. 150–1).
12 Alain de Benoist, 'Netzwerke funktionieren wie Viren', *Junge Freiheit*, 13 September 2002. De Benoist is a regular contributor to *Junge Freiheit*, and his books appear in German translation, often with an endorsement from Armin Mohler, who is widely regarded as the father of the German New Right.
13 Kurt Lenk, 'Ideengeschichtliche Dispositionen rechtsextremen Denkens', p. 13.
14 This is the basic tendency of much of the research on the New Right. For example, Armin Pfahl-Traughber may conclude correctly that Gessenharter's definition does not mark off the New Right from other extreme right-wing groups, nor even from democratic conservatism. He also argues that the New Right does not have a coherent ideology, yet he goes on to offer his own definition based on particular items of ideology, and relating these to the New Right's strong interest in the Conservative Revolution in the years of the Weimar Republic. Armin Pfahl-Traughber: *'Konservative Revolution' und 'Neue Rechte'*, pp. 157–61, 184.
15 Henning Eichberg, 'Kein Volk und keinen Frieden', *Wir selbst*, 1, 1995, 73–7. Gessenharter's definition of the New Right suggests it occupies a new place on the political spectrum, arguing that, compared with the Old Right and 'orthodox right-wing extremism' the New Right is something different, and it is also separate from conservatism. Wolfgang Gessenharter, 'Die intellektuelle Neue Rechte und die neue radikale Rechte in Deutschland', *Aus Politik und Zeitgeschichte*, B 9-10 (1998), 20–6 (p. 21).
16 Günter Rohrmoser, *Deutschlands Tragödie* (Munich: Olzog, 2002), p. 21.
17 Richard Stöss, 'Die "neue Rechte" in der Bundesrepublik', in *Die Wiedergeburt nationalistischen Denkens: Gefahr für die Demokratie*, ed. by Forschungsinstitut der Friedrich-Ebert-Stiftung (Bonn: Friedrich-Ebert-Stiftung, 1995), pp. 113–14.
18 See Gessenharter, *Kippt die Republik?* p. 43. Benthin dates the New Right from 1972, the year Siegfried Pöhlmann, one-time Deputy Chairman of the NPD, founded the *Aktion Neue Rechte* (Action New Right, ANR).

When Pöhlmann was defeated in his bid for the party leadership by Martin Mußgnug he left the party to set up the ANR, taking his supporters with him. (Rainer Benthin, *Die Neue Rechte in Deutschland*, p. 28; See also Angelika Königsreder, 'Zur Chronologie des Rechtsextremismus', in *Rechtsextremismus in Deutschland*, ed. by Wolfgang Benz (Frankfurt am Main: Fischer, 1996), pp. 246–315 (p. 258).

19 Wolfgang Strauss, 'Deutschlands Rechte und Hitler', *Europa vorn*, 92, 15 October 1995, 8–12 (p. 9).

20 Hartmut Lange, 'Existenz und Moderne: Über Selbsterkenntnis als Solidarität', in *Die selbstbewußte Nation*, pp. 436–7.

21 Siegfried Bublies, '20 Jahre wir selbst. Rückblick auf den Versuch einer publizistischen Topographie des Hufeisens', *Wir Selbst*, 4 (1999), 6–12 (p. 7).

22 Ibid.

23 The Federal Government, the Bundestag and the Bundesrat applied to the Federal Constitutional Court to have the NPD banned, claiming that its call for a *völkisch* collectivism was incompatible with the Basic Law's principle of equality. The case was abandoned in March 2003 after it was revealed that several senior NPD members were working as informers for the Office for the Protection of the Constitution.

24 Hajo Funke, *Paranoia und Politik. Rechtsextremismus in der Berliner Republik* (Berlin: Schiler Verlag, 2002), pp. 85–8.

25 Richard Stöss, 'Forschungs- und Erklärungsansätze – ein Überblick', in *Rechtsextremismus. Einführung und Forschungsbilanz*, ed. by Wolfgang Kowalsky and Wolfgang Schroeder (Opladen: Westdeutscher Verlag, 1994), pp. 23–66 (p. 39). Stöss sees the distinction between Old and New Right rather in the ways in which they justify their political views (ibid.). See also Gessenharter, *Kippt die Republik?* p. 60.

26 Amin Pfahl-Traughber, *'Konservative Revolution' und 'Neue Rechte'*, p. 161.

27 See Roger Woods, *The Conservative Revolution in the Weimar Republic* (Macmillan: Basingstoke; St Martin's Press: New York, 1996), esp. pp. 111–34.

28 Armin Pfahl-Traughber, *'Konservative Revolution' und 'Neue Rechte'*, p. 51. Stefan Breuer, *Anatomie der Konservativen Revolution* (Darmstadt: Wissenschaftliche Buchgesellschaft, 1993), p. 181.

29 Karlheinz Weißmann argues that the New Right does not exist as a homogeneous whole, and sees rather agreement among individuals. *Alles was recht(s) ist*, p. 245.

30 This approach is adopted by Armin Pfahl-Traughber in *'Konservative Revolution' und 'Neue Rechte'*, p. 153.

31 Pfahl-Traughber later acknowledges the absence of a coherent New Right ideology and criticises those who assume one exists (*'Konservative Revolution' und 'Neue Rechte'*, p. 161). He justifies not analysing the ideological differences within the New Right himself by defining his task as highlighting how the New Right is at odds with the values of a democratic constitutional state (ibid., p. 184).

32 Armin Pfahl-Traughber, 'Konservative Revolution' und 'Neue Rechte', p. 21.
33 Jürgen Habermas, The New Conservatism, pp. 254–5.
34 Hans-Joachim Veen, '"Rechtsextrem" oder "Rechtsradikal"?', Das Parlament, 15 April 1994, p. 1.
35 Armin Pfahl-Traughber; 'Konservative Revolution' und 'Neue Rechte', pp. 19–20. Pfahl-Traughber cites Armin Mohler's commitment to fascism and Bernhard Willms's commitment to a form of nationalism mit places the supposed interests of the nation above human rights and the constitution as reasons for locating the New Right on the extreme right (pp. 158–9).
36 See Dieter Stein, Moritz Schwarz, 'Mangel an Intellektualität. Interview mit Alexander von Stahl', Junge Freiheit, 3 January 2003, on the newspaper's legal action against North Rhine-Westphalia's Office for the Protection of the Constitution, seeking to end the observation. In the mid-nineties the Federal Office for the Protection of the Constitution classified Nation und Europa, a journal closely associated with the New Right as 'one of the most important theoretical and strategic publications of the extreme right'. Bundesamt für Verfassungsschutz, Entwicklungstendenzen im Rechtsextremismus (Cologne, l996), p. 3. It saw this and other New Right journals (Europa vorn, Staatsbriefe, Sleipnir) as providing the theories and strategies for the extreme right. Bundesamt für Verfassungsschutz, Rechtsextremismus in der Bundesrepublik Deutschland – Ein Lagebild, p. 18. In its 2003 report the Federal Office for the Protection of the Constitution does not refer to the New Right but rather to attempts to intellectualise the extreme right. It sees Junge Freiheit as a forum for extreme right-wing authors and gives the example of the political journalist Günter Maschke who elsewhere refers to himself as an enemy of the constitution and to the constitution itself as a prison. The report quotes Maschke in Junge Freiheit describing democratic values as 'cannibal humanity' and 'gypsy liberalism'. It also quotes an author in Junge Freiheit denying the Nazi regime's responsibility for the outbreak of the Second World War and seeking to justify the war against the Soviet Union. (Bundsesministerium des Innern, Verfassunsschutzbericht 2003 (Berlin, 2004), pp. 84–8).
37 Wolfgang Gessenharter, Kippt die Republik? p. 62.
38 Armin Pfahl-Traughber, 'Konservative Revolution' und 'Neue Rechte', p. 160. Pfahl-Traughber's idea of the bridge between conservatism and extremism does not sit easily with his simpler categorisation of the New Right as extremist. At various points Neaman attaches to the New Right the terms radical conservatism, the radical right, and extremism. Elliot Neaman, 'A New Conservative Revolution? in Antisemitism and Xenophobia in Germany after Unification, ed. by Hermann Kurthen, Werner Bergmann and Rainer Erb (New York, Oxford: OUP, 1997), pp. 190–208 (pp. 190–1).
39 Wolfgang Gessenharter, 'Die intellektuelle Neue Rechte und die neue radikale Rechte in Deutschland', p. 21. Gessenharter gives the example of a New Right appeal in the Frankfurter Allgemeine Zeitung which was

signed by Union politicians as well as extremists, and he takes this as a sign of the New Right's ability to draw in the political centre (p. 26).

40 Armin Pfahl-Traughber, 'Konservative Revolution' und 'Neue Rechte', p. 160.

41 Michael Minkenberg, 'German Unification and the Continuity of Discontinuities: Cultural Change and the Far Right in East and West', *German Politics*, 2 (1994), 169–92 (p. 178).

42 Wolfgang Gessenharter, *Kippt die Republik?* pp. 168–9.

43 Kurt Lenk, 'Ideengeschichtliche Dispositionen rechtsextremen Denkens', p. 13.

44 Gessenharter, *Kippt die Republik?* p. 128.

45 Rainer Benthin, *Die Neue Rechte in Deutschland*, p. 10.

46 Wolfgang Gessenharter, *Kippt die Republik?* p. 13. Stöss notes the definition of the New Right as a group of journals, including *Junge Freiheit, Criticón, Staatsbriefe, Nation und Europa*, organisations such as the Thule-Kreis and the Bund freier Bürger (League of Free Citizens), and prominent individuals such as Arnulf Baring, Alain de Benoist, Henning Eichberg, Hans-Magnus Enzensberger, Robert Hepp, Klaus Hornung, Gerd-Klaus Kaltenbrunner, Pierre Krebs, Heinrich Lummer, Armin Mohler, Klaus Motschmann, Ernst Nolte, Günter Rohrmoser, Caspar von Schrenck-Notzing, Karl Steinbuch, Botho Strauß, Wolfgang Strauss, Karlheinz Weißmann, Kurt Ziesel and Rainer Zitelmann. Richard Stöss, 'Die "neue Rechte" in der Bundesrepublik', p. 111.

47 Ibid., pp. 126–7.

48 See Gessenharter's analysis of the asylum debate: *Kippt die Republik?*, pp. 215–54. See also Uwe Worm on this point in *Die Neue Rechte in der Bundesrepublik* (Cologne: PappyRossa, 1995), p. 11.

49 Rainer Benthin, *Die Neue Rechte in Deutschland*, p. 65.

50 'Konservative Revolution' und 'Neue Rechte', p. 162.

51 The New Right theorist Günter Rohrmoser's 2002 study of the roots of National Socialism, *Deutschlands Tragödie*, was originally presented as a lecture course at the University of Stuttgart in the Summer Semester of 1994 (p. 16). Rohrmoser was a professor at the Pädagogische Hochschule Münster and Honorary Professor at the University of Cologne. He currently holds an academic post at the University of Hohenheim. The opening section of the book amounts to a lengthy plea for the New Right, with Rohrmoser arguing that when socialism collapsed there was already an embryonic New Right in Germany. Young, right-wing intellectuals spoke out and expected to be part of normal public debate. Rohrmoser sees it as the key question for Germany whether a democratic Right is allowed to exist (p. 22).

52 The Institut für Staatspolitik runs series of lectures in Berlin on topics broadly related to New Right concerns, and the speakers often have an academic connection. The Studienzentrum Weikersheim (Weikersheim Study Centre) runs annual workshops and conferences on political and cultural issues, a youth programme and evening discussion groups.

53 Wolfgang Gessenharter, 'Die intellektuelle Neue Rechte und die neue radikale Rechte in Deutschland', p. 26.
54 Stöss, 'Die "neue Rechte" in der Bundesrepublik', pp. 120–1.
55 Ansgar Graw, for example, who contributed to *Die selbstbewußte Nation*, writes for *Die Welt*. The co-editors of *Die selbstbewußte Nation*, Heimo Schwilk and Ulrich Schacht, are senior reporters for *Welt am Sonntag*. Schwilk's political views are apparent in his journalism, as, for example, when he writes about the decline of bourgeois society into selfishness and chaos, and the possible renaissance of a society based on notions of honour, duty and sacrifice. ('Der Bürger kehrt zurück', *Welt am Sonntag*, 30 September 2001).
56 The historian Ernst Nolte has been a speaker at the Institut für Staatspolitik, the social philosopher Günter Rohrmoser writes for *Junge Freiheit*, as does the political scientist Klaus Hornung. Hornung also serves on the executive committee of the Studienzentrum Weikersheim.
57 Gessenharter rightly comments that those who see the New Right purely as part of right-wing extremism are failing to see the links with and within the CDU and CSU. 'Die intellektuelle Neue Rechte und die neue radikale Rechte in Deutschland', pp. 21–2. For one observer the continuity with mainstream thought even stretches into the SPD with what is referred to as the Berlin Generation of politicians and journalists. Their journal *Berliner Republik* is said to offer a mix of concern at a moral crisis and growing individualism in society and the promotion of family, religion, and community. Richard Herzinger, *Republik ohne Mitte*, p. 90.
58 Rainer Benthin, *Die Neue Rechte in Deutschland*, pp. 76–7.
59 Ibid., p. 81.
60 Ibid.
61 Franz Schönhuber, *Die verbogene Gesellschaft: Mein Leben zwischen NS-Erziehung und US-Umerziehung* (Berg: VGB-Verlagsgesellschaft, 1996), p. 22. Schönhuber's image of the nose-ring is taken from Mohler's *Der Nasenring. Im Dickicht der Vergangenheitsbewältigung* (Essen: Heitz & Höffkes, 1987).
62 Similarly, Andreas Mölzer, editor-in-chief of the Austrian weekly *Zur Zeit*, is adviser to Jörg Haider.
63 New Right commentators themselves claim this link between political position and cultural context, for example 'Pankraz', who argues that Botho Strauß's views in his political essay 'Anschwellender Bocksgesang' were embedded in his philosophical attitudes ('Botho Strauß und der Fundamentalismus', *Junge Freiheit*, 11 October 2002).
64 Günter Rohrmoser, *Ideologie-Zerfall: Nachruf auf die geistige Wende* (Krefeld: Sinus, 1990), p. 38.
65 Karlheinz Weißmann, 'Maurice Barrès und der "Nationalismus" im Frühwerk Ernst Jüngers', in *Magie der Heiterkeit. Ernst Jünger zum Hundertsten*, ed. by Günter Figal and Heimo Schwilk (Stuttgart: Klett-Cotta, 1995), pp. 133–46 (p. 142).

66 Zygmunt Bauman, *Moderne und Ambivalenz. Das Ende der Eindeutigkeit* (Frankfurt am Main: Fischer, 1996), p. 22.

67 Hermann Glaser, 'Kultur und Identitäten', *Aus Politik und Zeitgeschichte*, B 50, 7 December 2001, 3–5 (p. 5).

68 Hajo Funke, *Paranoia und Politik*, p. 250.

69 Zygmunt Bauman, *Moderne und Ambivalenz*, p. 23. Similarly Glaser reflects that, despite its questioning nature, a critical culture can provide human existence with some sense of values and identity against a background of relativism. Hermann Glaser, 'Kultur und Identitäten', p. 4.

70 Wolfgang Gessenharter, 'Die intellektuelle Neue Rechte und die neue radikale Rechte in Deutschland', p. 26.

71 Jeffrey Herf, *Reactionary Modernism: Technology, culture and politics in Weimar and the Third Reich* (Cambridge, London: Cambridge University Press, 1984), p. 218.

72 John G.A. Pocock, *Politics, Language and Time: Essays on Political Thought and History* (New York: Atheneum, 1971), p. 37.

73 Ibid., p. 38.

74 Robert Darnton, 'Intellectual and Cultural History', in *The Past Before Us: Contemporary Historical Writing in the United States*, ed. by Michael Kammen (Ithaca, New York and London: Cornell University Press, 1980), pp. 327–54.

75 Dominick LaCapra, *Rethinking Intellectual History* (Ithaca: Cornell University Press, 1983), p. 14.

76 David Chaney, *The Cultural Turn* (London: Routledge, 1994), p. 1.

77 Victoria Bonnell, Lynn Hunt, *Beyond the Cultural Turn* (Berkeley, Los Angeles, London: University of California Press, 1999), p. 3.

Chapter 2   From Cultural Hegemony to Cultural Pessimism

1 Armin Mohler, 'Vorwort', in Alain de Benoist, *Kulturrevolution von rechts* (Krefeld: Sinus Verlag, 1985), p. 12.

2 Alain de Benoist, *Kulturrevolution von rechts*, p. 20.

3 Ibid., pp. 20–3.

4 Ibid., p. 44.

5 Ibid., p. 46. On de Benoist's interpretation of Gramsci see also Armin Pfahl-Traughber, '"Kulturrevolution von rechts". Definition, Einstellungen und Gefahrenpotential der Intellektuellen "Neuen Rechten"', *Mut*, 351 (1996), 36–57 (p. 42).

6 Alain de Benoist, *Kulturrevolution von rechts*, pp. 49–50.

7 Armin Mohler, *Liberalenbeschimpfung* (Essen: Heitz & Höffkes, 1990), p. 86.

8 Alain de Benoist, *Kulturrevolution von rechts*, p. 50.

9 Wolfgang Gessenharter, *Kippt die Republik?* p. 149.

10 Ibid., p. 166.

11 See 'Scheitert die "Intellektualisierung?"', *Junge Freiheit*, July/August 1989, pp. 1–2.

12 This strategy is quoted in a report on the website of the NPD youth organisation, the Junge Nationaldemokraten (Anon, 'Seminar mit Jürgen Schwab im Raum Heidelberg', http://www.jn-bw.de/aktionen/politik/seminar_20020713.htm, accessed 14 September 2004). The report is on a talk given on 13 July 2002 by Jürgen Schwab in a series on political theory.

13 Angelika Willig, 'Platon statt Judenwitze. Die NPD strebt eine Intellektualisierung an', *Junge Freiheit*, 15 June 2001.

14 For an overview of New Right publications see Siegfried Jäger (ed.), *Rechtsdruck: Die Presse der Neuen Rechten* (Berlin, Bonn: J.H.W. Dietz, 1988). On *Criticón* see Martin Dietzsch's chapter: 'Zwischen Konkurrenz und Kooperation. Organisationen und Presse der Rechten in der Bundesrepublik', pp. 31–80, esp. pp. 65–7.

15 Gerd Habermann, 'Die Debatte über den "letzten Menschen"', *Criticón*, April, May, June 1996, 79–81 (p. 80).

16 Friedrich Nietzsche, *Jenseits von Gut und Böse, Werke in drei Bänden*, 7th ed., ed. by Karl Schlechta (Munich: Carl Hanser, 1973), II, pp. 624, 787. These ideas are also taken up by Pierre Krebs of the New Right Thule-Seminar, who laments Germany's loss of its 'Germanentum' (Germanic self) and the ascendancy of the urge to reduce mankind which Nietzsche so courageously attacked. Pierre Krebs, 'Unser inneres Reich', *Elemente*, 1 (1986), p. 6.

17 Friedrich Nietzsche, *Werke in drei Bänden*, II, p. 786.

18 Pierre Krebs (ed.), *Mut zur Identität* (Struckum: Verlag für Ganzheitliche Forschung und Kultur, 1988), p. 21.

19 Ibid.

20 The Studienzentrum Weikersheim (http://www.studienzentrum-weikersheim.de.) has a similar profile of activities but is closer to the CDU/CSU in terms of its staff and guest speakers. In response to a parliamentary question (14/7931) the German government confirmed that over a ten-year period the Bundeszentrale für politische Bildung had paid 193,255 DM in support of the Study Centre's work.

21 Wolfgang Gessenharter, *Kippt die Republik?*, pp. 9–12.

22 Ibid., p. 17.

23 Franz Greß, Hans-Gerd Jaschke, Klaus Schönekäs, *Neue Rechte und Rechtsextremismus in Europa. Bundesrepublik – Frankreich – Großbritannien* (Opladen: Westdeutscher Verlag, 1990), p. 9.

24 Hajo Funke, *Paranoia und Politik*, pp. 246–7.

25 Interview with Dieter Stein, editor of *Junge Freiheit*, 14 February 2003. Funke similarly argues that the New Right sees its main task in providing the CDU and CSU with a nationalist ideology. This it does through series of publications such as *Edition Antaios* and *Junge Freiheit*, organisations such as the Institut für Staatspolitik and the Studienzentrum Weikersheim headed by Klaus Hornung and his Deputy, Jörg Schönbohm (CDU).

26 Günter Rohrmoser, *Ideologie-Zerfall*, p. 40.
27 Wolfgang Gessenharter, *Kippt die Republik?*, p. 134.
28 Hajo Funke, *Paranoia und Politik*, p. 248.
29 Ibid., pp. 17–18.
30 Ibid. See also Schönbohm's description of multi-culturalism as a 'left-wing heresy' in Dieter Stein, Moritz Schwarz, 'Interview mit Jörg Schönbohm', *Junge Freiheit*, 7 February 2003.
31 Hajo Funke, *Paranoia und Politik*, p. 243.
32 Ibid.
33 Dieter Stein, Moritz Schwarz, 'Interview mit Jörg Schönbohm'.
34 Hajo Funke, *Paranoia und Politik*, p. 243.
35 Karlheinz Weißmann, *Alles was recht(s) ist*, p. 250.
36 Ibid., p. 47.
37 The 'national revolutionary' journal *Neue Zeit* calls for a Conservative Revolution beyond the 'traditional clichées' of left or right, communism or capitalism. *Europa Vorn* laments the decline of the German right and declares that it lacks substance since the East/West antithesis became obsolete. Franz Schönhuber reported on a visit to France where he was able to follow the mighty upturn in the fortunes of the Front National and talk with Le Pen who expressed his regret at the splits among the patriotic groups in Germany. Franz Schönhuber, 'Die Nebel lichten sich', *Nation und Europa*, 46, Nov/Dec 1996, p. 13.
38 S. P., 'Eurorechte im Blickpunkt', *Nation und Europa*, 46, Nov/Dec 1996, p. 16. Gerwin Steinberger declares that opposition should not mean negation but an affirmation of what should replace those things the Right rejects. He concludes that the right has little or no idea about this. Gerwin Steinberger, 'Edgar Jung und der organische Staat', *Nation und Europa*, 9 September 1992, p. 50.
39 Dieter Stein, Hans-Ulrich Kopp, Goetz Meidinger, 'Der Zusammenbruch des Sozialismus führt zu einer Renaissance des Konservativen. Interview mit Günter Rohrmoser', *Junge Freiheit*, July/August 1991, p. 3.
40 'Interview mit Günter Rohrmoser', *Junge Freiheit*, March/April 1989, p. 3.
41 Roland Bubik, 'Herrschaft und Medien: Über den Kampf gegen die linke Meinungsdominanz', in *Die selbstbewußte Nation*, pp. 182–94 (p. 189).
42 Henning Eichberg, 'Kein Volk und keinen Frieden', *Wir selbst*, 1, 1995, pp. 73–7.
43 Angelika Willig 'Platon statt Judenwitze. Die NPD strebt eine Intellektualisierung an'.
44 Alain de Benoist, *Kulturrevolution von rechts*, pp. 9–11.
45 Jürgen Habermas describes this attitude among German conservatives who reacted with hostility to Daniel Goldhagen's book *Hitler's Willing Executioners: Ordinary Germans and the Holocaust* which appeared in 1996. Habermas links this hostility to Weikersheim, presumably to the New Right Study Centre there, and he also sees this attitude taking hold more generally in Germany since Unification. *Die postnationale Konstellation. Politische Essays* (Frankfurt am Main: Suhrkamp, 1998), pp. 50–1.

46 Jürgen Habermas, 'The New Intimacy between Culture and Politics', in *The New Conservatism*, ed. by Shierry Nicholson (Cambridge: Polity, 1989), pp. 196–205 (p. 201).

47 Stefan Ulbrich, 'Es entsteht eine neue Kultur', *Junge Freiheit*, 7 October 1992, p. 24. See also Seidel who takes a uniform culture as the basis of a New Right national identity in France and Great Britain. Gill Seidel, 'Culture, Nation and "Race" in the British and French New Right', in Ruth Levitas, *The Ideology of the New Right* (Cambridge: Polity, 1986), pp. 107–35 (p. 107).

48 Pierre Krebs, *Das unvergängliche Erbe* (Tübingen: Grabert, 1981), pp. 23–4.

49 Karlheinz Weißmann, 'Herausforderung und Entscheidung: Über einen politischen Verismus für Deutschland', in *Die selbstbewußte Nation*, pp. 309–26 (p. 315).

50 Pierre Krebs (ed.), *Mut zur Identität*, p. 12. Hajo Funke makes the point about the exclusivity of New Right culture with the following quotation from the 1981 Heidelberg Manifesto, in which a group of fifteen academics called for action to protect the German nation and German culture: 'We note with alarm the infiltration of the German people by means of an influx of millions of foreigners and their families, the foreignisation of our language, our culture and our national character'. *Paranoia und Politik*, p. 246.

51 Alfred Mechtersheimer, 'Nation und Internationalismus: Über nationales Selbstbewußtsein als Bedingung des Friedens', in *Die selbstbewußte Nation*, pp. 345–63 (pp. 357–8).

52 Alain de Benoist, *Kulturrevolution von rechts*, p. 69.

53 Ibid., p. 70. De Benoist does not stop short of national stereotypes as he quotes with no hint of criticism the idea that the Arabs of Saudi Arabia succumb to political fragmentation as soon as the absence of an iron hand allows them to abandon themselves to their temperament (pp. 71–2).

54 Ibid.

55 Alexander Gauland, 'Herkunft und Zukunft', *Criticón*, 167 (2000), pp. 24–5.

56 Karlheinz Weißmann quoting Arnold Gehlen in: *Alles was recht(s) ist*, p. 164. The point is echoed, albeit with a different purpose, by Habermas who argues that Modernity can no longer derive its standards from models offered by other epochs. Modernity sees itself as dependent exclusively upon itself – it has to draw on itself for its normativity. Jürgen Habermas, 'The New Obscurity', in *The New Conservatism*, pp. 48–70 (pp. 48–9).

57 Simone Satzger, 'Elemente', in *Wir 89er*, ed. by Roland Bubik (Frankfurt am Main, Berlin: Ullstein, 1995), pp. 35–49.

58 Günter Figal, 'Illusionslos sei das Leben und frei', *Die Welt am Sonntag*, 5 November 2002.

59 Ibid.

60 Ibid.

61 Karlheinz Weißmann, *Alles was recht(s) ist*, p. 36. Weißmann is quoting from Hielscher's 'Für die unterdrückten Völker' which appeared in *Arminius* (16 March 1927).

62 *Parteiprogramm 2002 der Republikaner*, http://www.rep.de (accessed 20 September 2004). Feelgood culture is also to be found in the political mainstream: for one observer the Brandenburg Minister of the Interior, Jörg Schönbohm (CDU), anchors an authoritarian and self-assured national identity in the culture, history and language of Germany, and this is taken as an example of a New Right tradition being continued. See Hajo Funke, *Paranoia und Politik*, p. 243.

63 Anon, 'Untergang des Abendlandes? Die Folgen eines EU-Beitritts der Türkei', *National-Zeitung*, 12 September 2003.

64 Section 1 of the NPD's party programme. http://www.npd.de/npd_startseiten/programme.html (accessed 10 September 2004).

65 See, for example, Karlheinz Weißmann, 'Den Konfliktfall denken', *Junge Freiheit*, 3 November 2000. Weißmann quotes Bassam Tibi, a Syrian political scientist based at Göttingen University, who coined the term 'Leitkultur' to stress that integration of immigrants is not a mere legal formality. It should mean acknowledging and accepting certain cultural forms. Weißmann comments that Tibi fears Europeans have lost the will to protect their identity in the face of Muslim immigrants. They cannot decide on what can reasonably be expected of others, but tolerance should not mean sacrificing oneself.

66 Botho Strauß, *Der Unterstehende auf Zehenspitzen* (Munich, Vienna: Carl Hanser, 2004), p. 77. Michael Wiesberg quotes Strauß's version of *Leitkultur* in 'In tiefer Stille gegen die Welt leben', *Junge Freiheit*, 9 July 2004.

67 Botho Strauß, *Der Unterstehende auf Zehenspitzen*, p. 78.

68 Ibid. Strauß's image of Frau Welt is originally medieval and exemplified in the statue at Worms Cathedral dating from 1298. Strauß's ambiguous attitude towards the two-sided culture he describes is summed up in his comment that 'only an impotent rationalist would fail to acknowledge the rich temptations of the woman when viewed from the front' (ibid.).

69 Karlheinz Weißmann, *Alles was recht(s) ist*, p. 170.

70 Ibid., p. 170.

71 Ibid., p. 174.

72 Roland Bubik, 'Der Standort des Jungen Konservatismus', *Junge Freiheit*, December/January 1992–93, p. 13.

73 Günter Rohrmoser, *Ideologie-Zerfall*, p. 38.

74 Ibid., p. 159.

75 Günter Rohrmoser, *Deutschlands Tragödie*, p. 174. Rohrmoser also sees the collapse of the socialist Utopian project resulting in a 'vacuum of meaning' (*Ideologie-Zerfall*, p. 17).

76 Marcel Reding, 'Zum Begriff Tradition', in *Rekonstruktion des Konservatismus*, ed. by Gerd-Klaus Kaltenbrunner, 3rd edn (Bern and Stuttgart: Haupt, 1978), pp. 561–81 (p. 561).

77 Ibid., p. 561.
78 Jochen Schaare, 'Ein Lob der Skepsis', *Junge Freiheit*, 30 August 2002.
79 Weißmann sees this process at the heart of 're-education' in Germany.
    Karlheinz Weißmann, *Rückruf in die Geschichte* (Frankfurt am Main and
    Berlin: Ullstein, 1992), p. 33.
80 Botho Strauß, *Beginnlosigkeit: Reflexionen über Fleck und Linie* (Munich:
    dtv, 1997), p. 11. (The first edition was published in 1992). The essay
    'Anschwellender Bocksgesang' was first published in February 1993 in
    Der Spiegel, and the following year it was given pride of place in the
    volume of essays, *Die selbstbewußte Nation*.
81 Ernst Jünger, *Der Kampf als inneres Erlebnis* (Berlin: Mittler, 1922), p. 68.
82 Botho Strauß, *Beginnlosigkeit*, p. 16.
83 Ernst Jünger, 'Alfred Kubin', *Neues Forum*, 154, October 1966, 629–32
    (p. 629). Stefan Breuer comments that Conservative Revolutionary arro-
    gance was a facade concealing a basic mood of fear which Heidegger
    raised to an existential level. *Anatomie der Konservativen Revolution*,
    p. 44.
84 Ernst Jünger, 'Zu Kubins Bild: Der Mensch', in *Ernst Jünger, Alfred Kubin
    Eine Begegnung* (Frankfurt aM: Propyläen, 1975), p. 13. Quoted by
    Heimo Schwilk in *Ernst Jünger. Leben in Bildern und Texten*, ed. by Heimo
    Schwilk (Stuttgart: Klett-Cotta, 1988), p. 90.
85 Ernst Jünger, *Sturm* (Olten: Oltener Liebhaberdruck, 1963. First
    published in 1923), pp. 44–5.
86 Botho Strauß, *Beginnlosigkeit*, p. 41.
87 Ibid., p. 62.
88 Angelika Willig, editor of the cultural section of *Junge Freiheit*,
    comments that Strauß's book shows the individual cast adrift and the
    impossibility of grasping reality through reason. Willig takes this
    predicament to be what has been described over the last 150 years
    as a crisis of meaning, loss of centre or nihilism. 'Botho Strauß:
    "Beginnlosigkeit": Das Geräusch des Toastkauens', *Junge Freiheit*,
    October 1992, p. 15.
89 Botho Strauß, *Beginnlosigkeit*, p. 67.
90 Ibid., p. 55.
91 Botho Strauß, *Die Fehler des Kopisten* (Munich and Vienna: Hanser,
    1997), p. 36.
92 Hartmut Lange, 'Existenz und Moderne: Über Selbsterkenntnis als
    Solidarität', in *Die selbstbewußte Nation*, pp. 432–43 (pp. 441–2).
93 Hajo Funke, *Paranoia und Politik*, pp. 249–50.
94 Karlheinz Weißmann, *Alles was recht(s) ist*, p. 147.
95 Pierre Krebs (ed.), *Mut zur Identität*, p. 25.
96 Karlheinz Weißmann, 'Herausforderung und Entscheidung', p. 312.
97 Karlheinz Weißmann, 'Maurice Barrès und der "Nationalismus" im
    Frühwerk Ernst Jüngers' in *Magie der Heiterkeit. Ernst Jünger zum
    Hundertsten*, pp. 133–46 (p. 142).
98 Hartmut Lange, 'Existenz und Moderne', p. 441.
99 Ibid., p. 437.

100 Günter Figal, *Für eine Philosophie von Freiheit und Streit* (Stuttgart, Weimar: Metzler, 1994), p. 96.
101 Ibid., p. 97.
102 Ibid., p. 99.
103 Ernst Jünger, *Der Kampf als inneres Erlebnis*, p. 68. For an examination of the type in Jünger's work see Roger Woods, *Ernst Jünger and the Nature of Political Commitment* (Stuttgart: Akademischer Verlag Hans-Dieter Heinz, 1982), pp. 50–4.
104 Baal Müller, 'Jenseits von Leid- und Lightkultur', *Junge Freiheit*, 24 November 2000.
105 Ibid.
106 Heimo Schwilk, *Wendezeit – Zeitenwende: Beiträge zur Literatur der achtziger Jahre* (Bonn, Berlin: Bouvier, 1991), p. 142.
107 Botho Strauß, 'Anschwellender Bocksgesang', in *Die selbstbewußte Nation*, p. 25.
108 Jürgen Habermas, 'The New Intimacy between Culture and Politics', p. 201.
109 Botho Strauß, *Der Aufstand gegen die sekundäre Welt* (Munich, Vienna: Hanser), 1999, pp. 37–53.
110 Botho Strauß, *Die Fehler des Kopisten*, p. 19.
111 Heimo Schwilk, *Wendezeit – Zeitenwende*, p. 11.
112 Jochen Schaare, 'Ein Lob der Skepsis'.
113 Rüdiger Safranski, 'Der Wille zum Glauben oder die Wiederkehr der Götter', *Magie der Heiterkeit*, pp. 243–54 (p. 251).
114 Roger Griffin, 'Interregnum or Endgame? Radical Right Thought in the "Postfascist" Era', first published in *The Journal of Political Ideologies*, vol. 5, no. 2, July 2000, pp. 163–78. Accessed online 26 June 2006 at: http://ah.brookes.ac.uk/history/staff/griffin/interregnum.pdf.
115 Armin Mohler, *Die Konservative Revolution in Deutschland 1918–1932*, 3rd edn, 2 vols (Darmstadt: Wissenschaftliche Buchgesellschaft, 1989), 1, p. 16.
116 Ibid.
117 Alain de Benoist, Charles Champetier, 'The French New Right In The Year 2000', http://www.alphalink.com.au/%7Eradnat/debenoist/alain9.html, accessed 26 June 2006.
118 Gessenharter's analysis of the asylum debate suggests a consensus among New Right thinkers on such issues which can be traced back to Carl Schmitt (*Kippt die Republik?* pp. 215–16).
119 Günter Rohrmoser, *Deutschlands Tragödie*, p. 37.
120 Karlheinz Weißmann, *Rückruf in die Geschichte*, pp. 158–9.
121 Stefan Maninger, 'Die Volkskrise', Report on the Summer Academy 2000, http://www.staatspolitik.de, accessed 1 July 2003.
122 Matthias Bath, 'Von der Negation zum neuen Denken', *Junge Freiheit*, 13 November 1998.
123 Quoted by Michael Wiesberg in 'Der Westen muß sich wehren', *Junge Freiheit*, 6 September 2002.
124 Ibid.

125 Heinrich Lummer, 'Nur keine Eile', *Junge Freiheit*, 19 July 2002.
126 Rolf Stolz, 'Integration als Existenzgrundlage', *Junge Freiheit*, 5 July 2002.
127 Pierre Krebs, *Die europäische Wiedergeburt* (Tübingen: Grabert, 1982), p. 33.
128 Pierre Krebs, *Mut zur Identität*, pp. 7, 18.
129 Guillaume Faye, 'Die neuen ideologischen Herausforderungen', in *Mut zur Identität*, ed. by Pierre Krebs, pp. 185–265 (p. 192). Gessenharter points out that mainstream political parties can use similar arguments, and he gives the example of the February 1998 draft document revising the laws on foreigners in Germany. The document came from the Ministry of the Interior and discussed foreigners as a threat to the homogeneity of society. The shared history, tradition, language and culture of Germany would lose its power to draw together and shape the people, and the Federal Republic would become a multi-national community burdened in the long term with problems of minorities. The document saw it as a legitimate goal of a nation to preserve the national character for the sake of domestic peace and the national interest. Gessenharter points out that the document was withdrawn almost as soon as it appeared, but views it as a sign of a shift towards the ideas of Carl Schmitt among the political class (*Kippt die Republik?* pp. 216–17.
130 Alain de Benoist, *Kulturrevolution von rechts*, pp. 55, 64–5.
131 http://www.thule-seminar.org/HTML/RAHMEN/rahmen-start.htm, accessed 4 April 2004.
132 Pierre Krebs, 'Ethnokraten der Welt, Vereinigt Euch!: Interview mit Günter Schwab', *Deutsche Stimme*, May 2001.
133 Martin Schwarz, 'Globalisierung und Spaßgesellschaft. Die sogenannte Ausländerfrage in Europa und der Islam', speech to Synergon Deutschland, March 2002, www.eisernekrone.tk, accessed 20 June 2004.
134 Peter Meier-Bergfeld, 'Deutschland und Österreich', in *Die selbstbewußte Nation*, pp. 195–226 (p. 224) The quotation is taken from Meinhard Miegel and Stefanie Wahl, *Das Ende des Individualismus* (Bonn: Bonn aktuell, 1993), p. 120.
135 Hartmut Lange, 'Existenz und Moderne: Über Selbsterkenntnis als Solidarität', in *Die selbstbewußte Nation*, p. 441.
136 Botho Strauß, 'Anschwellender Bocksgesang', in *Die selbstbewußte Nation* p. 22.
137 Martin Schwarz, 'Globalisierung und Spaßgesellschaft'.
138 Ibid.
139 Günter Rohrmoser, *Deutschlands Tragödie*, p. 166. Rohrmoser is quoting from Nietzsche's *Unzeitgemäße Betrachtungen*.
140 Ibid., p. 171.
141 Ibid., p. 171n.
142 Hans-Dietrich Sander, 'Wie und unter welchen Umständen kann eine niedergegangene Kultur erneuert werden? Thesen und Glossare', *Staatsbriefe*, 11, 2000.

143 Günter Rohrmoser, *Deutschlands Tragödie*, p. 70. Funke points to Carl Schmitt's 'homogeneous nation' as the psychological counterbalance to the fear of chaos and disorder which paved the way for racism: 'Homogeneity appears to banish persistent doubts and the paranoid fear of chaos. The path from this homogeneity to uniformity and, by 1933, to racial identity is not a long one'. Hajo Funke, *Paranoia und Politik*, p. 260.

144 Günter Figal, 'Philosophische Zeitkritik im Selbstverständnis der Modernität', in *Selbstverständnis der Moderne*, ed. by Günter Figal and Rolf-Peter Sieferle (Stuttgart: Metzler, 1991), pp. 100–32 (pp. 102–3).

145 Günter Rohrmoser, *Ideologie-Zerfall*, pp. 54–5.

Chapter 3   A Cultural Interpretation of National Socialism

1 Wolfgang Strauss, 'Deutschlands Rechte und Hitler', *Europa Vorn*, 15 October 1995, 8–12 (p. 9).

2 Pfahl-Traughber does however refer to Armin Mohler's apologia in *Der Nasenring* for the Leuchter Report. The report, written by the American engineer Fred A. Leuchter, set out to prove that the gassing of Jews in the extermination camps was not possible on purely technical grounds. Armin Pfahl-Traughber, 'Konservative Revolution' und 'Neue Rechte', p. 169.

3 Franz Schönhuber, *Ich war dabei* (Munich: Langen Müller), 1981.

4 Armin Mohler, *Die Konservative Revolution in Deutschland 1918–1932*, 3rd edn, 2 vols (Darmstadt: Wissenschaftliche Buchgesellschaft, 1989), II, p. 103.

5 Karlheinz Weißmann, *Alles was recht(s) ist*, pp. 179–85.

6 Ibid., pp. 18–45. This passage is also quoted by Mohler, *Die Konservative Revolution in Deutschland 1918–1932*, II, p. 116.

7 Karlheinz Weißmann, *Alles was recht(s) ist*, p. 185.

8 Armin Mohler, *Die Konservative Revolution in Deutschland 1918–1932*, II, p. 107. Mohler is quoting from Zeev Sternhell, *Ni droite ni gauche. L'idéologie fasciste en France* (Paris: Éditions du Seuil, 1983), p. 293.

9 'Ich bin ein Faschist', *Leipziger Volkszeitung*, 25–6 November 1995. Mohler explains in this interview how his application to join the Waffen-SS was turned down.

10 Franz Schönhuber, *Die verbogene Gesellschaft: Mein Leben zwischen NS-Erziehung und US-Umerziehung*, pp. 34–5.

11 Ibid.

12 Armin Mohler, *Liberalenbeschimpfung*, p. 86.

13 Armin Mohler, 'Ich bin ein Faschist'.

14 Ibid.

15 Ibid.

16 Johannes Schwefel, 'Leserbrief', *Junge Freiheit*, 30 August 2002.

17 Wilhelm Kleinau, 'Mussolini über Verfassungen und Programme', in: *Die Standarte*, 14 August 1927, p. 339.

18 Oswald Spengler, *Jahre der Entscheidung* (Munich: Beck, 1933), pp. 134–5.

19 Günter Maschke, 'Der Zauberlehrling Machiavellis: Benito Mussolini', *Erste Etappe*, 1, 1988, pp. 63–71. This idea is particularly significant when one considers that it was put forward in the first issue of the journal *Etappe* where one might expect to read some kind of programmatic statement or set of goals. Mohler also takes up this line of thought in Sternhell's work. Mohler quotes Sternhell on Maurice Barrès (for Mohler one of the fathers of fascism): 'For a man like Barrès it is not a matter of which doctrine is the correct one, but rather which force will enable one to act and to be victorious'. Mohler also picks out Sternhell quoting Sorel on myth in order to prove that fascism is not to be judged by how true it is. *Die Konservative Revolution in Deutschland 1918–1932*, II, p. 116.

20 Rüdiger Safranski, *Wieviel Wahrheit braucht der Mensch? Über das Denkbare und das Lebbare* (Munich, Vienna: Carl Hanser, 1990), p. 198.

21 Karlheinz Weißmann, *Rückruf in die Geschichte*, p. 86.

22 Günter Rohrmoser, *Deutschlands Tragödie*, p. 130.

23 Ibid., p. 131.

24 Ibid., pp. 140–3.

25 Rüdiger Safranski, *Wieviel Wahrheit braucht der Mensch?*, pp. 143–4.

26 Ibid., p. 144.

27 Richard Herzinger, *Republik ohne Mitte*, pp. 68–9.

28 Jürgen Habermas, *The New Conservatism*, p. 234.

29 Ibid., p. 234.

30 Ibid., p. 235.

31 Günter Rohrmoser, *Deutschlands Tragödie*, p. 52. In his preface to the book Michael Grimminger adds that for Rohrmoser a great injustice is done to the German people if it is suggested that they knew at the time or could have known how things would end (p. 10). Similarly, Karlheinz Weißmann, who was controversially commissioned to produce the volume on National Socialism in the Propyläen series on the history of Germany, argues in *Rückruf in die Geschichte* that voters did not flock to Hitler because of his 'Lebensraum imperialism' or his rabid anti-Semitism (p. 86).

32 Karlheinz Weißmann, *Rückruf in die Geschichte*, pp. 29–31.

33 Ibid., p. 31.

34 Ulrich Schacht, 'Stigma und Sorge: Über deutsche Identität nach Auschwitz', p. 64.

35 Wolfgang Venohr, 'Vor 50 Jahren: Der Kulminationspunkt wird überschritten', *Junge Freiheit*, September 1992, p. 15. Quoted by Elliot Neaman in 'A New Conservative Revolution?: Neo-nationalism, Collective Memory, and the New Right in Germany since Unification', in *Antisemitism and Xenophobia in Germany after Unification*, ed. by Hermann Kurthen, Werner Bergmann, Rainer Erb (New York, Oxford: OUP, 1997), pp. 190–208 (p. 203).

36 Armin Mohler, *Liberalenbeschimpfung*, pp. 90–1.

37 Wolfgang Venohr, 'Vor 50 Jahren', *Junge Freiheit*, 1–2, January/February, 1992, p. 15.
38 Ibid.
39 Ibid.
40 Ibid., p. 15.
41 Günter Rohrmoser, *Deutschlands Tragödie*, p. 42.
42 Ibid., p. 39.
43 Alexander Barti, 'Die Schlammschlacht geht weiter', *Junge Freiheit*, 20 July 2001.
44 Erich Vad, 'Eine ganze Generation unter Generalverdacht', *Junge Freiheit*, 11 January 2002.
45 Brigitte Seebacher-Brandt 'Norm und Normalität: Über die Liebe zum eigenen Land', in *Die selbstbewußte Nation*. pp. 43–56 (p. 50).
46 See, for example, Stefan Scheil, 'Argumentation mit der Brechstange', *Junge Freiheit*, 11 April 2003.
47 'Immer von ihrem Gewissen geführt. Interview mit Oberst Kleyser', *Junge Freiheit*, 20 July 2001.
48 Günter Rohrmoser, *Deutschlands Tragödie*, pp. 66–7.
49 Ibid., p. 68.
50 Ibid., p. 69.
51 Franz Schönhuber, 'Endzeit', *Nation und Europa*, January 1997, 9–12 (p. 9).
52 Botho Strauß, 'Anschwellender Bocksgesang', p. 35.
53 Wolfgang Bialas, 'Die selbstbewußte Nation und ihre Intellektuellen', *Berliner Debatte. Initial*, 8 (1997), 214–24 (p. 220). Strauß gives a bitter account of the effect his association with the New Right has had on his life: 'What a tiny fall: from famous to infamous! Etymologically insignificant. Some people who spit at me today used to like coming to visit, and one said as he entered my home: let me take a deep breath. I must absorb the whole atmosphere…Today he writes in the newspapers: Hang him!' *Die Fehler des Kopisten*, p. 118.
54 *Die Fehler des Kopisten*, pp. 107, 114.
55 Günter Rohrmoser, *Deutschlands Tragödie*, p. 26.
56 Ibid., pp. 37–8.
57 Peter Meier-Bergfeld, 'Deutschland und Österreich', in *Die selbstbewußte Nation*, pp. 195–226 (pp. 215–16).
58 Wolfgang Saur, 'Neurose oder Selbstbehauptung', *Junge Freiheit*, 11 October 2002.
59 Bernard-Henry Lévy, 'Allemagne année zéro?', *Le Monde*, 6–8 February 1999. Similarly, Jürgen Habermas says one group in the Historikerstreit has a functionalist understanding of the public use of history. They dispense the slogan of 'national consciousness instead of guilt consciousness'. The other group promotes enlightenment, and they 'trust above all a national self-consciousness that draws its strength solely from the critical appropriation, educated by Auschwitz, of our traditions, which, fortunately, are not lacking in unambiguous models'. *The New Conservatism*, pp. 247–8.

Notes 161

60 Wolfgang Saur, 'Neurose oder Selbstbehauptung'.
61 Günter Rohrmoser, *Deutschlands Tragödie*, p. 26.
62 Hajo Funke, *Paranoia und Politik*, pp. 247–8.
63 Quotation from the Holocaust Memorial in Berlin website: http://www.holocaust-denkmal-berlin.de, accessed 4 June 2003. The decision to build the memorial was preceded by over a decade of public debate, and in 1999 the Bundestag resolved that the memorial should be erected. Its purpose was to 'honour the murder victims, to keep alive the memory of an unimaginable event and to warn all future generations never again to interfere with human rights, always to defend the democratic constitutional state, to preserve the equality of people before the law and to resist dictatorship and tyranny'. 'Beschluss des Bundestages vom 25. Juni 1999 zum Holocaust-Denkmal'.
64 Doris Neujahr, 'Wie bei Hempels unterm Sofa', *Junge Freiheit*, 19 March 2004.
65 Oliver Busch, 'Identität durch Irritation: Berliner Denkmalpläne: Es hätte schlimmer kommen können', *Junge Freiheit*, 21 January 2005.
66 Hans-Helmuth Knütter, 'Servilität', *Junge Freiheit*, 2 July 1999.
67 Ulrich Schacht, 'Stigma und Sorge: Über deutsche Identität nach Auschwitz', p. 65.
68 Ibid., p. 66.
69 Quoted by Schacht, ibid.
70 Karlheinz Weißmann, *Rückruf in die Geschichte*, pp. 27–8.
71 Ibid., p. 28.
72 Wolfgang Venohr, *Patrioten gegen Hitler, Der Weg zum 20. Juli 1944* (Bergisch Gladbach: Lübbe, 1994), p. 5.
73 Karlheinz Weißmann, *Rückruf in die Geschichte*, p. 49.
74 See, for example, Armin Pfahl-Traughber, '*Konservative Revolution*' und '*Neue Rechte*', p. 13.
75 Karlheinz Weißmann, *Alles was recht(s) ist*, p. 27.
76 Hugo von Hofmannsthal, 'Das Schrifttum als geistiger Raum der Nation' (Munich: Bremer Presse, 1927), p. 31.
77 Angelika Willig, 'Abschied von rechts', *Junge Freiheit*, 16 October 1998.
78 Armin Mohler, *Die Konservative Revolution in Deutschland 1918–1932*, 1, p. 9.
79 Frank Como, 'Organisch, faustisch, grenzenlos: Oswald Spenglers ästhetische Theorie', *Etappe*, 12, June 1996, 136–9 (p. 136).
80 Günter Rohrmoser, *Deutschlands Tragödie*, p. 88.
81 Oswald Spengler, *Briefe 1913–1936*, ed. by A.M. Koktanek (Munich: Beck, 1963), p. 749.
82 See Roger Woods, *The Conservative Revolution in the Weimar Republic*, pp. 127–32.
83 Observers generally do not pursue this deeper link between the Conservative Revolution and National Socialism, and their comments can suffer from vagueness as a result. Pfahl-Traughber writes, for example, that it is true that some representatives of the Conservative Revolution not only actively opposed the Nazi state, they were also

murdered by the Nazis. Pfahl-Traughber concludes that while this makes the Conservative Revolutionaries opponents of National Socialism to some extent, it does not necessarily make them democrats. (*'Konservative Revolution' und 'Neue Rechte'*, p. 189).

84 Wolfgang Venohr, *Patrioten gegen Hitler*, p. 87.

85 Documents of the Preußische Geheime Staatspolizei (R58/243), Bundesarchiv. See also Robert Gellately, *The Gestapo and German Society: Enforcing Racial Policy 1933–1945* (Oxford: Clarendon, 1990), p. 50.

86 Albrecht Erich Günther (ed.), *Was wir vom Nationalsozialismus erwarten* (Heilbronn: Eugen Salzer, 1932).

87 See documents on Albrecht Erich Günther at the Berlin Document Center (hereafter BDC).

88 Letter from Head of the Regional Personnel Office of 18 March 1941 to the President of the Reich Chamber of Literature. A letter from the Hamburg Gestapo of 24 May 1941 to the President of the Reich Chamber of Literature draws attention to his anti-Semitism, but also to the fact that he has been criticised in the Nazi press for his conservatism. (Documents on Wilhelm Stapel, BDC).

89 Quoted in Kurt Sontheimer, *Antidemokratisches Denken in der Weimarer Republik* (Munich: Nymphenburger, 1968), p. 283.

90 Dieter Stein, 'Streit, Aufbruch und Selbstkritik', *Junge Freiheit*, supplement, 14 June 1996, p. 8, quoted by Armin Pfahl-Traughber, *'Konservative Revolution' und 'Neue Rechte'*, p. 189.

91 Karlheinz Weißmann, *Alles was recht(s) ist*, pp. 33–42.

92 Günter Rohrmoser, *Deutschlands Tragödie*, pp. 86–7.

93 Ibid., p. 91.

94 Ibid., p. 285.

95 Günter Rohrmoser, *Ideologie-Zerfall*, p. 49.

96 Henning Eichberg, 'Der Unsinn der "Konservativen Revolution". Über Ideengeschichte, Nationalismus und Habitus', *Wir selbst*, 1, 1996, 6–33 (p. 9).

97 Karlheinz Weißmann, *Alles was recht(s) ist*, p. 17.

98 Ibid., p. 11.

99 Ibid., pp. 11–13.

100 Ibid., p. 14.

101 Ibid., p. 15.

102 Heimo Schwilk, Ulrich Schacht (eds), *Die selbstbewußte Nation*, pp. 63, 67; Karlheinz Weißmann, *Alles was recht(s) ist*, p. 11.

103 Harald Holz, 'Die Tragik der deutschen Geschichte', in *Criticón*, 135, January/February 1993, p. 39.

104 Rainer Zitelmann, 'Position und Begriff', in Heimo Schwilk, Ulrich Schacht (eds), *Die selbstbewußte Nation*, p. 166. Peter Bochinski takes the same line: 'The political demands that Stauffenberg and those who thought as he did put down on paper would be regarded by today's standards in the Federal Republic as "(extreme) right-wing"'. 'War Stauffenberg ein Nazi?', *Nation und Europa*, 47, 50–2 (p. 52).

105 Wolfgang Venohr, *Patrioten gegen Hitler*, p. 285.
106 Wolfgang Venohr, *Stauffenberg. Symbol der deutschen Einheit* (Frankfurt am Main and Berlin: Ullstein, 1986), p. 9.
107 Ibid., pp. 39–40.
108 Ibid., p. 50.
109 Ibid., pp. 73–4.
110 Günter Rohrmoser, *Deutschlands Tragödie*, p. 177.
111 Martin Greiffenhagen, *Das Dilemma des Konservatismus in Deutschland*, (Munich: Piper, 1977), pp. 195–6.

Chapter 4   Values and Programmes

1 Pierre Krebs, 'Eine Epoche in der Krise', *Elemente*, Hauptausgabe, 1990, 8–19 (p. 8).
2 Pierre Krebs, *Das Thule-Seminar: Geistesgegenwart der Zukunft in der Morgenröte des Ethnos* (Kassel, Vienna: Weecke, 1994), pp. 26–7.
3 Karlheinz Weißmann, *Alles was recht(s) ist*, p. 247.
4 Alain de Benoist, *Kulturrevolution von rechts*, p. 61.
5 Ibid., p. 75.
6 *Nation und Europa*, September 1998, p. 20.
7 Franz Schönhuber, 'Schweigen ist keine Antwort', *Nation und Europa*, March 1998, 11–14 (p. 14).
8 Anon, 'Editorial', *Wir Selbst*, 2, 1990, p. 5.
9 Hans P., '"…gegen die Plage der bürgerlichen Welt". Ein Gespräch mit einem Nationalrevolutionär', *Wir Selbst*, 3, 1999, 68–73 (p. 72).
10 Ibid.
11 Karlheinz Weißmann, *Rückruf in die Geschichte*, pp. 113–14.
12 Ibid., p. 115.
13 Henning Eichberg, 'Der Unsinn der "Konservativen Revolution"': Über Ideengeschichte, Nationalismus und Habitus', p. 9.
14 Ibid., p. 10.
15 Uwe Worm, *Die Neue Rechte in der Bundesrepublik*, p. 37. For a general discussion of nationalism as a characteristic of right-wing extremism see Hans-Joachim Veen, 'Rechtsextrem' oder 'Rechtsradikal?', p. 1. Gessenharter detects some of the problems the New Right experiences with nationalism, however, in his account of the New Right author Gerd-Klaus Kaltenbrunner's nationalism: Kaltenbrunner acknowledges a destructive radicalisation of nationalism in the past, but concludes that the nation and the multiplicity of nations are a reality. Gessenharter sees Kaltenbrunner's argument culminating in a view of the nation as 'beyond all doubt', as if it were the unproblematic object of commitment that the New Right can suggest it is. Wolfgang Gessenharter, *Kippt die Republik?*, pp. 98–100.
16 Kurt Lenk, 'Ideengeschichtliche Dispositionen rechtsextremen Denkens', p. 13.
17 Hajo Funke, *Paranoia und Politik*, p. 267.

18 Klaus Fritzsche, *Politische Romantik und Gegenrevolution: Fluchtwege in der Krise der bürgerlichen Gesellschaft: Das Beispiel des 'Tat'–Kreises* (Frankfurt a.M.: Suhrkamp, 1976), p. 327.
19 Karlheinz Weißmann, *Rückruf in die Geschichte*, p. 135.
20 Ibid., p. 20. Weißmann goes on to quote the dramatist Wolfgang Borchert on the post-war mood in Germany: 'We are the generation without God, for we are the generation without bonds, without a past, without any recognition.' (p. 26).
21 Günter Rohrmoser, *Ideologie-Zerfall*, pp. 196–7.
22 Pierre Krebs, 'Deutsch und europäisch: grenzenlos', *Elemente*, Hauptausgabe 1990, 4–6 (p. 4).
23 Ibid.
24 Karlheinz Weißmann, *Rückruf in die Geschichte*, p. 26. Weißmann goes on to quote the Conservative Revolutionary Ernst Niekisch who wrote in a pamphlet published after Germany's defeat: 'Germany's misspent life: the yield from the whole of German history turns out to be a terrible nothing'. (Ibid.).
25 Karlheinz Weißmann notes that Germanophobia is not just in evidence among non-Germans; within Germany's borders he detects a strong national self-hatred, and he refers to Alfred von Tirpitz's description of a 'suicidal corner in the soul of the people'. He also notes that some of the demonstrators on the streets in the run-up to unification were chanting 'Down with Germany' and 'Germany never again'. *Rückruf in die Geschichte*, p. 165.
26 Karlheinz Weißmann, *Rückruf in die Geschichte*, p. 95.
27 Ibid., p. 12. Weißmann is quoting from *Newsweek*, 26 February 1990.
28 Ibid., p. 12.
29 Dieter Stein, Jürgen Lanter, 'Macht sich in Deutschland ein neuer Wilhelminismus breit? Interview mit Günter Maschke', *Junge Freiheit*, June 1991, p. 3.
30 Rainer Zitelmann, 'Position und Begriff', in *Die selbstbewußte Nation*, pp. 163–81 (pp. 174–5).
31 Alain de Benoist, 'Netzwerke funktionieren wie Viren', *Junge Freiheit*, 13 September 2002.
32 Richard Schröder, 'Wie weit verbindet die Deutschen die gemeinsame Nation?', *Wir Selbst*, 3, 1999, 8–13 (p. 12).
33 Ibid., p. 13.
34 Michael Hageböck, 'Endzeit', in *Wir 89er*, ed. by Roland Bubik (Frankfurt am Main, Berlin: Ullstein, 1995), pp. 145–62 (pp. 150–1).
35 Ansgar Graw, 'Dekadenz und Kampf' in *Die selbstbewußte Nation*, pp. 281–90 (p. 285).
36 Botho Strauß, 'Anschwellender Bocksgesang', p. 22.
37 Botho Strauß, *Beginnlosigkeit*, p. 125.
38 Botho Strauß, 'Anschwellender Bocksgesang', p. 25.
39 Peter Osborne, *The Politics of Time. Modernity and Avant-Garde* (London, New York: Verso, 1995), p. 164.
40 Gunnar Sohn, 'Freiheit und Konservatismus', *Criticón*, 139, Sept/Oct 1993, 246–7 (p. 246).

41 Ibid., pp. 246–7.
42 Tilman Krause, 'Innerlichkeit und Weltferne', in *Die selbstbewußte Nation*, pp. 134–41. The essay had already appeared elsewhere under the ominous title 'Deutsche Abgründe. Westliche Wurzeln allein werden unserer Kultur nicht gerecht' (German chasms. Western roots alone do not match up to our culture). See the bibliographical note in *Die selbstbewußte Nation*, p. 478.
43 Edgar Jung, *Sinndeutung der deutschen Revolution* (Oldenburg: Stalling, 1933), p. 20.
44 G, 'Reaktion', *Deutsches Volkstum*, 9 (1927), 8–12.
45 Heimo Schwilk, 'Ernst Jünger – Prophet der Globalisierung', *Criticón*, 168, Winter 2000, pp. 26–30.
46 Ibid., pp. 26–30.
47 Günter Figal, 'Nochmals über die Linie', in *Magie der Heiterkeit*, pp. 25–40 (p. 26).
48 Ibid.
49 Ibid., p. 27.
50 Ibid.
51 Matthias Bath, 'Von der Negation zum neuen Denken'.
52 Roland Bubik, 'Die Kultur als Machtfrage', *Junge Freiheit*, October 1994, p. 23.
53 Hans P., '"…gegen die Plage der bürgerlichen Welt". Ein Gespräch mit einem Nationalrevolutionär', pp. 72–3.
54 Franco Volpi 'Praktische Vernunft inmitten ihrer technischen Entmachtung', in *Magie der Heiterkeit*, pp. 72–83.
55 Ansgar Graw, 'Dekadenz und Kampf', pp. 282–3.
56 Alain de Benoist, Charles Champetier, 'The French New Right in the Year 2000', accessed 26 June 2006.
57 Karlheinz Weißmann, 'Herausforderung und Entscheidung: Über einen politischen Verismus für Deutschland', pp. 313–14.
58 'Interview mit dem CDU/CSU-Fraktionsvorsitzenden Wolfgang Schäuble', *Süddeutsche Zeitung*, 28 December 1994, p. 8.
59 Pierre Krebs, 'Eine Epoche in der Krise', pp. 8–19.
60 Eberhard Straub, 'Individuum und Gesellschaft: Über die Enteignung des Eigentums' in *Die selbstbewußte Nation*, pp. 416–31 (pp. 421–2).
61 Paul Berlin, 'Liberalismus bis zum Volkstod', *Nation und Europa*, 47, 1, 1997, 5–8 (p. 5).
62 Alain de Benoist, *Kulturrevolution von rechts*, p. 28.
63 Günter Rohrmoser, *Deutschlands Tragödie*, p. 187.
64 Günter Rohrmoser, *Ideologie-Zerfall*, p. 157.
65 Klaus Motschmann, 'Krise und Kritik: Alte Irrtümer in neuer Gestalt – diesmal in der Grundrechtscharta Europas', *Criticón*, 168, Winter 2000, pp. 4–5.
66 Botho Strauß, *Die Fehler des Kopisten*, pp. 44–5.
67 Günter Rohrmoser, *Ideologie-Zerfall*, pp. 36–7.
68 Ibid., p. 50.
69 Ibid., p. 192.
70 Günter Rohrmoser, *Deutschlands Tragödie*, pp. 435–6.

71 Günter Rohrmoser, *Deutschlands Tragödie*, p. 436. New Right differences over religion may be acknowledged by commentators but the differences are seen as ideological differences between individual thinkers rather than as a complex process of cause and effect whereby religion can be dismissed but then revived as a value. Pfahl-Traughber thus points to the ideological differences within the New Right, but he explains those relating to religion in terms of positions of individuals rather than as a process (*'Konservative Revolution' und 'Neue Rechte'*, p. 163). Pfahl-Traughber points to the fact that Karlheinz Weißmann is an ex-theology student who believes in Christianity, quoting him saying: 'As a Protestant I believe that all nations are thoughts of God' (179).

72 Michael Wiesberg, 'Botho Strauß: Die Fehler des Kopisten: Verschmelzung von Einst und Jetzt', *Junge Freiheit*, 9 May 1997.

73 Botho Strauß, *Die Fehler des Kopisten*, pp. 46–9.

74 See Wolfgang Bialas, 'Die selbstbewußte Nation und ihre Intellektuellen', pp. 214–24, and Bergfleth's essay in *Die selbstbewußte Nation*, pp. 101–23.

75 Gerd Bergfleth, 'Erde und Heimat', pp. 104–17.

76 Ibid., pp. 119–23.

77 Botho Strauß, *Die Fehler des Kopisten*, p. 54.

78 Karlheinz Weißmann, *Alles was recht(s) ist*, p. 166.

79 Jürgen Habermas, *The New Conservatism*, p. 34.

80 Rüdiger Safranski, *Wieviel Wahrheit braucht der Mensch?*, p. 17.

81 Ibid., p. 34.

82 Wolfgang Gessenharter, *Kippt die Republik?*, p. 160. Similarly, Hajo Funke emphasises ethnocentric nationalism and the authoritarian state as the 'ideological core' of the New Right. *Paranoia und Politik*, p. 18. Pfahl-Traughber examines some of what he refers to as the New Right's basic ideological positions, in particular as they contrast with the values of modern democracies. For Pfahl-Traughber the New Right looks back to the anti-democratic Conservative Revolution in the Weimar Republic as the source of ideas on politics as essentially to do with decision-making rather than establishing norms, rejection of individualism and support for collectivism. The New Right also regards 1989 as a call to history and a rejection of Germany's ties with the West. *'Konservative Revolution' und 'Neue Rechte'*, p. 188.

83 Wolfgang Gessenharter, *Kippt die Republik?*, pp. 168–9.

84 Rainer Benthin, *Die Neue Rechte in Deutschland und ihr Einfluß auf den politischen Diskurs der Gegenwart*, pp. 27–37.

85 Parteiprogramm der Nationaldemokratischen Partei Deutschlands (NPD), Section 8. http://www.npd.de/npd_startseiten/programme.html, accessed 25 August 2004. Uwe Worm suggests that it was one-time NPD member Wolfgang Strauß who coined the term ethnopluralism in the first place (*Die Neue Rechte in der Bundesrepublik*, p. 38).

86 Chapter 1 of the May 2002 party programme, http://www2.rep.de/, accessed 25 August 2004.

87 DVU programme, http://www.dvu.de/DVU-Programm/dvu-programm-2.html, accessed 25 August 2004.

88 http://www.npd.de, accessed 25 August 2004.

89 Armin Pfahl-Traughber: *'Konservative Revolution' und 'Neue Rechte'*, p. 38.

90 Quoted by Armin Pfahl-Traughber: *'Konservative Revolution' und 'Neue Rechte'*, p. 157. Pfahl-Traughber criticises definitions of the New Right based on anti-liberalism since all extremist right-wing movements share this stance (p. 158).

91 Hajo Funke, *Paranoia und Politik*, pp. 247–8. Jaschke summarises: 'The New Right sets the bonds with the national community ('Volksgemeinschaft'), the natural inequality of people and races and the creation of heroic elites against the principles of freedom, equality and fraternity'. (Hans-Gerd Jaschke, 'Nationalismus und Ethnopluralismus. Zum Wiederaufleben von Ideen der "Konservativen Revolution"', p. 7.

92 Alain de Benoist, *Kulturrevolution von rechts*, pp. 14–15.

93 Armin Mohler, 'Vorwort', in Alain de Benoist, *Kulturrevolution von rechts*, pp. 16–17.

94 Cited in Roger Eatwell, 'Towards a New Model of the Rise of Right-Wing Extremism', *German Politics*, 6 (December 1997), 166–84 (p. 181). Eatwell is quoting from Moreau's contribution to *Extremism in Europe*, ed. by Jean-Yves Camus (Paris: Edition de l'aube/CERA, 1997).

95 Gessenharter quotes this point from Schmitt's *Die geistesgeschichtliche Lage des heutigen Parlamentarismus* (*Kippt die Republik?*, pp. 77–8). See also Hajo Funke, *Paranoia und Politik*, p. 260. In his analysis of the asylum debate Gessenharter suggests that the New Right's position can be traced back to Carl Schmitt (*Kippt die Republik?*, pp. 217–20).

96 Armin Mohler, *Georges Sorel: Erzvater der Konservativen Revolution* (Bad Vilbel: Edition Antaios, 2000), p. 52.

97 Ibid., p. 53.

98 Quoted by Mohler, ibid.

99 Karlheinz Weißmann, 'Es gibt keine Geschichtsphilosophie', in *Georges Sorel: Erzvater der Konservativen Revolution*, pp. 87–99 (p. 90).

100 Gerwin Steinberger, 'Edgar Jung und der organische Staat', *Nation und Europa*, 9 September 1992, p. 50.

101 Martin Greiffenhagen, *Das Dilemma des Konservatismus in Deutschland*, pp. 195–6.

102 Ernst Niekisch, *Das Reich der niederen Dämonen* (Hamburg: Rowohlt, 1953), p. 67. Niekisch wrote this work between 1935 and 1936. Niekisch traces this idea back to Carl Schmitt and argues that it takes political form in fascist activism. He describes this activism as militant nihilism which found expression in the work of Ernst Jünger (ibid., p. 68).

103 Ernst Jünger, 'Nationalismus und Nationalismus', *Das Tagebuch*, 21 September 1929, 1552–8. Otto-Ernst Schüddekopf, *Nationalbolschewismus in Deutschland 1918–1933* (Frankfurt am Main, Berlin, Vienna: Ullstein, 1973), notes the more abstract, 'metaphysical' politics of the last years of the Republic (pp. 233–5).

104 Ernst Niekisch, *Gewagtes Leben 1889–1948: Erinnerungen eines deutschen Revolutionärs*, 2 vols (Cologne: Wissenschaft und Politik, 1974), 1, p. 191.

105 Heimo Schwilk, 'Auf der Suche nach der Einheit – Träume bei Ernst Jünger und Carl Gustav Jung', *Criticón*, January/February/March 1996, 45–9 (p. 45).

106 See also Gerwin Steinberger, 'Edgar Jung und der organische Staat', p. 50.

107 Alain de Benoist, 'Ideologie: Es kommt zum Endkampf', *Elemente*, Jan/March 1987, 13–18 (p. 13).

108 Johanna Christina Grund, 'Euro-Gesellschaft statt Volk', *Nation und Europa*, 46, November–December 1996, 39–40.

109 Armin Pfahl-Traughber, *'Konservative Revolution' und 'Neue Rechte'*, p. 192.

110 Alain de Benoist, *Kulturrevolution von rechts*, pp. 82–5.

Conclusion: From Exemplary Thinkers of Modernity to Living without Absolutes

1 Karlheinz Weißmann, *Alles was recht(s) ist*, pp. 163–4.

2 Heimo Schwilk, *Wendezeit – Zeitenwende: Beiträge zur Literatur der achtziger Jahre*, pp. 17–18.

3 Jürgen Habermas, *The New Conservatism*, pp. 36–7. In this connection Richard Wolin refers to Weber's theory of the 'differentiation of the spheres'. For Weber modernity is characterised by the proliferation of independent logics in the spheres of science and technology, morality, law and art. 'Introduction', in *The New Conservatism*, pp. vii–xxxi (p. xxii).

4 Günter Figal, 'Philosophische Zeitkritik im Selbstverständnis der Modernität', pp. 102–3.

5 Ibid., p. 11.

6 Günter Rohrmoser *Deutschlands Tragödie*, p. 70.

7 Ibid., p. 70n.

8 Ibid., p. 152.

9 Botho Strauß, *Beginnlosigkeit*, p. 41.

10 Rüdiger Safranski, *Wieviel Wahrheit braucht der Mensch?* p. 40.

11 Ibid., p. 41.

12 Ibid.

13 Fritz Stern, *The Politics of Cultural Despair*, 2nd edn (Berkeley, Los Angeles, London: University of California, 1974), pp. ix–x.

14 Stuart Hall, 'Introduction: Who needs "Identity"', in, *Questions of Cultural Identity*, ed. by Stuart Hall and Paul Du Gay (London: Sage, 1996), pp. 1–17 (p. 1).

15 Ibid., pp. 2–3.

16 Ibid., p. 4.

17 Zygmunt Bauman, 'From Pilgrim to Tourist – or a Short History of Identity', in *Questions of Cultural Identity*, pp. 18–36 (p. 19). More gen-

erally, Anthony Giddens argues that Modernity is a post-traditional order, but not one in which the sureties of tradition and habit have been replaced by the certitude of rational knowledge. Doubt is a pervasive feature of modern critical reason and it forms a general existential dimension of the contemporary social world. Modernity institutionalises the principle of radical doubt and insists that all knowledge takes the form of hypotheses. *Modernity and Self-Identity: Self and Society in the Late Modern Age*, 4th edn, (Cambridge: Polity Press, 1994), p. 3.

18 Richard Herzinger, *Republik ohne Mitte*, pp. 83–4.
19 Ibid., p. 17.
20 Fritz Stern, *The Politics of Cultural Despair*, pp. xi–xii.
21 Botho Strauß, *Die Fehler des Kopisten*, pp. 82–3.
22 Richard Herzinger, *Republik ohne Mitte*, pp. 7–21.
23 Scott Lash, Brian Wynne, 'Introduction', in Ulrich Beck, *Risk Society* (London: Sage, 2002), pp. 2–8 (p. 2).
24 Richard Herzinger, *Republik ohne Mitte*, p. 37.
25 Zygmunt Bauman, *Moderne und Ambivalenz. Das Ende der Eindeutigkeit*, pp. 23–30.
26 Ibid., p. 22.
27 Hermann Glaser, 'Kultur und Identitäten', pp. 3–4.
28 See Jürgen Kocka, 'Die Zukunft der Gerechtigkeit', *Berliner Republik*, 3/2003.
29 In July 2002 a Bundestag Commission of Enquiry submitted its report on the subject of citizens' involvement in the community. The report showed that 20 million citizens were involved in one form or another of voluntary work for their community. SPD Bundestag and Commission member Lothar Binding commented: 'With the help of these citizens the bonds and understanding between all members of society will be strengthened. People who are involved in the community create an atmosphere of solidarity'. Michael Bürsch, SPD Chairman of the Commission of Enquiry, commented similarly: 'In our initial resolution the most important point is that involvement in the community is absolutely essential for society's cohesion'. 'Interview mit Götz Planer-Friedrich und Jürgen Wandel: Der richtige Weg in die Zukunft', *Zeitzeichen* 6/2001, pp. 32–5.
30 See the issue of *Aus Politik und Zeitgeschichte* devoted to this topic, B 44, 26 October 2001.
31 See Richard Stöss, 'Soziale Gerechtigkeit. Die ostdeutsche Perspektive', http://www.polwiss.fu-berlin.de/osz/dokumente/PDF/Sozgerla.pdf: Accessed 4 September 2004.
32 See, for example, Axel Honneth, *Kampf um Anerkennung* (Frankfurt am Main: suhrkamp, 2003).
33 Heimo Schwilk, *Wendezeit – Zeitenwende: Beiträge zur Literatur der achtziger Jahre*, p. 19.
34 Rüdiger Safranski, *Wieviel Wahrheit braucht der Mensch?*, pp. 206–7.

Bibliography

Internet sources

New Right websites

Deutschland-Bewegung: http://www.deutschland-bewegung.de
Institut für Staatspolitik: http://www.staatspolitik.de
Studienzentrum Weikersheim: http://www.studienzentrum-weikersheim.de
Thule-Seminar: http://www.thule-seminar.org

Other websites

Holocaust Memorial website: http://www.holocaust-denkmal-berlin.de
Nationaldemokratische Partei Deutschlands, http://www.npd.de

Selection of New Right Journals with websites

Criticón, http://www.criticon-magazin.de/
Junge Freiheit, http://www.jungefreiheit.de/
Nation und Europa, http://www.nationeuropa.de
Sleipnir, http://www.sleipnir.netfirms.com/
Staatsbriefe, http://www.staatsbriefe.de/start.htm
Wir selbst, http://www.wirselbst.de/

Books and articles

Anon, 'Editorial', *Wir Selbst*, 2, 1990, p. 5
Anon, 'Scheitert die "Intellektualisierung?"', *Junge Freiheit*, July/August 1989, pp. 1–2
Anon, 'Seminar mit Jürgen Schwab im Raum Heidelberg', http://www.jn-bw.de/aktionen/politik/seminar_20020713.htm, accessed 14 September 2004
Anon, 'Untergang des Abendlandes? Die Folgen eines EU-Beitritts der Türkei', *National-Zeitung*, 12 September 2003
Backes, Uwe, 'Rechtsextremismus in Deutschland. Ideologien, Organisationen und Strategien', *Aus Politik und Zeitgeschichte*, B 9-10 (1998), 27–35
Barti, Alexander, 'Die Schlammschlacht geht weiter', *Junge Freiheit*, 20 July 2001
Bath, Matthias, 'Von der Negation zum neuen Denken', *Junge Freiheit*, 13 November 1998

Bauman, Zygmunt, 'From Pilgrim to Tourist – or a Short History of Identity', in *Questions of Cultural Identity*, ed. by Stuart Hall and Paul Du Gay (London: Sage, 1996), pp. 18–36

Bauman, Zygmunt, *Moderne und Ambivalenz. Das Ende der Eindeutigkeit* (Frankfurt am Main: Fischer, 1996)

de Benoist, Alain and Charles Champetier, 'The French New Right in the Year 2000', http://www.alphalink.com.au/%7Eradnat/debenoist/alain9.html

de Benoist, Alain, 'Ideologie: Es kommt zum Endkampf', *Elemente*, January/March 1987, 13–18

de Benoist, Alain, *Kulturrevolution von rechts* (Krefeld: Sinus Verlag, 1985)

de Benoist, Alain, 'Netzwerke funktionieren wie Viren', *Junge Freiheit*, 13 September 2002

Benthin, Rainer, *Die Neue Rechte in Deutschland und ihr Einfluß auf den politischen Diskurs der Gegenwart* (Frankfurt am Main: Lang, 1996)

Bergfleth, Gerd, 'Erde und Heimat', in *Die selbstbewußte Nation*, pp. 104–17 (see under Schwilk)

Berlin, Paul, 'Liberalismus bis zum Volkstod', *Nation und Europa*, 47, 1, 1997, 5–8

Bialas, Wolfgang, 'Die selbstbewußte Nation und ihre Intellektuellen', *Berliner Debatte. Initial*, 8 (1997), 214–24

Bochinski, Peter, 'War Stauffenberg ein Nazi?', *Nation und Europa*, 47, 50–2

Bonnell, Victoria Lynn Hunt, *Beyond the Cultural Turn* (Berkeley, Los Angeles, London: University of California Press, 1999)

Breuer, Stefan, *Anatomie der Konservativen Revolution* (Darmstadt: Wissenschaftliche Buchgesellschaft, 1993)

Bubik, Roland, 'Herrschaft und Medien: Über den Kampf gegen die linke Meinungsdominanz', in *Die selbstbewußte Nation*, pp. 182–94 (see under Schwilk)

Bubik, Roland, 'Die Kultur als Machtfrage', *Junge Freiheit*, October 1994, p. 23

Bubik, Roland, 'Der Standort des Jungen Konservatismus', *Junge Freiheit*, December/January 1992–93, p. 13

Bublies, Siegfried, '20 Jahre wir selbst. Rückblick auf den Versuch einer publizistischen Topographie des Hufeisens', *Wir selbst*, 4 (1999), 6–12

Bundesamt für Verfassungsschutz, *Entwicklungstendenzen im Rechtsextremismus* (Cologne, l996)

Bundesamt für Verfassungsschutz, *Rechtsextremismus in der Bundesrepublik Deutschland – Ein Lagebild* (Cologne, September 1996)

Bundesministerium des Innern, *Verfassungsschutzbericht 2003* (Berlin, 2004)

Busch, Oliver, 'Identität durch Irritation: Berliner Denkmalpläne: Es hätte schlimmer kommen können', *Junge Freiheit*, 21 January 2005

Buttlar, Horst von, '"Neue Rechte" in Deutschland: Braune in Nadelstreifen', *Der Spiegel*, 10 October 2003

Camus, Jean-Yves (ed.), *Extremism in Europe* (Paris: Edition de l'aube/CERA, 1997)

Chaney, David, *The Cultural Turn* (London: Routledge, 1994)

Como, Frank, 'Organisch, faustisch, grenzenlos: Oswald Spenglers ästhetische Theorie', *Etappe*, 12, June 1996, 136–9

Darnton, Robert, 'Intellectual and Cultural History', in *The Past Before Us: Contemporary Historical Writing in the United States*, ed. by Michael Kammen (Ithaca, New York and London: Cornell University Press, 1980), pp. 327–54

Dietzsch, Martin, 'Zwischen Konkurrenz und Kooperation. Organisationen und Presse der Rechten in der Bundesrepublik', in *Rechtsdruck: Die Presse der Neuen Rechten*, ed. by Siegfried Jäger (Berlin, Bonn: J.H.W. Dietz, 1988), pp. 31–80

DVU programme, http://www.dvu.de/DVU-Programm/dvu-programm2.html, accessed 25 August 2004

Eatwell, Roger, 'Towards a New Model of the Rise of Right-Wing Extremism', *German Politics*, 6 (December 1997), 166–84

Eichberg, Henning, 'Der Unsinn der "Konservativen Revolution". Über Ideengeschichte, Nationalismus und Habitus', *Wir selbst*, 1, 1996, 6–33

Eichberg, Henning, 'Kein Volk und keinen Frieden', *Wir selbst*, 1, 1995, 73–7

Faye, Guillaume, 'Die neuen ideologischen Herausforderungen', in *Mut zur Identität*, ed. by Pierre Krebs, pp. 185–265

Figal, Günter, *Für eine Philosophie von Freiheit und Streit* (Stuttgart, Weimar: Metzler, 1994)

Figal, Günter, 'Illusionslos sei das Leben und frei', *Die Welt am Sonntag*, 5 November 2002

Figal, Günter, 'Nochmals über die Linie', in *Magie der Heiterkeit. Ernst Jünger zum Hundertsten*, ed. by Günter Figal and Heimo Schwilk (Stuttgart: Klett-Cotta, 1995), pp. 25–40

Figal, Günter, 'Philosophische Zeitkritik im Selbstverständnis der Modernität', in *Selbstverständnis der Moderne*, ed. by Günter Figal and Rolf-Peter Sieferle (Stuttgart: Metzler, 1991), pp. 100–32

Fischer, Jörg and Frank Philip, 'Europa: Treffen von Haider, Lega Nord und Vlaams Blok', *Junge Freiheit*, 9 August 2002

Fritzsche, Klaus, *Politische Romantik und Gegenrevolution: Fluchtwege in der Krise der bürgerlichen Gesellschaft: Das Beispiel des 'Tat'-Kreises* (Frankfurt a.M.: suhrkamp, 1976)

Funke, Hajo, *Paranoia und Politik. Rechtsextremismus in der Berliner Republik* (Berlin: Schiler Verlag, 2002)

G, 'Reaktion', *Deutsches Volkstum*, 9 (1927), 8–12

Gauland, Alexander, 'Herkunft und Zukunft', *Criticón*, 167 (2000), pp. 24–5

Gellately, Robert, *The Gestapo and German Society: Enforcing Racial Policy 1933–1945* (Oxford: Clarendon, 1990)

Gessenharter, Wolfgang, 'Die intellektuelle Neue Rechte und die neue radikale Rechte in Deutschland', *Aus Politik und Zeitgeschichte*, B 9-10 (1998), 20–6

Gessenharter, Wolfgang, *Kippt die Republik? Die Neue Rechte und ihre Unterstützung durch Politik und Medien* (Munich: Knaur, 1994)

Giddens, Anthony, *Modernity and Self-Identity: Self and Society in the Late Modern Age*, 4th edn (Cambridge: Polity Press, 1994)

Glaser, Hermann, 'Kultur und Identitäten', *Aus Politik und Zeitgeschichte*, B50, 7 December 2001, 3–5

Graw, Ansgar, 'Dekadenz und Kampf' in *Die selbstbewußte Nation*, pp. 281–90 (see under Schwilk)

Greiffenhagen, Martin, *Das Dilemma des Konservatismus in Deutschland* (Munich: Piper, 1977)

Greß, Franz, Hans-Gerd Jaschke, Klaus Schönekäs, *Neue Rechte und Rechtsextremismus in Europa. Bundesrepublik – Frankreich – Großbritannien* (Opladen: Westdeutscher Verlag, 1990)

Griffin, Roger, 'Interregnum or Endgame? Radical Right Thought in the "Postfascist" Era', http://ah.brookes.ac.uk/history/staff/griffin/interregnum.pdf. Accessed 26 June 2006

Grund, Johanna Christina, 'Euro-Gesellschaft statt Volk', *Nation und Europa*, 46, November–December 1996, 39–40

Günther, Albrecht Erich (ed.), *Was wir vom Nationalsozialismus erwarten* (Heilbronn: Eugen Salzer, 1932)

Habermann, Gerd, 'Die Debatte über den "letzten Menschen"', *Criticón*, April, May, June 1996, 79–81

Habermas, Jürgen, *The New Conservatism*, ed. by Shierry Nicholson (Cambridge: Polity Press, 1989)

Habermas, Jürgen, 'The New Intimacy between Culture and Politics', in *The New Conservatism*, pp. 196–205

Habermas, Jürgen, *Die postnationale Konstellation. Politische Essays* (Frankfurt am Main: Suhrkamp, 1998)

Hageböck, Michael 'Endzeit', in *Wir 89er*, ed. by Roland Bubik (Frankfurt am Main, Berlin: Ullstein, 1995), pp. 145–62

Hall, Stuart, 'Introduction: Who needs "Identity"', in *Questions of Cultural Identity*, ed. by Stuart Hall and Paul Du Gay (London: Sage, 1996), pp. 1–17

Herf, Jeffrey, *Reactionary Modernism: Technology, culture and politics in Weimar and the Third Reich* (Cambridge, London: Cambridge University Press, 1984)

Herzinger, Richard, *Republik ohne Mitte* (Berlin: Siedler, 2001)

Hielscher, Friedrich, 'Für die unterdrückten Völker', *Arminius*, 16 March 1927

Hofmannsthal, Hugo von, 'Das Schrifttum als geistiger Raum der Nation' (Munich: Bremer Presse, 1927)

Holz, Harald, 'Die Tragik der deutschen Geschichte', in: *Criticón*, 135, January/February 1993, p. 39

Honneth, Axel, *Kampf um Anerkennung* (Frankfurt am Main: suhrkamp, 2003)

'Interview mit Günter Rohrmoser', *Junge Freiheit*, March/April 1989, p. 3

'Interview mit Oberst Kleyser: Immer von ihrem Gewissen geführt', *Junge Freiheit*, 20 July 2001

Jäger, Siegfried (ed.), *Rechtsdruck: Die Presse der Neuen Rechten* (Berlin, Bonn: J.H.W. Dietz, 1988)

Jaschke, Hans-Gerd 'Nationalismus und Ethnopluralismus. Zum Wiederaufleben von Ideen der "Konservativen Revolution"', *Aus Politik und Zeitgeschichte*, B 3-4 (1993), 3–10

Jesse, Eckhard, 'Fließende Grenzen zum Rechtsextremismus? Zur Debatte über Brückenspektren, Grauzonen, Vernetzungen und Scharniere am rechten Rand – Mythos und Realität', in *Rechtsextremismus: Ergebnisse und*

Perspektiven der Forschung, ed. by Jürgen W. Falter, Hans-Gerd Jaschke, and Jürgen R. Winkler (Opladen: Westdeutscher Verlag, 1996), pp. 514–29

Jung, Edgar, *Sinndeutung der deutschen Revolution* (Oldenburg: Stalling, 1933)

Jünger, Ernst, 'Alfred Kubin', *Neues Forum*, 154, October 1966, 629–32

Jünger, Ernst, *Der Kampf als inneres Erlebnis* (Berlin: Mittler, 1922)

Jünger, Ernst, 'Nationalismus und Nationalismus', *Das Tagebuch*, 21 September 1929, 1552–8

Jünger, Ernst, *Sturm* (Olten: Oltener Liebhaberdruck, 1963)

Jünger, Ernst, 'Zu Kubins Bild: Der Mensch', in *Ernst Jünger, Alfred Kubin Eine Begegnung* (Frankfurt aM: Propyläen, 1975), p. 13

Kleinau, Wilhelm, 'Mussolini über Verfassungen und Programme', in *Die Standarte*, 14 August 1927, p. 339

Knütter, Hans-Helmuth, 'Servilität', *Junge Freiheit*, 2 July 1999

Kocka, Jürgen, 'Die Zukunft der Gerechtigkeit', *Berliner Republik*, 3/ 2003

Königsreder, Angelika, 'Zur Chronologie des Rechtsextremismus', in *Rechtsextremismus in Deutschland*, ed. by Wolfgang Benz (Frankfurt am Main: Fischer, 1996), pp. 246–315

Krause, Tilman, 'Innerlichkeit und Weltferne', in *Die selbstbewußte Nation*, pp. 134–41 (see under Schwilk)

Krebs, Pierre, *Das Thule-Seminar: Geistesgegenwart der Zukunft in der Morgenröte des Ethnos* (Kassel, Vienna: Weecke, 1994)

Krebs, Pierre, *Das unvergängliche Erbe* (Tübingen: Grabert, 1981)

Krebs, Pierre, 'Deutsch und europäisch: grenzenlos', *Elemente*, Hauptausgabe 1990, 4–6

Krebs, Pierre, *Die europäische Wiedergeburt* (Tübingen: Grabert, 1982)

Krebs, Pierre, 'Eine Epoche in der Krise', *Elemente*, Hauptausgabe, 1990, 8–19

Krebs, Pierre, 'Ethnokraten der Welt, Vereinigt Euch!: Interview mit Günter Schwab', *Deutsche Stimme*, May 2001

Krebs, Pierre (ed.), *Mut zur Identität* (Struckum: Verlag für Ganzheitliche Forschung und Kultur, 1988)

Krebs, Pierre, 'Unser inneres Reich', *Elemente*, 1 (1986), p. 6

LaCapra, Dominick, *Rethinking Intellectual History* (Ithaca: Cornell University Press, 1983)

Lange, Hartmut, 'Existenz und Moderne: Über Selbsterkenntnis als Solidarität', in *Die selbstbewußte Nation*, pp. 436–7 (see under Schwilk)

Lash, Scott, Brian Wynne, 'Introduction', in Ulrich Beck, *Risk Society* (London: Sage, 2002), pp. 2–8

Lenk, Kurt, 'Ideengeschichtliche Dispositionen rechtsextremen Denkens', *Aus Politik und Zeitgeschichte*, B 9-10 (1998), 13–19

Lévy, Bernard-Henry, 'Allemagne année zéro?', *Le Monde*, 6–8 February 1999

Lummer, Heinrich, 'Nur keine Eile', *Junge Freiheit*, 19 July 2002

Maninger, Stefan, 'Die Volkskrise', Report on the Summer Academy 2000, http://www.staatspolitik.de, accessed 1 July 2003

Maschke, Günter, 'Der Zauberlehrling Machiavellis: Benito Mussolini', *Erste Etappe*, 1, 1988, pp. 63–71

Mechtersheimer, Alfred, 'Nation und Internationalismus: Über nationales Selbstbewußtsein als Bedingung des Friedens', in *Die selbstbewußte Nation*, pp. 345–63 (see under Schwilk)

Meier-Bergfeld, Peter, 'Deutschland und Österreich', in *Die selbstbewußte Nation*, pp. 195–226 (see under Schwilk)

Miegel, Meinhard and Stefanie Wahl, *Das Ende des Individualismus* (Bonn: Bonn aktuell, 1993)

Minkenberg, Michael, 'German Unification and the Continuity of Discontinuities: Cultural Change and the Far Right in East and West', *German Politics*, 2 (1994), 169–92

Mohler, Armin, *Der Nasenring. Im Dickicht der Vergangenheitsbewältigung* (Essen: Heitz & Höffkes, 1987)

Mohler, Armin, *Die Konservative Revolution in Deutschland 1918–1932*, 3rd edn, 2 vols (Darmstadt: Wissenschaftliche Buchgesellschaft, 1989)

Mohler, Armin, *Georges Sorel: Erzvater der Konservativen Revolution* (Bad Vilbel: Edition Antaios, 2000)

Mohler, Armin, 'Ich bin ein Faschist', *Leipziger Volkszeitung*, 25–26 November 1995

Mohler, Armin, *Liberalenbeschimpfung* (Essen: Heitz & Höffkes, 1990)

Mohler, Armin, 'Vorwort', in Alain de Benoist, *Kulturrevolution von rechts*, pp. 16–17

Motschmann, Klaus, 'Krise und Kritik: Alte Irrtümer in neuer Gestalt – diesmal in der Grundrechtscharta Europas', *Criticón*, 168, Winter 2000, pp. 4–5

Müller, Baal, 'Jenseits von Leid-und Lightkultur', *Junge Freiheit*, 24 November 2000

Neaman, Elliot, 'A New Conservative Revolution? in *Antisemitism and Xenophobia in Germany after Unification*, ed. by Hermann Kurthen, Werner Bergmann and Rainer Erb (New York, Oxford: OUP, 1997), pp. 190–208

Neujahr, Doris, 'Wie bei Hempels unterm Sofa', *Junge Freiheit*, 19 March 2004

Niekisch, Ernst *Gewagtes Leben 1889–1948: Erinnerungen eines deutschen Revolutionärs*, 2 vols (Cologne: Wissenschaft und Politik, 1974)

Niekisch, Ernst, *Das Reich der niederen Dämonen* (Hamburg: Rowohlt, 1953)

Nietzsche, Friedrich, *Werke in drei Bänden*, 3 vols, 7th edn, ed. by Karl Schlechta (Munich: Carl Hanser, 1973)

P., Hans, '"…gegen die Plage der bürgerlichen Welt". Ein Gespräch mit einem Nationalrevolutionär', *Wir selbst*, 3, 1999, 68–73

Pankraz, 'Botho Strauß und der Fundamentalismus', *Junge Freiheit*, (11 October 2002)

Parteiprogramm 2002 der Republikaner, http://www.rep.de (accessed 20 September 2004)

Parteiprogramm der Nationaldemokratischen Partei Deutschlands (NPD), http://www.npd.de/npd_startseiten/programme.html (accessed 25 August 2004)

Pfahl-Traughber, Armin, *'Konservative Revolution' und 'Neue Rechte'. Rechtextremistische Intellektuelle gegen den demokratischen Verfassungsstaat* (Opladen: Leske und Budrich, 1998)

Pfahl-Traughber, Armin, '"Kulturrevolution von rechts". Definition, Einstellungen und Gefahrenpotential der Intellektuellen "Neuen Rechten"', *Mut*, 351 (1996), 36–57

Planer-Friedrich, Götz, 'Interview mit Götz Planer-Friedrich and Jürgen Wandel: Der richtige Weg in die Zukunft', *Zeitzeichen* 6/2001, pp. 32–5

Pocock, John G.A., *Politics, Language and Time: Essays on Political Thought and History* (New York: Atheneum, 1971)

Reding, Marcel, 'Zum Begriff Tradition', in *Rekonstruktion des Konservatismus*, ed. by Gerd-Klaus Kaltenbrunner, 3rd edn (Bern and Stuttgart: Haupt, 1978), pp. 561–81

Rensmann, Lars, 'Four Wings of the Intellectual New Right', unpublished manuscript, 2003

Rohrmoser, Günter, *Deutschlands Tragödie* (Munich: Olzog, 2002)

Rohrmoser, Günter, *Ideologie-Zerfall: Nachruf auf die geistige Wende* (Krefeld: Sinus, 1990)

S. P., 'Eurorechte im Blickpunkt', *Nation und Europa*, 46, November/December 1996, p. 16

Safranski, Rüdiger, 'Der Wille zum Glauben oder die Wiederkehr der Götter', *Magie der Heiterkeit*, pp. 243–54

Safranski, Rüdiger, *Wieviel Wahrheit braucht der Mensch? Über das Denkbare und das Lebbare* (Munich, Vienna: Carl Hanser, 1990)

Sander, Hans-Dietrich, 'Wie und unter welchen Umständen kann eine niedergegangene Kultur erneuert werden? Thesen und Glossare', *Staatsbriefe*, 11, 2000

Satzger, Simone, 'Elemente', in *Wir 89er*, ed. by Roland Bubik (Frankfurt am Main, Berlin: Ullstein, 1995), pp. 35–49

Saur, Wolfgang, 'Neurose oder Selbstbehauptung', *Junge Freiheit*, 11 October 2002

Schaare, Jochen, 'Ein Lob der Skepsis', *Junge Freiheit*, 30 August 2002

Schacht, Ulrich, 'Stigma und Sorge: Über deutsche Identität nach Auschwitz', in *Die selbstbewußte Nation*, pp. 432–43 (see under Schwilk)

Schäuble, Wolfgang, 'Interview mit dem CDU/CSU-Fraktionsvorsitzenden Wolfgang Schäuble', *Süddeutsche Zeitung*, 28 December 1994, p. 8

Scheil, Stefan, 'Argumentation mit der Brechstange', *Junge Freiheit*, 11 April 2003

Schönhuber, Franz, 'Die Nebel lichten sich', *Nation und Europa*, 46, November/December 1996, p. 13

Schönhuber, Franz, *Die verbogene Gesellschaft: Mein Leben zwischen NS-Erziehung und US-Umerziehung* (Berg: VGB-Verlagsgesellschaft, 1996)

Schönhuber, Franz, 'Endzeit', *Nation und Europa*, January 1997, 9–12

Schönhuber, Franz, *Ich war dabei* (Munich: Langen Müller), 1981

Schönhuber, Franz, 'Schweigen ist keine Antwort', *Nation und Europa*, March 1998, 11–14

Schröder, Richard 'Wie weit verbindet die Deutschen die gemeinsame Nation?', *Wir selbst*, 3, 1999, 8–13

Schüddekopf, Otto-Ernst, *Nationalbolschewismus in Deutschland 1918–1933* (Frankfurt am Main, Berlin, Vienna: Ullstein, 1973)

Schwarz, Martin, 'Globalisierung und Spaßgesellschaft. Die sogenannte Ausländerfrage in Europa und der Islam', March 2002, www.eisernekrone.tk, accessed 20 June 2004

Schwefel, Johannes, 'Leserbrief', *Junge Freiheit*, 30 August 2002

Schwilk, Heimo, 'Auf der Suche nach der Einheit – Träume bei Ernst Jünger und Carl Gustav Jung', *Criticón*, January/February/March 1996, 45–9

Schwilk, Heimo, 'Der Bürger kehrt zurück', *Welt am Sonntag*, 30 September 2001

Schwilk, Heimo and Ulrich Schacht, (eds), *Die selbstbewußte Nation. 'Anschwellender Bocksgesang' und andere Beiträge zu einer deutschen Debatte* (Berlin: Ullstein, 1994)

Schwilk, Heimo (ed.), *Ernst Jünger. Leben in Bildern und Texten* (Stuttgart: Klett-Cotta, 1988)

Schwilk, Heimo, 'Ernst Jünger – Prophet der Globalisierung', *Criticón*, 168, Winter 2000, pp. 26–30

Schwilk, Heimo, *Wendezeit – Zeitenwende: Beiträge zur Literatur der achtziger Jahre* (Bonn, Berlin: Bouvier, 1991)

Seebacher-Brandt, Brigitte, 'Norm und Normalität: Über die Liebe zum eigenen Land', in *Die selbstbewußte Nation*. pp. 43–56 (see under Schwilk)

Seidel, Gill, 'Culture, Nation and "Race" in the British and French New Right', in Ruth Levitas, *The Ideology of the New Right* (Cambridge: Polity, 1986), pp. 107–35

Sohn, Gunnar, 'Freiheit und Konservatismus', *Criticón*, 139, September/ October 1993, 246–7

Sontheimer, Kurt, 'Die Kontinuität antidemokratischen Denkens', in *Die Neue Rechte – eine Gefahr für die Demokratie?*, ed. by Wolfgang Gessenharter and Thomas Pfeiffer (Wiesbaden: Verlag für Sozialwissenschaften, 2004), pp. 19–29

Sontheimer, Kurt, *Antidemokratisches Denken in der Weimarer Republik* (Munich: Nymphenburger, 1968)

Spengler, Oswald, *Briefe 1913–1936*, ed. by A.M. Koktanek (Munich: Beck, 1963)

Spengler, Oswald, *Jahre der Entscheidung* (Munich: Beck, 1933)

Spengler, Oswald, *Nation und Europa*, September 1998, p. 20

Stein, Dieter, Hans-Ulrich Kopp, Goetz Meidinger, 'Der Zusammenbruch des Sozialismus führt zu einer Renaissance des Konservativen. Interview mit Günter Rohrmoser', *Junge Freiheit*, July/August 1991, p. 3

Stein, Dieter, Moritz Schwarz, 'Interview mit Jörg Schönbohm', *Junge Freiheit*, 7 February 2003

Stein, Dieter, Jürgen Lanter, 'Macht sich in Deutschland ein neuer Wilhelminismus breit? Interview mit Günter Maschke', *Junge Freiheit*, June 1991, p. 3

Stein, Dieter, Moritz Schwarz, 'Mangel an Intellektualität. Interview mit Alexander von Stahl', *Junge Freiheit*, 3 January 2003

Stein, Dieter, 'Streit, Aufbruch und Selbstkritik', *Junge Freiheit*, supplement, 14 June 1996, p. 8

Steinberger, Gerwin, 'Edgar Jung und der organische Staat', *Nation und Europa*, 9 September 1992, p. 50

Bibliography 179

Stern, Fritz, *The Politics of Cultural Despair*, 2nd edn (Berkeley, Los Angeles, London: University of California, 1974)

Sternhell, Zeev, *Ni droite ni gauche*. *L'idéologie fasciste en France* (Paris: Éditions du Seuil, 1983)

Stolz, Rolf, 'Integration als Existenzgrundlage', *Junge Freiheit*, 5 July 2002

Stöss, Richard, 'Die "neue Rechte" in der Bundesrepublik', in *Die Wiedergeburt nationalistischen Denkens: Gefahr für die Demokratie*, ed. by Forschungsinstitut der Friedrich-Ebert-Stiftung (Bonn: Friedrich-Ebert-Stiftung, 1995)

Stöss, Richard, 'Forschungs- und Erklärungsansätze – ein Überblick', in *Rechtsextremismus. Einführung und Forschungsbilanz*, ed. by Wolfgang Kowalsky and Wolfgang Schroeder (Opladen: Westdeutscher Verlag, 1994), pp. 23–66

Stöss, Richard, 'Soziale Gerechtigkeit. Die ostdeutsche Perspektive', http://www.polwiss.fu-berlin.de/osz/dokumente/PDF/Sozgerla.pdf

Straub, Eberhard, 'Individuum und Gesellschaft: Über die Enteignung des Eigentums' in *Die selbstbewußte Nation*, pp. 416–31 (see under Schwilk)

Strauß, Botho, *Beginnlosigkeit: Reflexionen über Fleck und Linie* (Munich: dtv, 1997)

Strauß, Botho, *Der Aufstand gegen die sekundäre Welt* (Munich, Vienna: Hanser), 1999

Strauß, Botho, *Der Untenstehende auf Zehenspitzen* (Munich, Vienna: Carl Hanser, 2004)

Strauß, Botho, *Die Fehler des Kopisten* (Munich and Vienna: Hanser, 1997)

Strauss, Wolfgang, 'Deutschlands Rechte und Hitler', *Europa vorn*, 92, 15 October 1995, 8–12

Ulbrich, Stefan, 'Es entsteht eine neue Kultur', *Junge Freiheit*, 7 October 1992, p. 24

Vad, Erich, 'Eine ganze Generation unter Generalverdacht', *Junge Freiheit*, 11 January 2002

Veen, Hans-Joachim, '"Rechtsextrem" oder "Rechtsradikal"?', *Das Parlament*, 15 April 1994, p. 1

Venohr, Wolfgang, *Patrioten gegen Hitler, Der Weg zum 20. Juli 1944* (Bergisch Gladbach: Lübbe, 1994)

Venohr, Wolfgang, *Stauffenberg. Symbol der deutschen Einheit* (Frankfurt am Main and Berlin: Ullstein, 1986)

Venohr, Wolfgang, 'Vor 50 Jahren', *Junge Freiheit*, 1–2, January/February, 1992, p. 15

Venohr, Wolfgang, 'Vor 50 Jahren: Der Kulminationspunkt wird überschritten', *Junge Freiheit*, September 1992, p. 15

Volpi, Franco, 'Praktische Vernunft inmitten ihrer technischen Entmachtung', in *Magie der Heiterkeit*, pp. 72–83 (see under Figal)

Weißmann, Karlheinz *Alles was recht(s) ist: Ideen, Köpfe und Perspektiven der politischen Rechten* (Graz, Stuttgart: Leopold Stocker Verlag, 2000)

Weißmann, Karlheinz, 'Den Konfliktfall denken', *Junge Freiheit*, 3 November 2000

Weißmann, Karlheinz, 'Es gibt keine Geschichtsphilosophie', in *Georges Sorel: Erzvater der Konservativen Revolution*, ed. by Armin Mohler (Bad Vilbel: Edition Antaios, 2000), pp. 87–99

Weißmann, Karlheinz, 'Herausforderung und Entscheidung: Über einen politischen Verismus für Deutschland', in *Die selbstbewußte Nation*, pp. 309–26 (see under Schwilk)

Weißmann, Karlheinz, 'Maurice Barrès und der "Nationalismus" im Frühwerk Ernst Jüngers' in *Magie der Heiterkeit*, pp. 133–46 (see under Figal)

Weißmann, Karlheinz, *Rückruf in die Geschichte* (Frankfurt am Main and Berlin: Ullstein, 1992)

Wiesberg, Michael, 'Botho Strauß: Die Fehler des Kopisten: Verschmelzung von Einst und Jetzt', *Junge Freiheit*, 9 May 1997

Wiesberg, Michael, 'Der Westen muß sich wehren', *Junge Freiheit*, 6 September 2002

Wiesberg, Michael, 'In tiefer Stille gegen die Welt leben', *Junge Freiheit*, 9 July 2004

Willig, Angelika, 'Abschied von rechts', *Junge Freiheit*, 16 October 1998

Willig, Angelika, 'Botho Strauß: "Beginnlosigkeit": Das Geräusch des Toastkauens', *Junge Freiheit*, October 1992, p. 15

Willig, Angelika, 'Platon statt Judenwitze. Die NPD strebt eine Intellektualisierung an', *Junge Freiheit*, 15 June 2001

Wolin, Richard, 'Introduction', in *The New Conservatism*, pp. vii–xxxi (see under Habermas)

Woods, Roger, *The Conservative Revolution in the Weimar Republic* (Macmillan: Basingstoke; St Martin's Press: New York, 1996)

Woods, Roger, *Ernst Jünger and the Nature of Political Commitment* (Stuttgart: Akademischer Verlag Hans-Dieter Heinz, 1982)

Worm, Uwe, *Die Neue Rechte in der Bundesrepublik* (Cologne: PappyRossa, 1995)

Zabel, Wolfram, 'Editorial', *Criticón*, 167, Sept 2000, p. 3

Zitelmann, Rainer, 'Position und Begriff', in *Die selbstbewußte Nation* (see under Schwilk)

Index